OUR
VIOLENT
SOCIETY

OUR VIOLENT SOCIETY

David Abrahamsen, M.D.

Funk & Wagnalls   New York

This book is dedicated to the youth of America—
that they may build a better life for everyone

Acknowledgments

The years of extreme violence, 1963–1969, during which I have been writing to my view the first comprehensive book about violence in our society, have required both presence and distance in order to evaluate correctly our violent behavior. During the time of this turmoil I have had many discussions with social scientists, judges of the courts, psychiatrists, and historians which were instrumental in elucidating my own viewpoints. In particular, I would like to mention the many conferences I have had as a member of the Board of Overseers of the Lemberg Center for the Study of Violence, Brandeis University, ably directed by John Spiegel, M.D.

I am grateful for the assistance given me by Thomas J. Kelly, Assistant Director of the United States Secret Service, Washington, D.C., and to the Probation Department of the United States District Court, Southern District of New York, which made available to me records of violent behavior.

I am grateful to Bernard Pacella, M.D., Associate Professor of Clinical Psychiatry, Department of Psychiatry, Columbia University, for the many suggestions he gave about Lee Harvey Oswald. Thanks go to Dr. Gunnar Myrdal, Professor of the University of Stockholm, Institute of International Economic Studies, for his fundamental book, *The American Dilemma,* and for the illuminating discussions I have had with him on the violent American society. I would also like to express my thanks to the Library of the New York Academy of Medicine for its always prompt service in securing for me sources about violence which otherwise were not available, and to *The New York Times,* in particular A. M. Rosenthal, Managing Editor, which made it possible for me to study the many millions of words in the Warren Commission's volumes on Lee Harvey Oswald. Chapter VI of this book, "Lee Harvey Oswald—Psychological Capability of Murder," has been printed in the *Bulletin of the New York Academy of Medicine,* Second Series, Vol. 43, No. 10, pp. 861-888, October 1967.

I appreciate deeply the help extended to me by my son-in-law, Dr. William Foltz, Associate Professor of Political Sciences, Yale University, through his painstaking review and constructive ideas he gave about the manuscript.

One last word—writing a book requires patience, spirit, and discipline, not only on the part of the writer but also on the part of those around him. This book was made possible only because of my wife Lova's enduring patience and spirit. For this, more than words can express, "I thank you."

—D.A.

Contents

	Introduction	1
I	Manifest Violence	5
II	Hidden Violence	35
III	Racial Violence	61
IV	Sex—An Instrument of Violence	92
V	Instinctive and Learned Aggression	109
VI	Lee Harvey Oswald: Psychological Capacity for Violence and Murder	129
VII	The Political Assassin in America	161
VIII	The American Dream—Inspiration or Deception?	181
IX	Detecting the Potentially Violent Person	209
X	Are We Able to Prevent Violence?	237
	Notes	273
	Bibliography	284
	Index	291

OUR
VIOLENT
SOCIETY

Introduction

In 1963, following the assassination of President John F. Kennedy, I felt that a special inquiry had to be made into the violent personality and the society that fosters it. Here was a challenging task indeed. As a medical researcher, trained in psychoanalysis and the social sciences, I was certain that a clear understanding of the violence in and around us required more than the recording of surface manifestations. To study violence in our society and to uncover the underlying motivations for our behavior demanded an examination of our unconscious feelings and fantasies, hopes and fears. The method of study that evolved was much like a case study of a human being in a dilemma, in need of help.

When a patient comes for help, a psychiatrist may let him "tell it like it is." But the psychiatrist knows that it will be next to impossible for him to do so, because the patient, driven more by unconscious than by conscious feelings, distorts reality. In the same way, when we try to describe our society's problem, we do not express our real feelings about it, since this might reveal some deep vulnerability in us or endanger our image as a group. Sometimes we honestly do not know what our feelings are. Yet these hidden or unrecognized feelings often determine our behavior, and may, therefore, be the real cause of our problem.

In trying to evaluate the pattern of turbulence in our country, we are apt to conclude that violence in our society is becoming normalized. The question arises: Has it always been that way or has it become so recently? Or is our American life part of a larger pattern of violent behavior present in all societies?

Although all Americans today decry the prevalence of violence and many ask whether ours is a sick society (hoping to be reassured that it is not), few have noticed the many subtle gradations of individual and mass violence that have become so closely allied to our cultural life that they have germinated and existed without our being aware of them.

Stretching like an almost unending thread through our history has been one particular form of violence—hidden violence—which so far has been largely overlooked but is pervasive on all levels.

This book is based upon my research findings, drawing from my own investigations and teaching in the field of violence and crime at the Psychiatric Institute, Columbia University, as Consultant to the Department of Mental Hygiene in the State of New York, as Research Psychiatric Consultant to the Research Center for the Study of Social Change, Roosevelt Hospital; and as a psychiatric consultant in the state and Federal courts.

In chapters dealing with the roots of violence on the

individual level, using case histories for illustration, I have
described the link between sex and violence, and on the
mass level I have examined the unconscious psychosexual
emotions that lie beneath our bitter racial conflict. I have
also included a detailed case history of Lee Harvey Oswald to show those elements of the human personality
which could conceivably, under certain conditions, pre-
dispose an individual to violence and murder.

One important aspect of our violent society is the political assassin or would-be assassin, many of whom I have
had the opportunity to examine and whose life histories
are published here for the first time. Closely allied is the
detection of the potentially violent person.

An individual's emotional past determines his behavior
to a great extent. Similarly, influenced in part through
the American Dream, America has an emotional past that
in many ways has determined our national attitude and
present-day life style. Since we all are largely dependent
upon our environmental conditioning and instinctual
impulses, the success of our attempt at counteracting our
violent behavior depends upon the degree to which we
are able to change our own feelings toward ourselves and
others.

Psychological insight tends to widen and deepen our
understanding and tolerance of ourselves and of one another. Constructive individual and group long-range programs to cope with violence in our country can be formulated only on the basis of sound psychological and
sociological principles. This formula has been followed
here. But are we ready to be educated for this task? Are
we emotionally able to prevent violence? Notwithstand-

ing this dim outlook, we must take steps to temper our violent impulses.

This book, then, is an attempt to bring us to our senses —a call to move us into awareness.

If these critical times do not permit long-range goals, still the urgency to recognize them and pursue them is clear.

Let us man the barricades!

—*David Abrahamsen,* M.D.
New York, N.Y.
March, 1969

Manifest Violence

Throughout our country, people are murdered rampantly. There are mass random shootings and riots in many of our cities. There are student revolts during which teachers are attacked. There are tumultuous demonstrations and counterdemonstrations provoking violent police action during which innocent newspaper men and onlookers are clubbed. The slums thrive as breeding grounds of racial violence, ghetto uprisings, and vicious battles. Crime syndicates operating under cover terrorize and corrupt our citizens and institutions. Extremist groups under the guise of patriotism advocate and activate hatred. Our President, our Vice President, and other government officials receive daily a flood of threatening letters and telephone calls from would-be assassins.

Three high points in American violence seem to have been reached in the 1963 assassination of John F. Kennedy—one of four presidents to be murdered within the span of one hundred years—and in the 1968 murders of

Martin Luther King, Jr., and Senator Robert F. Kennedy.

A confrontation has taken place here in the United States between people on many levels, in the government, on streets, and between students on university campuses. Lawlessness has resulted from the acting out of hostile aggression by the individual or the group, leading to *manifest* violence, which has caused sudden damage or destruction of person or property.

Manifest violence occurs under all kinds of conditions. It can be produced by a mob acting more or less justifiably in response to social or legal abuse, or it can be caused by an emotionally disturbed individual. But whatever the motivation, conflicts between individuals and between groups become violent when people feel threatened or frustrated and have lost faith in society's ability to protect them or to satisfy their grievances.

Although we cannot always equate lawlessness with violence, we must ask whether there may exist within the American geographical, emotional, and social environments certain indigenous fear- and hate-producing elements that foster and perpetuate our human tendencies toward destructive behavior. If we can assume that all human beings, on the instinctual level, are capable of about the same proportion of conscious or unconscious fear and hate, which elicit violence, we must then inquire whether or not such feelings produce violence more often in America than in other countries.

Although recent years have shown a considerable increase in violence committed by adults—a significant fact in itself—there has also been an alarming acceleration of the rate and degradation in the nature of violence and crime among children and adolescents. While many of our youth have always been involved in pranks—such as petty thievery and other relatively innocent kinds of crimes—today more than a few commit vicious criminal acts.

Killings have become markedly bizarre in nature. A notable example is an eight-year-old boy's stabbing of his parents during their sleep. The police, despite careful efforts, could find no sign that the house had been broken into. The boy reported several versions of the murders, one of which was that a man with a white mask had sneaked into the house, stabbed his parents, and then tried to choke him. The detail of the white mask was suspicious: a person who disguises himself usually wears a dark mask, not a white one. This detail, combined with the fact that the boy's father was a surgeon and that it would be natural for his son to imagine the intruder as wearing a white mask similar to the one his father wore during operations, focused suspicion on the child. He soon confessed the crime (which he later denied), was examined psychiatrically and found to be mentally ill.

Until comparatively recently, youthful murderers were rare. I can well remember how shocked most people were when early in the 1950s three adolescent boys in Brooklyn—the "thrill killers," as they were called—tortured an old man by burning his toes and the soles of his feet with a cigarette butt, then drowned him in the river.

During the last twenty years, however, such a grotesque episode has become anything but unique. An eighteen-year-old boy murdered a mother and her four children who had befriended him. On Long Island a fourteen-year-old boy wiped out almost his entire family—his mother, his sister, and finally himself. A young man shot fifteen people to death from a university tower in Austin, Texas. In Chicago a man slew eight young nurses.

This overwhelming rise in juvenile crimes reflects the extreme forms of violence to which our society has resorted. While juveniles were responsible for three-quarters of a million crimes in 1958,[1] they accounted for more than one million of the four and a half million arrests made in 1963.[2] Nineteen percent of these arrests were for murder committed by youths under twenty-one years of age.[3] In 1965, 65 percent of these arrests were of people under twenty-five years of age, and of these, 20 percent were adolescents.[4] From 1960 to 1967, police arrests in the ten-to-seventeen age group jumped 72 percent, while the corresponding increase in the population was only 22 percent.[5]

When this enormous wave of juvenile crime and violence first became evident, a cry of horror and disgust went up from the citizenry. As time has gone by, an even greater increase in wanton murder has developed, but the cry has become more and more feeble.

Statistics seem to confirm our suspicion that there is more violence in America than in other nations. The highest rate of murder—the most definitive act of violence in the civilized world—is found in the United States. According to the FBI, we had an estimated 13,650 murders in 1968, which when compared to the 12,090 murders in 1967, represents an increase of 1,560 murders—12 percent, the largest absolute rise over any prior year in the 1960's.[6] In the first nine months of 1968, there was an increase of 15 percent. The rate of murder in 1968 amounted to an incredible 6.8 murder victims per 100,000 population, in contrast to 1967, when it was 6. In England and Wales in 1965 there were 0.4 murders per 100,000 population—less than one-tenth the United States rate. In Scandinavia the rate was even lower.

Some sociologists have disputed the FBI statistics,[8] citing, among other reasons, that they do not account for population growth (for example, the increase in the seventeen-to-twenty-four age group, the "war babies," who now account for 70 percent of serious crimes) and the fact that there is a greater efficiency in police crime-reporting. However, this criticism has now been blunted, particularly since the 1967 crime rise was led by a 28 percent increase in robberies, which include muggings, stick-ups, bank robberies, and thefts involving a threat of bodily harm. The first nine months of 1968 saw an increase of 32 percent. This jump in robberies is significant because robbery is a key indicator of violence.[9]

There is criticism, too, of the role of television, radio, and the press in exaggerating and "playing up" crime and criminal activities to achieve audience excitement and greater reader and viewer reaction to violence. Many people believe that a calmer view on the part of the media would result in a lessening of violent activity, but the problem with such an approach is its possible effect upon children, most of whom are unable to distinguish between fantasy and reality. This effect will be discussed in later chapters.

When we scrutinize recent crime statistics, we find one obvious reason for the high number of murders in this country—the easy availability of firearms. There has been a dramatic increase in the production and importation of hand guns (pistols and revolvers) from 380,462 in 1951 to 973,823 in 1965. In 1966 there was an increase to 1.1 million and in 1967 to 1.6 million. For the first six months in 1968, the total was put at 1.2 million. While the overall total of manufactured and imported weapons in 1951 was 2.4 million, in 1967 it was 4.7 million, and in the first half of 1968 it was 3 million.[10]

A comparison of the number of gun murders here to that in other countries shows a definite correlation between easy access to firearms and manifest violence. Only 10 percent of the murders committed in England in 1962 were committed with firearms. In 1962 in England and Wales (which have one-fourth the population of the United States), there were 29 murders by gunfire,[11] while in the United States, 7,000 killings were carried out with guns.[12] In 1967, 7,700, or 63 percent, of the 12,090 people murdered were shot to death.

A regional examination of homicides in the United States in 1966 shows that New England had the lowest incidence (2.1 per 100,000 population), while the highest rates were shared between two regions, the East North Central and the South Atlantic (8.8 and 8.4 per 100,000 respectively). In the Mountain States, the rate was 4.7 per 100,000; in the Middle Atlantic States, 4.0. The incidence for the Pacific States was 4.2, and in the West South Central States it was 8.6.[13] One-half of the murders reported, 49 percent to be exact, occurred in the Southern States,[14] which represent 30 percent of the country's population.

The incidence of homicide in large cities, as could be expected, varies in correspondence with the geographic location. In 1967 in Boston the homicide rate was 3.2 per

100,000 population; in New York, 7.0; in Los Angeles, 7.0; in Chicago, 9.5; and in Dallas, 11.1. Only Southern cities had a murder rate of over 12 per 100,000: Birmingham, 12.4; Houston, 16.9; and New Orleans, 14.2. Charlotte, North Carolina, had the highest rate in the country: 17.0.[16]

Gun murders in 1967 followed a regional pattern consistent with that of earlier years. Firearms were used in 44.5 percent of the willful killings in the Northeastern States, 59.2 percent in the Western States, 65.9 percent in the North Central States, and 72.2 percent in the Southern States.[15]

The easy availability of firearms is an inducement to violent acts and outbreaks. Shooting to kill in "self-defense" is often a rationalization, idealized and enforced in the image of the free-wheeling, gun-slinging American. We have forgotten that the "right to bear arms" is no longer necessary to the security of a free state.

The geographical differences seem to be in direct correlation with firearms-control laws, which differ from state to state. Firearms, for instance, are not so strictly controlled in Texas as they are in Massachusetts, Connecticut, or New York. But this is not by any means the full story. In the Southern and Southeastern parts of the country, force and violence have always been considered more justifiable than in other parts of the country. A gun in the glove compartment of the Southerner's automobile is often thought of as standard equipment. Eighty years ago, however, Knut Hamsun wrote of *all* America that "the gun is the national murder weapon."[17] It remains so to this day.

As interesting as it is to note the high incidence of

murder in general, perhaps even more important is the
frequency with which murder erupts within the family.
There were 637 family murders in New York City in
1964 (a 16 percent increase over the previous year).*
The FBI has reported that in 1965 killings within the
American family made up of 31 percent of all murders
(and 48 percent took place between acquaintances). Almost one out of every five criminal homicides in the
Western States was a "spouse killing," a considerably
higher ratio than in other geographic regions. In addition,
killing of children by their parents was higher in the
West than in other areas of the country.[19]

Because of our glorification of the gun and our easy
access to it, we should not be surprised that murder
within the family is more prevalent in the United States
than in other countries.

Closely related to murder in the family is the high
incidence of physical cruelty exercised by parents against
their own children—a matter largely unsuspected by most
people today. There has always been some brutality to-

* These 637 murders included:
>   Sixteen husbands killed by their wives
>   Twenty-seven wives killed by their husbands
>   Nine sons killed by their mothers
>   Five sons killed by their fathers
>   One son killed by both parents
>   Twelve daughters killed by their mothers
>   Four daughters killed by their fathers
>   Four fathers killed by their sons
>   One stepson killed by his stepfather
>   One stepdaughter killed by her stepfather
>   Two brothers and two sisters killed by their brothers
>   One brother and one sister killed by their sisters
>   Four brothers-in-law killed by their brothers-in-law
>   Eighteen common-law husbands killed by their wives
>   Twenty-nine common-law wives killed by their husbands.[18]

ward children, but it has increased alarmingly during
the last few years. Throughout the nation, it is estimated
that up to 10,000 children each year are victimized by
their parents. "If we had true figures on the incidence
of maltreatment of children," says Dr. Vincent J. Fontana, "this disease would probably be listed as the
most common cause of death among children. Of the
small victims, at least ten percent die from such brutality
every year and at least one percent suffers 'irreversible
brain damage.' Most of these unfortunate, helpless children
are under three years old. In 1962 more small children
died from abusive treatment than died from leukemia,
cystic fibrosis, and muscular dystrophy combined." [20]
Complete numbers of these cases are lacking because
doctors and hospitals are reluctant to record them. They
fear the parents will take legal action against them. Nonetheless, examples of this kind of violence are, unfortunately, not too difficult to find.*

The battered-child syndrome is characterized by brain
damage on the child perpetuated by often mentally re-
tarded, psychotic, or emotionally disturbed mothers or
fathers. Such a parent, preoccupied with his own problems, may become furious when his child tries to attract
his attention, and retaliate by burning him with cigarettes,
breaking his arms and legs, immersing him in hot water,

* "A severely beaten two-year-old boy died in Paterson General Hospital after the boy's father, according to the police, walked the child to
the hospital. Bleeding from the head and body, the youngster died in the
emergency room ten minutes after arrival." [21]
"In Washington, D.C., a blond, blue-eyed four-year-old girl was admitted unconscious to one of the hospitals. An examination disclosed a
fractured skull, and lacerations covered her back, face, arms and legs.
When questioned, she is reported to have told the doctors in her childish
way: 'Mama kept hitting me with a big black stick.' " [22]

banging his head against a radiator, or throwing him down a flight of stairs.

In view of the sadistic nature of these acts, we may suspect that there is more to the battered-child syndrome than is usually known. In examining women who have killed their children, we have often found that unconscious seduction wishes or incest have played a large role. The estimate of incest in the United States, according to Dr. Roger Olive, has grown from one case in 500,000 persons in 1963 to a higher rate in recent years.[23] There may be a correlation between this estimate and the rise in the incidence of child-battering, since sexuality, as we shall see, is a predominant element of all forms of violence.

This increase of child-battering by adults parallels the overwhelming increase of general violence and crime that reflects a definite behavior pattern in our society. While in 1941 we had a little more than 1.5 million serious crimes (murder, negligent manslaughter, forcible rape, robbery, and aggravated assault),[24] in 1968 the total rose to almost 4.50 million.[25] It is significant that serious crimes during the first quarter of 1967 were 20 percent higher than those reported for the same period in 1966, the most dramatic increase for the first three months in any year since the FBI quarterly reports [26] began in 1958. From 1960 until 1967 the volume of serious crimes went up 88 percent, although the nation's population grew only about 10 percent. In other words, crime outpaced population growth by almost nine times. During that same period crimes of violence as a group increased 72 percent.[27] The most telling point illustrating the insidious growth of violence and crime is that 8,000,000 citizens of the United States (the population of New York City) have criminal records, and of every 100,000 people here, 118 were in prisons in 1964—the highest rate of any Western country.[28] Moreover, out of every 1,000 Americans, 14 were victims of some crimes in 1965.[29]

Our hostile aggressions turn inward as well as outward. It is estimated that 25,000 Americans take their own lives every year. Suicide is the tenth greatest killer in the United States. Among college students, it is the third most frequent cause of death.

Our cynicism toward violence has unwittingly grown. An example is Truman Capote's *In Cold Blood*, an account of a most gruesome crime, the killing of an entire family of four in Kansas in 1959.[30] The author describes in minute detail every occurrence, every feeling surrounding the life and murder of the Clutter family to such an extent that both author and reader become participants in the slaughter. It is Capote's fascination with the surface of reality that gives the book its compelling quality. The reader is drawn into the crime through accumulation of objective detail. Characteristic of Capote's attempt to stand aside and simultaneously participate in the crime is the way he describes the fatal moment of the first murder with the killer's own words: "I thought he (Clutter) was a very nice man. (Softspoken) I thought so right up to the moment I cut his throat." Capote keeps aloof from evaluating because then he would become involved—he mght be sentimental, and that would reduce the force of the moment.

To many of us the killing of the Clutter family was aimless and senseless (although to the murderers themselves it had a dubious meaning—they thought they were going to find money). Trying to keep himself at a distance from the killers while involving the reader emotionally, Capote gives the impression of such cynicism that one wonders if he unconsciously condones killing. He shares, however, his fascination with murders and murderers with thousands of others, as testified to by the colossal book sale.

How differently Theodore Dreiser treated murder when he wrote his novel *An American Tragedy*. At the moment when Clyde Griffiths permits his pregnant girl friend to drown, the author releases waves of images, feelings, and ideas, attempting to capture the reality and the meaning of this violent act.

To Capote's excuse, we can say that he dealt with a factual murder while Dreiser's case, although at least in part suggested by an actual murder, was fictional, enabling him to seek more readily for meaning and motivation. Nevertheless, we are still left with the question of Capote's resistance to comment on the Clutter murders. The reason for it, I believe, lies in the temper of our time, of which the author himself and millions of other people are victims.

Times have changed since the mid-twenties when *An American Tragedy* was written. We have gone through a second devastating World War in which millions of people were killed, not to mention six million Jews wantonly exterminated in the gas chambers at the hands of the Nazis. The Korean War again drew attention to killing. One young man said to me at that time, "My country teaches me to kill," an idea repeated to me verbatim a little while ago when another young man was drafted to fight in Vietnam. While these statements may be, in part, rationalizations, nevertheless the fact remains that we are living through a bloody and violent time in which our entire civilization is on trial.

Violence is a traditional expression of American behavior, particularly during periods of economic and social change. When such changes take place, there is always a measure of turbulence, upheaval, and tension—in the individual and in society. It is easy to be nonviolent when everything is going smoothly; the real test of our mettle comes in the way we react under pressure. Despite many efforts to ignore or disregard our violent impulses as merely incidental manifestations of "human nature," we must remember that there is *nothing* normal about excess, be it of violence or of anything else.

Much of our history has been a chronicle of stress and strain in spite of and because of our American Dream, which led so many to believe that the land was there for the taking and that everyone would be automatically rich and happy. Force, often leading to violence, became a substantial ingredient of the budding American society. We tend to think of this violence as cyclical in nature, forgetting about the daily acting out of aggression in our lives. Violent events—riots, demonstrations, or war —do not take place only because of environmental elements, but are often triggered by the emotional makeup of an individual. The turbulent events that have occurred throughout our history are tied together through the minds of the men who set them off.

Vigilante movements, which began first in South Carolina in 1767, have periodically fanned the fires of American violence. In 1786 Shays' Rebellion, a series of mob actions by debt-ridden farmers in Massachusetts, broke up courts, finally compelling the legislature to desist from imposing any direct tax. Violent action was here established as a means to a desired end, setting the pattern for much of our later behavior.

The fomenting pioneer society required determination and ruthless action, often ending in death. During the period 1820–33, when Indiana and Illinois were still very much Indian territory, the wagon route of the pioneers was the main route west. Through robbery and murder it became a veritable trail of death. An Indiana physician has described this era.

It was not the incredible hardships of pioneer life, not the deadly danger of disease, not the threat of the Indians that brought the most terror to the pioneers of what is now Tennessee, Kentucky, Indiana, Illinois, Missouri, and Arkansas. It was a group of psychopathic murderers from their own ranks, who lived among them. . . . There has probably never been a more terrible crime wave, population considered, than one that occurred in the area just mentioned, in that period between the Revolution and the Civil War.[31]

In 1834, for the first time, Federal troops had to be called in to restore order among rioting Irish laborers constructing the Chesapeake & Ohio Canal, while the bloody 1844 anti-Irish riots in Philadelphia brought about considerable extralegal violence—particularly the formation of vigilante committees, a particular form of lawlessness in which people, in order to protect their life, property, and community values, banded together to take the law into their own hands.

Vigilante activity, which, contrary to popular opinion, took place in the Eastern part of the United States as

well as the Western frontier, has strongly contributed to our history of cyclical violence. It was the response to the absence of law and order in an undeveloped society where the usual institutions, such as courts, schools, and churches, expressing the esteem and power of the community were nonexistent. Vigilantes went after not only criminals or outlaws but also no-gooders or people in bad repute. Their taking the law into their own hands most often resulted in the unlawful killing of those who threatened whatever civilized values there were. Whenever outlaws were caught, justice was fast. In the early days of the vigilance movement offenders were merely expelled from the community, but from the 1850s on, hanging became the usual form of punishment. One noteworthy vigilance committee was established in 1851 and reorganized in 1856 in San Francisco, where many people, including criminals, were lured following the discovery of gold. Threatened by these desperados and trying to bring order to the Barbary Coast, this vigilance committee arrested, tried, and hanged four persons and banished about thirty others. Similar lawless mob rule took place in 1863 and 1864 in mining districts of Idaho and Montana, where twenty-four outlaws were hanged within a few months.

The cyclical manifestations of violence have always been nurtured by an undercurrent of savage impulses. What we see occur in the open is an explosion of frustrated, force-filled ambitions and hostility deep within the people. This was clear during the draft riots in the working-class quarters of New York City in 1863, where an estimated twelve hundred people were killed during four days of pillaging and Negro lynching.[32] This violent outbreak grew out of *individual* frustration and griev-

ances: anyone with $300 could avoid the draft, while the
rioters, who were poor workers, had no money to buy
their way out.

The poverty of laborers during wartime was not an
exclusively American phenomenon; the wage scale for
workers at that time was low throughout the world. But
the United States at the time of the Civil War was a young
country, fomenting, expanding, and undeveloped, and
the draft riots may also be seen as an effect of the gulf
between what people had expected—the fulfillment of
the promises of the American Dream—and what they in
reality had achieved. Many had emigrated from the
greatly troubled Europe of the 1840s and 50s, expecting
to find not only "streets paved with gold" but a more
trouble-free existence than that from which they had
escaped. Instead, they found sweatshops, child labor, and
compulsory conscription for service in a Civil War that
had no meaning to them.

More significant to this study than the draft rioting,
however, was the Civil War itself, which must not be
considered an isolated phenomenon, but studied in its relationship to previous and subsequent outbursts of American prototypes of violence. While it is beyond the scope
of this book to pin down the causes of the Civil War, it is
worth remembering that this was a young nation with
unusual opportunities for anyone with the brains and the
guts to do something with his life. And yet immigrants
were often compelled to struggle merely to survive. How
could they dispel the horror of fighting for their very
existence? Is it far-fetched to assume that they consciously or unconsciously may have turned what could have
been constructive energies to a destructive prupose—as
if they were unconsciously seeking an excuse for fight-

ing? The abolition of slavery, the resultant economic problem, and the desire for secession were important motivations, but not the only ones. A fratricidal war of such dimensions, in which close to a million people were killed or wounded and cities and countryside were burned and laid desolate, reflects ferocious underlying emotions of fear and hate.

A diary entry of John Hay, Assistant Secretary to President Lincoln, describing Elmer Ellsworth, who had won national renown from the performance of a Chicago military company which he had trained, and who had become even more of a celebrity through the President's known fondness for him, gives vent to these emotions:

May 2, 1861. Tonight Ellsworth and his stalwart group arrived. He was dressed like his men—red cap, red shirt, grey breeches, grey jacket. In his belt a sword, a very heavy revolver, and what was still more significant of the measures necessary with the turbulent spirits under his command, an enormously large and bloodthirsty looking bowie knife, more than a foot long in the blade and with body enough to go through a man's head from crown to chin as you would split an apple.[33]

These words were written during a time of war, it is true, and may not reflect Hay's peacetme feelings. Whatever the case, however, the entry cannot be regarded as simply a result of direct observation. Hay's dormant fantasies of violence were awakened by the sight of Ellsworth. In how many other Americans, both in the North and the South, were such fantasies triggered off when the emotional climate became too hot?

How combustible the climate was can be seen in the Reverend J.W.T. McMullen's response to Senator Douglas' query, "Are we *in our hearts* prepared for war with our brethren and kindred?" Reverend McMullen published the following prayer in the Indianapolis *Sentinel*:

I pray God that I may be one of the men who will pull the rope to hang Jeff Davis, and that the spirits of Washington, Jefferson, Jackson and Adams may look over the battlements of Heaven down upon the bleaching carcass, as the flesh drops from the bones, and listen to the winds whistling Hail Columbia and Yankee Doodle through the decaying ribs which once enclosed his corrupt and treacherous heart. Amen.[34]

Against a backdrop of environmentally produced anger, fear, and frustration, a parallel may be drawn between the Civil War and the intrafamily violence we have already seen as prevalent in our society. Deep-seated aggression and confusion exploded when the North's demand for the abolition of slavery came into conflict with the South's resolve to remain free to decide its own way of life without being encroached upon by a more or less distant Federal authority. Slavery had become a vital part, a practical labor system in the structure of Southern society, and an emotional relationship between master and slave had come to be one significant foundation of that society. A symbiosis had developed between them: the one could not live without the other. Although the Negro had no personal identity, his whole family living in an environment where the owner was the father, the provider, the final authority, his emotional need for the white man in this sadistic-masochistic relationship was as strong as the white man's need— emotional *and* economic—for him. While Southern life seemed more simple, it had a psychological complexity the Northerner was ill-equipped to understand.

The tremendous clash that shook the country's foundations when North and South attacked each other was not unlike the often violent and hateful battles between family members, each of whom acts out his own emotional need with no awareness or tolerance of that of his antagonist. Judging from the divided emotions and loyalties, particularly in the border states where brothers of the same family fought on opposing sides, the Civil War was a true replica of intrafamily violence.

Of course, other countries have also had their Civil War, but outside forces have often taken part in the conflict. In the bloody Spanish Civil War of 1936, where thousands of people were killed and towns and cities were burned, one faction was supported by the superior Nazi and Fascist armed forces, who indiscriminately bombed Spanish towns (including Picasso's Guernica) into ruins and massacred many of the inhabitants. We wrought our own destruction.

Following the Civil War, the emerging labor unions brought about such outbreaks of mass violence as the Tompkins Square Riot of 1874; the ten "Molly Maguires," people who were hanged for murder while others were sentenced to prison in 1875; the Pittsburgh railroad strikes of 1877, during which twenty-six men were killed and the mob tore up railroad tracks and damaged property valued at five to ten million dollars; the Haymarket Massacre of 1886, during which seven policemen were killed; the Homestead Massacre of 1892, during which seven were killed and Henry Clay Frick was shot and stabbed; and the Pullman strike of 1894. Throughout the following years more labor unrest followed, climaxing in 1937 with the Memorial Day Massacre, in which four people were killed and eighty-four injured.

While there has been an ebb and flow in this sort of

mass violence, the underlying fear for the future is constant, and havoc can erupt at any time.

Nurtured, as we have seen, by our physical and cultural environment and our belief in the American Dream, we Americans have always been, to some extent at least, a fighting people. This does not negate our good characteristics; we are, among other things, friendly, imaginative, highly constructive, industrious, and productive. We spend our energies and our fighting spirit willingly and easily when our "cause," whatever it may be, is important. But our refusal to give in, perhaps an admirable trait in itself, can, when colored by stubbornness, lead us into disaster.

Consider Wild Bill Hickok's reputed attitude toward killing in the Old West, as reported in *Harper's Magazine*.

WILD BILL, HAVING SHOT HIS MAN, TURNS ON THE CROWD

When George Ward Nichols was in Springfield, Missouri, in 1866, "Wild Bill" Hickok (or Hitchcock, as Nichols called him) had just shot a man named Tutt in a "duel" which consisted simply in seeing which could draw and fire quickest. Many in the crowd were friends of Tutt's, and the moment Bill fired they started to draw their pistols. But Bill wheeled around without waiting to see if he had hit Tutt, and they put up their guns.

Later Nichols questioned Bill about the shooting. Here is his account as given in "Wild Bill," *Harper's*, February 1867:

" 'Do you not regret killing Tutt? You surely do not like to kill men?'

" 'As ter killing men,' he replied, 'I never thought much about it. The most of the men I have killed it was one or t'other of us, and at sich times you don't stop to think; and what's the use after it's all over? As for Tutt, I had rather not have killed him, for I want ter settle down quiet here now. But thar's been hard feelings between us a long while. I wanted ter keep out of that fight; but he tried to degrade me, and I couldn't stand that, you know, for I am a fighting man, you know.'

"A cloud passed over the speaker's face for a moment as he continued:

" 'And there was a cause of quarrel between us which people around here don't know about. One of us had to die, and the secret died with him.'

" 'Why did you not wait to see if your ball had hit him? Why did you turn round so quickly?'

"The scout fixed his gray eyes on mine, striking his leg with his riding whip, as he answered.

" 'I knew he was a dead man. I never miss a shot. I turned on the crowd because I was sure they would shoot me if they saw him fall.'

" 'The people about here tell me you are a quiet civil man. How is it you get into these fights?'

" 'D – – – – d if I can tell,' he replied, with a puzzled look which at once gave place to a proud, defiant expression as he continued—'but you know a man must defend his honor.' " [35]

Wild Bill Hickok contributed to the American brand of violence, and his mythical life style is an example of it. "He tried to degrade me," he said, "and I could not stand it, you know, for I am a fighting man." These last words—"I am a fighting man"—reflect a characteristic attitude of ours. Wild Bill was and remains an American folk hero. Our adoration of this type of hero is clear evidence that we identify with such personalties; we think of ourselves as "fighting men." When President

Franklin Delano Roosevelt said in his famous Philadelphia speech in 1944, "I'm an old fighter, and I love a good
fight," the audience chuckled approvingly.

The tradition of the "fighting man" goes back to our
very origins as a nation—to the American colonials, whose
patriots like Patrick Henry and James Otis have been
called "muscular radicals" by British historians Law-
rence Henry Gipson and Charles M. Andrews,[36] a term
that, besides indicating the willingness and preparedness
of those patriots to fight, shows the European disdain for
the kind of revolutionary the early American environment
produced. What should not be forgotten, though, is
that in this early environment were embodied the hopes
and aspirations—and the resulting frustrations—that lin-
gered in the promise of the New World. Because these
frustrations have not disappeared from our society, Wild
Bill Hickok represents much of what many of us would
like to do or be if only we dared carry out our belligerent
impulses. When we are challenged, this fighting and
assertive mood emerges to the surface, our inhibitions
cave in, and our emotions are all too easily mobilized for
ruthless action.

It would be wrong to think that Wild Bill or any fighting man is of necessity a psychiatric case, although sometimes he is. As we shall see later, this fighting attitude
reflects an emotional need in most Americans that comes
to the fore as a character trait. At times, however, this
spirit can get out of hand, particularly when people overcome by real or imagined fear band together to protect
themselves. Although we have witnessed such distortion
of the fighting spirit many times in our complex, varied
history, it is possibly most clearly exemplified by the Ku
Klux Klan.

The Ku Klux Klan has always been known as a fear-instilling organization in our country. A persistent and disruptive force upon the American democratic process of law, it set out to protect the community and its values from threats, be they from white or black people. Resorting to illegal actions, it became an exponent of the lawlessness that had gone on at the frontier and that later began to polarize in the South. There the movement received an added impetus through the failure of the Reconstruction Period, as a result of which Negroes and whites became more defensive and fearful of one another. The whites' defensive reaction, combined with their position of superior strength, frequently resulted in the sort of lawless and barbarous activity that has become special to the American scene.

The Ku Klux Klan is not the only secret society in the United States, nor is it the only organization formed to combat the real or imagined evils that seem to threaten its goals, its beliefs, and its own existence. For the KKK the enemy has become the black man and the liberals who they fear would force him on them as neighbor, as co-worker, as brother- or son-in-law.

The Minutemen visualize another, albeit no less potent, enemy—Communism and its threat to their American beliefs and goals, their existence as "free men." Their defensive aggression, like the Klansmen's, stems from the fear of being overcome by a powerful enemy, one who must constantly be suppressed.

The primary purpose of the Minutemen is to prepare their members to overthrow the government through illegal means in the event it is taken over by Communists. The danger is, of course, that *they* will decide when the takeover has occurred. Basing their right to buy and store arms for the coming insurrection on Article II of the Bill of Rights, they are, according to the FBI, obsessed with armaments, including machine guns, rocket-launchers, explosives, and the like. Says J. Edgar Hoover:

The obsession with violence and expressed intent to make the determination as to the occurrence of a Communist takeover are indicative of the dangerous nature of such extremist groups as the Minutemen. They would act as vigilantes, a law unto themselves.[37]

Closely allied to the heart of these aggressive threats born of fear were the violent race riots during World Wars I and II in which 138 were shot, burned, or lynched, many others beaten, and houses and furniture looted, vandalized, and destroyed. In East St. Louis in 1917, nine white people and thirty-nine Negroes were killed; in Chicago in 1919, fifteen white people and thirty-three Negroes were killed; and in Detroit in 1943, nine white people and twenty-five Negroes were killed.[38] These are the official statistics, but it is safe to say that the number of casualties was much higher. The present-day mass race riots in many of our great cities, North and South, have taken on a revolutionary quality, as characterized by the Black Power movement. Once again the confrontation of frustration and fear threatens to rip America asunder.

Violence, an intrinsic part of individual hostile aggression to the point of criminality, has become an essential component of organized crime, which never could have gained its present stronghold in our country without the use of force. Organized crime in America has had its periods of ebb and flow, but never has it gone out of business. Its ubiquity is illustrated by J. Edgar Hoover's conservative estimate in 1969 that the yearly cost of crime was an astronomical $31 billion.[39] The greatest part of this can be attributed to organized criminal activities —gambling, narcotics traffic, robbery, "skimming," extortion, prostitution, loan sharking, fraudulent arson, kidnapping, and murder. It has been estimated that the income of organized crime is $22 billion a year. Meyer Lansky, the financial wizard of America's largest organized crime syndicate, said, "We're bigger than U.S. Steel."[40]

The Law of Prohibition, that reflection of American puritanism which may now be seen as an error in judgment, left the door wide open for racketeers, but it was the average citizen, eager to circumvent the law and purchase liquor illegally or patronize the speakeasies, who really gave the open sesame to organized crime. By condoning it he condoned his own transgression—his own lawlessness.

The notorious gangsterism promoted by Al Capone, who is estimated to have "earned" about $30 million a year at the height of his reign, by Dillinger, and by others during the Prohibition period heralded a new era of violence. The gangs moved on from smuggling, distilling, and hijacking liquor to gambling, prostitution, and narcotics—and from there to murder.

Among the most infamous of crime syndicates was Murder Incorporated,* which specialized in professional

* Murder Incorporated started in New York City in the 1930s, then branched out to offices in Chicago, Detroit, and San Francisco under the leadership of gangsters like Benjamin ("Bugsy") Siegel, later killed; Charles ("Lucky") Luciano, finally deported to Italy; and Louis ("Lep-

killing. Through skilled manipulation, it acquired restaurants, bars, hotels, and nightclubs, and eventually
infiltrated a number of labor unions. Murder for hire
then became a "legitimate" way of eliminating competi-
tors or others who were "in the way." Using some of the
most bestial methods known to man, Murder Incorporated killed sixty-three men in New York between 1931
and 1940 and more in other cities. The gangland war
waged in Boston from 1965 to 1967 resulted in the
murders of forty-five people.[43]

Today powerful crime syndicates spreading violence
and terror flourish within our society. Most notorious are
the Mafia and the Cosa Nostra, which control vast illegal operations in prostitution, labor-union racketeering,
gambling, and narcotics traffic. The Mafia was involved
in a $150 million heroin smuggling ring which operated
between 1956 and 1960 in the United States, France, Italy,
and Canada. During those years large quantities of
heroin were smuggled into the United States and Canada in the luggage of often unwitting immigrants.

The Mafia were originally a group of brigands hired by
Sicilian landlords to prevent peasants from claiming or
settling down on the land in their absence. These brigands later became autonomous and began to strongarm
their former employers as well as the peasants. Calling
themselves *Mafiosi*, they soon established a reign of terror—murder, extortion, rape, robbery, and kidnapping—

---

ke") Buchalter, electrocuted at Sing Sing.[41] Other leaders were Joe
Adonis, Albert Anastasia, and Abe ("Kid Twist") Reles. The latter, held
by the police as a material witness, either was pushed or fell to his death
from a window in 1941, implicating the police themselves.[42]

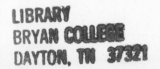

throughout their province.[44] Their terroristic reign flour-
ished to such an extent that the Fascist government felt
compelled to try to stamp them out. The attempt was not
completely successful, however, and as a matter of fact,
the United States government turned to some of the
Mafia leaders for assistance in Italy during World War
II.[45] Emigrating to the United States, members of the
Mafia found a rich environment in which to expand and
develop their illegal activities.

The first recorded instances of Mafia activity in the
United States occurred in 1890, when the Mafia was
accused of the murder of the New Orleans Chief of
Police, and eleven Italians were lynched. After the Second World War the organization, sometimes known as
the Black Hand, spread throughout the country.

Encouraged by their success in illicit activities, international crime syndicates have now invaded legitimate
businesses such as sanitation, book publishing (through
pirating books), restaurants, nightclubs, and entertainment enterprises. At times they have replaced their direct
violent actions by infiltrating corporations and stealing
stock shares. The public is wrong in its belief that gangsters become legitimate businessmen. Once they become
partners in any business, it becomes illegal, since at their
core they are criminals, whether they are thieves, extor-
tionists, or killers.

Organized crime has found people's weaknesses and
exploited them as much as the traffic can bear. One of
these weaknesses is the avarice for money. With the almost limitless supply of money at their disposal, they fix
their operations with police, executives in business, and

governmental officials on all levels. But the fix is not their only tool. Another one, as described in *Life*, is the cover-up.

[It] is of equal importance to public officials who allow themselves to be fixed or who ignore fixes. Case in point: the censoring of the official report on organized crime of President Johnson's own crime commission. As an apparent result of political pressure, specific findings relating to official corruption were watered down or omitted.

Here for the first time are some of the suppressed items:

The success of the Chicago group [of the Mob] has been primarily attributable to its ability to corrupt the law enforcement processes, including police officials and members of the judiciary. . . .

Control, sometimes direct, has been exercised over local, state, and federal officials and representatives. Men have been told when to run or not to run for office or how to vote or not to vote on legislative issues or [for judges] how to decide motions to suppress evidence or for judgments of acquittal.[46]

One reason it has been so difficult to come to grips with crime syndicates like the Mafia and the Cosa Nostra is that the leaders themselves do not actively participate in the crimes they direct and our court decisions have prevented admission of evidence obtained through listening devices. In November, 1957, more than sixty of the Mafia's alleged leaders were discovered at a conference at Apalachin, New York. Twenty were convicted in 1959 of "obstructing justice," but the convictions were reversed a year later on appeal.

Another difficulty is that the members do not "squeal" on each other, even at the risk of being punished or imprisoned. (A notable exception to this rule was Joseph Valachi, who "sang" to the 1963 Senate Rackets Committee, divulging information about the Cosa Nostra that had been previously totally unknown.) One reason for the reluctance to inform is the threat of retaliation, if not directed toward the member himself, then directed toward his family. It is characteristic of these kinds of organizations that the families of the members are under control equal to that of the members themselves. What may be more important, however, is the dependency (oral dependence) each member has upon the other, a fact that is instrumental in forcing the members to keep "mum" (oral inhibition) and not inform on their fellows. This mutual dependency is more prevalent in a criminal organization than in any other group.

Organized crime has become almost a law unto itself. Each member of the Mafia and the Cosa Nostra is blood brother to every other. Since membership is hard to come by, any member is proud and honored to belong. Anyone who does not follow the dictates of the leader is shot or burned to death.[47]

We may ask why organized crime has become such a predominant manifestation in American life, more so than in any other country. A fundamental factor is our own attitude. Organized group and individual violence and crime owe much of their continuing existence to the indifference or fear of most of our citizens. The crime syndicates, since they are much more powerful and persistent than any protection the police can provide, operate so openly because they can intimidate many of their victims into silence through violence or threats of violence.

Another factor is the affluence of our society. In a land where everything is within reach, greater opportunities are offered for those who want to move ahead through honest and hard work. At the same time, however, there are greater opportunities for moving ahead through illegal means, through threats and violence. Our proffered abundance has also created an unusually high degree of competition, giving rise to an almost merciless struggle for power and success. While on the one hand, our material resources have become an important stimulus for American wealth and success, on the other hand these very material resources have become a significant foundation for group and individual violence and crime. Since all behavior, including aggressive acting out, is rooted in our emotional needs, which are related to our kind of society, our environmental affluence can be seen to contribute to the emotional atmosphere that has promoted the spread of violence and crime.

Again we see an American phenomenon of violence, which we have created, and which has been nurtured by the physical environment and emotional climate of our society.

The many manifestations of individual and mass violence that we have observed, which are constantly festering and erupting within our civilization, weaving themselves practically unchecked through the fabric of American life, must lead us to the conclusion that violence is part and parcel of our existence.

Hidden
Violence

"They used to say that there was an impulse to see and enjoy violence vicariously in all of us.

"Ladies and gentlemen, we do not only tolerate violence, we love it. We put it on the front pages of our newspapers. One-third or one-fourth of our television programs use it for the amusement of our children. Condone! My dear friends, we love it." [1]

Thus spoke Dr. Karl Menninger.

Wittingly or unwittingly, we do more than condone violence in our lives. To put it bluntly, we seek it out. If we stop to think of what most excites us when we read the newspapers, we will have to admit that it is not always the accounts of international, political, and economic news. Rather, it is the latest lurid accounts of divorce scandal, suicide, rape, and murder which, although we may not read them first, we certainly devour with a great degree of fascination and relish. In this way we express our hidden violence.

By hidden violence I refer to the dormant hostile and aggressive feelings present in us that, when activated, may manifest themselves as destructive acts. These latent hostile emotions can also be stirred up through a kind of contagion when someone else is hurt or killed, although we have had no part in the violent act.

Familiar to us from newspaper accounts is the image of a crowd on a sidewalk gazing up at a solitary figure on a ledge of a high building, waiting impatiently and urging the figure, with strident screams, to jump. We need not look too closely to notice the savage and sadistic inclinations of this crowd who have already fantasized the would-be suicide hurtling to his death and would be profoundly disappointed if he changed his mind.

Similarly, many people are gleeful on hearing that a prisoner has been sentenced to death. Witness Caryl Chessman's painful last days and execution, which were eagerly followed in the newspapers with unashamed fascination by sensation-hungry people.

We find ourselves unable to pass the scene of an accident or fire without stopping to ferret out from the gathered curiosity seekers every possible detail of the tragic event. Although sympathy may form a part of our reaction, we are largely motivated by an unconscious fascination for that which is violent and sadistic—a simultaneous attraction and revulsion. We are, in a sense, hypnotized by it, much like the child who covers his eyes and screams, "I can't look! I can't look!" while he peers through his fingers at the witch in the dramatized fairy tale.

At best, we tolerate violence, and this in itself indicates concealed or unconscious hatred. The apathy on the part of bystanders when a person is attacked or killed in front of them mirrors the same vicarious gratification of latent sadistic impulses.

A case in point is that described by A. M. Rosenthal of the young woman who was killed in Queens, New York City, while many onlookers stood passively by.[2] Fascinated when they saw the woman being killed, they repressed the significance of seeing a murder. That they unconsciously enjoyed watching the killing is shown by the fact that thirty-eight people came forth and confessed that they had observed it without doing anything about it. These confessions were in actuality attempts to get rid of the feelings of guilt aroused by their unconscious enjoyment of the act. It is true that they might have been afraid of exposing themselves to the murderer. It is also sadly evident that they acted as people in a crowd, who, because of lessened responsibility, are always apt to think that someone else will take care of an emergency. Many people feel it embarrassing to be concerned, anxious, or upset at a catastrophe. In this dramatic instance, however, *everyone* was a passive onlooker, each acting as though nothing wrong were taking place. Since none of them came to the aid of the dying woman, the act of murder must have reflected their true feelings.

This is, unfortunately, not an isolated incident. The fascination and, at best, apparent unconcern with people's acute suffering is appalling. The following case, not from New York City but from Buffalo, New York, tells the same story:

"I never knew people could be so cruel," said a young nurse today. She said 20 persons had stood and watched a 66-year-old man bleed to death moments after he had been stabbed 22 times.

The nurse, Mrs. Joan White of Buffalo, helped Joseph Osinski, a liquor store owner, after he had been attacked by a man attempting to rob his store Saturday.

"I've heard about bystanders refusing to get involved in incidents in New York City—I never thought I'd see it in Buffalo," she said. . . .

"I always thought any human being would try to help another in trouble," she said. "People just let him lie there like an animal.

"I used to think people would help even an animal. Several were gazing through a restaurant window like they were watching a movie.

"It makes me sick to my stomach.

"No one offered to call help or offered to give me a dime," she added.

Mrs. White called an ambulance and accompanied Mr. Osinski to the hospital.[3]

It may be true that society hates its criminals, but it is equally true that people love their crimes.

While most of us are intimidated by criminals, racketeers, or juvenile gangs, our own apathy, which acts as a strong stimulus to their activities, indicates that we derive secret satisfaction from them.

We do not often realize the significance of the willing patronage on the part of a good many of our otherwise respectable citizens that wittingly or unwittingly helps to maintain the crime syndicates. Were it not for these people, who actively seek ways to give a bribe, to purchase narcotics, to place an illegal bet, or to get a bargain price on stolen goods, criminals would have far fewer outlets for their trade. Our ethical principles have so degenerated that organized crime is now run not only by seasoned criminals but often by "average" citizens. A visible difference between organized crime today and that of previous years is the extent to which it has infiltrated legitimate business and made the average citizen a more or less willing partner. The practice so implicitly and often openly accepted by business firms themselves—the undercover system of kickbacks, bribery, padding of expense accounts, etc—testifies to this fact.

As if the reality of violence and crime today were not grim enough, we relive the theme in books. The "In Cold Blood" phenomenon has been discussed. And Andrew Turnbull said of Hemingway: "Another source of his wide appeal was a strain of violence that spoke to something in the American temper, and a style which, on the simplest level, had a good deal in common with the sock and biff of journalism." [4]

An example of how hidden violent impulses can be mobilized is well described in the following selection from a report in the *New Yorker* magazine:

A couple of weeks ago, I heard there was to be a parade starting here in support of our troops in Vietnam, and since I hold some rather anxious opinions—shared, I should add, by a great many of my friends—on how our troops might best be supported at this time, I rummaged around and found an old shirt cardboard from the laundry and lettered a message on it with a felt pen. "SUPPORT," I wrote in large red letters, and in smaller letters, "Our Troops Through a Negotiated" and then a large "PEACE." Below this, I added, "STOP BOMBING." Then I propped the sign in a window facing the street. I did not expect, of course, that this act would win me any particular approbation, or even that it would make converts. It was merely a gesture, but one that it somehow seemed important for me to make. I was more or less prepared for the angry boos that rose from below whenever the sign was noticed by members of the early groups in the parade. I was less prepared,

I must admit, to see swarms of men and women, of all ages, shaking their fists and making obscene gestures at me and my wife and children whenever we glanced out the window. In time, there were unmistakable invitations for me to come down to the street and subject myself to violence. As more and more marchers crowded into our block (it was a big parade), the sounds of anger increased, and then there was a clank and a roar of pleasure as the first full beer can banged against a sill and splattered our window with beer. Within minutes, the air was full of flying stuff. Bottles splintered against the front of the house, and shattered eggs and more beer ran down the window panes. I removed the sign. I was frightened that morning. I was frightened by the faces down there—by a look I had never seen or expected to see on my street or in my city. As I peered down and saw missiles being heaved at me out of a sea of American flags, it came to me—as it must have come to many other people that day and the next day, when they learned of other and far more serious incidents of violence during the parade—that I had been too comfortable behind my windows, too sure of my right to put up a bit of cardboard with my scrap of opinion on it. But what stays with me now is not just that unhappy new knowledge, or the knowledge that the mob silenced me. *Most of all, it is the memory of how I felt at that last moment when I looked down at those people through my smeared windows. I hated them. All I wanted at that moment was a flamethrower; I wanted to destroy them. They had carried the day. They made me one of them.*[5]

When we look at our national sports, we find violent impulses at play. In boxing, primitive hostile aggressions are put into action while the sole purpose is to knock out the adversary, giving vent to the instinct for destruction. The result has all too often been severe brain damage or

death. Is it coincidental that most of the boxing cham-
pions have been Americans?

Another sport that threatens, not without reason, to
become the "national pastime" is football. While, of
course, strategy and tactics are very important to the
game, in the final analysis, twenty-two men on a field are
slamming into each other at each play. It is a contest of
forces—the moment for which the fascinated spectators
have been waiting. It is noteworthy that interest in baseball has been waning lately because it is considered too
tame, while fascination with football has increased. One
reason may be the drama that football displays on television, where baseball is hard to follow: the camera can
focus down on a specific skirmish, catapulting the viewer
into the melee. The homosexual leanings that may come
to the fore during the close physical contact between the
players may be another factor, as it is in the enjoyment
of wrestling. More important, however, is the thrill the
spectators experience, the outlet for their own hostile aggressions, the vicarious pleasure derived from watching
how one player can prevent the other from keeping the
ball by force.

The popularity of war toys is another expression of
our hidden violent impulses. There is hardly a boy who
does not spend much of his time playing with toy guns
—gifts from family or friends. War toys and toys designed for "make-believe" violence fill the stores. A recent
addition to the war-toy arsenal is a toy bomb that, when
dropped on a toy airplane, simulates an explosion. Thus
do we inject hidden violent attitudes not only into our
own amusements but also into our children's games.

One theory holds that we can release hostile aggression through play or games in much the same way children do in "make believe." In order to satisfy our appetite for violence, we resort to substitutes. We flock to the movies and sit glued to TV programs that glorify brutality. We forget, though, that this "make-believe" violence is not child's play to children, who cannot recognize the difference between fantasy and reality. Few parents today even screen the films and TV programs their children may see, although many voices have been raised in protest against the preponderance of barbarousness displayed on these media.

The New York *Herald Tribune,* for example, reported that "Los Angeles has the highest crime rate in the world —on TV." In monitoring the city's seven television stations during the week of June 21, 1964, the article continued, the National Association for Better Radio and Television counted "501 electronic killings in 192 telecasting hours, or more than 2½ premeditated slayings per hour. Other TV crimes: 394 attempted murders, 61 robberies, 40 kidnappings, 5 suicides, murder conspiracies and arson. Mrs. Clara S. Logan, NAF-BRAT president, noted that more than two-thirds of the crimes were committed during the children's hours before 9 P.M." [6]

One mother, at least, questioned the networks' programming of terror cartoons under the headline "Horror in the Morning":

In my opinion—as the mother of two children, aged two and three—the networks should neither want nor be allowed to televise the horror cartoons aimed at children. Since these shows are on when the older kids are at school, I must deduce that "horror" cartoons are meant for those under five. On the few occasions my three-year-old has sat through these cartoons, he has been confused as to whether they were real or make-believe. I've since worked out which he can watch. But what about the children whose parents are glad to see them sitting quietly and not squabbling with each other or cluttering up the house with toys? These poor children are in a dilemma as to what is right and what is wrong.[7]

People in general and parents in particular are not aware that when we are face to face with violent acts, whether real or presented through the entertainment media, our resistance to our own violent inclinations is lowered. Alexander Pope's words come to mind:

> Vice is a monster of so frightful mien,
> As to be hated needs but to be seen;
> Yet seen too oft, familiar with her face,
> We first endure, then pity, then embrace.

The great storehouse of latent, invisible violence that has worked its way gradually and pervasively into our lives portends as much potential harm to ourselves and our society as does manifest violence. The line between hidden and manifest violence is often imperceptible. The emotional and mental elements of both are similar, and their destructive aftermaths are not so dissimilar as one would think. Violence to our feelings, to our senses, can be in many cases as devastating as physical violence. Hidden hatred and aggression do not kill, but they inflict a kind of living death.

The human mind is an elusive entity. Unable to sound its depths, we live in a sea of unconscious emotions and impulses whose nature we may feel but whose significance we are oblivious to. Hidden violence closely connected to unconscious hatred is often expressed indirectly. Cutthroat business operations, the high divorce rate, and such self-destructive tendencies as alcoholism and reckless driving are manifestations of the same instinctual forces that lead to criminal acts.

Our dormant violent impulses find open—and often socially accepted—expression in the activities of the various hate groups prevalent in our society. It is estimated that in 1939, simultaneous with the growing Nazi menace in Germany, America had more than five hundred varied Fascist and anti-Semitic groups.[8] This was was heyday of such organizations as the German-American Bund, which branched out to practically every large city in America, and the Reverend Charles E. Coughlin's National Union for Social Justice.

During the post-World War II era many of the organized hate groups waned considerably or disbanded. But there was much lingering resentment among Americans toward the Germans, the Japanese, and the refugees from Europe; and even though many Negroes, Jews, and Catholics had gained greater status through participating in the war and in jobs they had an opportunity to fill as a result of wartime personnel shortages, prejudice and discrimination was as prevalent as before, although not always in an organized form. The strongest wave of hate during this period was promoted by Senator Joseph McCarthy, who created an atmosphere of fear and intimidation that lasted several years.

No sooner had McCarthy been dethroned than hate found a new outlet. The United States Supreme Court's 1954 decision outlawing segregation not only revived the old Ku Klux Klan but also brought thirty new segregationist groups into being. While early in 1954 some thirty-five definite hate groups existed, by the end of that year they numbered seventy-five.[9] And in 1964, "in addition to the clearly definable hate groups, approximately 250 organizations, radical rightist in outlook, were in operation. Twenty-five radical rightist groups may be considered national in scope."[10]

As the right-wing hate groups increased in size and number, they grew in power, as indicated by the funds they spent:

An exhaustive study by Group Research, Inc., using the public portions of reports of tax-exempt groups to the Internal Revenue Service and other data, produced an estimate that conservative organizations, from the John Birch Society to the National Defense Committee of the Daughters of the American Revolution, spent $30 million in 1963.

Officials of the Washington research organization, which often surveys right-wing activities said this week that figures available so far in 1964 had indicated the trend was continuing.[11]

In 1966, the right wing raised and spent between forty and fifty million dollars, according to Group Research.[12]

The power these radical groups wield today is shown by the extent of the propaganda they disseminate. A searing attack upon President Johnson was contained in the book *A Texan Looks at Lyndon, A Study in Illegitimate Power*, written by wealthy Texas rancher and historian J. Evetts Haley, who heads a group called Texans for America. Sales of this $1 paperback, which was distributed through outlets specializing in radical right-wing literature put out by such groups as the John Birch Society and the Christian Crusade, were estimated to have reached nearly one million copies throughout the country after it had been out for only a month.* One organization, Constructive Action, Inc., distributed about three million copies of ultraconservative books during the Presidential election of 1964.[14]

While much of this propaganda took place during a Presidential election, a time when tempers traditionally run high, hate propaganda from the same sources has continued with unabated force. *Every week*, through radio and television alone, countless audiences are exposed to at least seven thousand programs (which have multiplied rapidly from fewer than five hundred in 1958[15]) produced or sponsored at an estimated cost of $10 million by extremist groups in all fifty states. To measure the impact of such extensive propaganda is impossible.

Of course, everyone has a right to advocate his political views. But when they are charged with fear and hate, a high degree of emotional involvement is indicated, which may tend to distort viewpoints and release hidden violent impulses. This is reflected in the ultraconservatives' intense preoccupation with furthering their cause. A recent study by political scientists has shown that ultraconservatives are far more active in partisan politics than is common for people of their educational and social backgrounds.[16]

Why is ultraconservatism, the aggressive expression of

* Other books and pamphlets flooding the market from obviously extremist right sources were John A. Stormer's *None Dare Call It Treason* and Phyllis Schafly's *A Choice Not An Echo*. One bookstore near Los Angeles claims to have sold some 55,000 copies of *Treason*—mostly in lots of a thousand or more—to doctors and lawyers who distributed the book to clients and colleagues.[13]

unfounded fears, more prevalent in the United States than in any other country? One reason is that ours is a land of immigrants or descendants of immigrants against whom the "old comers" have always had to defend themselves. When they saw their way of life threatened and the American Dream menaced, it was natural that they would defend their existence with all the means at their disposal. It may perhaps sound strange that our attitudes and social institutions are considered conservative, since we are known to be a pragmatic people, known to experiment, known for bringing up new ideas and forms to better our lot. Yet on a deeper level, the emotional one, the conservative feeling still holds, particularly intensified by the fact that the United States was originally an agrarian society—as for instance, was France—the sort that has traditionally fostered such an attitude.

Another contributing factor is that our social structure was originally built upon beliefs and ideas in the greater part stemming from Puritans who were unwilling to accept beliefs other than their own. The Indians were killed off or put on reservations, and the Negroes were either enslaved or excluded from our community life, producing a closed social system.

The mobility of our society has been instrumental in reinforcing our conservatism. Thanks to the vastness and richness of our country, people have moved around from place to place, as well as up and down the ladder of social status. Although our society has become industrialized, our instinctive patterns of behavior have not changed. While technology made life easier for us, instinctively we have remained the same human beings, unsure about our future and wanting to hold onto what we had. Isn't it therefore natural to believe that especially in a mobile society such as ours, people would try to keep their way of life as it had always been? Wouldn't they be defensive, and more often than not, when threatened, put into motion their hidden violent impulses?

A group of extremists that has catapulted itself into the limelight in recent years is the John Birch Society, founded in 1958, who cloak their fearful, hostile feelings under a veil of patriotism designed to create the impression that they are saving America from certain disaster at the hands of the Communists. Laudable as it is to protect our country by exposing any group that seeks to overthrow the government, this group, feeling threatened, operates almost exclusively from a base of anger generated by fear. In return, those whom they threaten become insecure and, therefore, equally angry. Hidden violent aggressions are aroused on both sides, and the opposition is personified in both cases as "total evil." The emotional climate pictured here is well described by Matthew Arnold:

> We are here as on a darkling plain
> Swept with confusing alarms of struggle and flight
> Were ignorant armies clash by night.

The John Birch Society's thinking is expressed in *The Politician,* written by Robert Welch, founder of the society, and published by him in 1963.* Copies of the un-

---

* In the epilogue of the published edition, page xvii, Welch states that the manuscript ". . . was begun in December 1954 and, with repeated additions, finished in June 1958." On this same page, Welch indicates that the purpose of the epilogue was to add evidence covering the period from the completion of the manuscript through 1962, because:

Although we are still too close to the picture to attempt to fix republished manuscript were originally given by Welch to selected members of the Society and later withdrawn, apparently going underground. As a result, many people doubted the existence of the book. It does, indeed, exist,* and deals primarily with Welch's accusations of Communism against former President Dwight D. Eisenhower, John Foster Dulles, Earl Warren, and many other prominent Americans. Following is an excerpt from these pages:

At this stage of the manuscript, however, perhaps it is permissible for me to take just a couple of paragraphs to support my own belief. And, it seems to me that the explanation of sheer political opportunism, to account for Eisenhower's Communist-aiding career, stems merely from a deep-rooted aversion to any American to recognizing the horrible truth. Most of the doubters, who go all the way with me except to the final logical conclusion, appear to have no trouble whatever in suspecting that Milton Eisenhower is an outright Communist. Yet they draw back from attaching the same suspicion to his brother for no other reason than that one is a professor and the other a President. While I too think that Milton Eisenhower is a Communist, and has been for 30 years, this opinion is based largely on general circumstances of his conduct. But my firm belief that Dwight Eisenhower is a dedi-

---

sponsibility on individuals in the new Administration by cumulative evidence, as we can now do for the period from 1952-1960, it is clear that there has been no change in the course or purpose of our Government as a whole. It still remains, as it became under Eisenhower, the most powerful force promoting the world-wide Communist advance. The copyright page bears the following imprint at the bottom: "Privately printed for Robert Welch, Belmont 78, Massachusetts."

* As a matter of fact, thirteen pages of the original text (which was somewhat revised in the published manuscript) were printed into the *Congressional Record of the United States Senate* on April 12, 1961.

cated, conscious agent of the Communist conspiracy is based on an accumulation of detailed evidence so extensive and so palpable that it seems to me to put this conviction beyond any reasonable doubt.

The arguments used by Welch are also illustrated in two succeeding paragraphs from the same tract:

This inevitably prompts the third question, as to how a man born in the American Midwest who went through the U.S. Military Academy could ever become a convert to communism (or even to the service of communism for personal glory. . . .

Those converts are most likely to occur among warped but brilliant minds, which have acquired either by inheritance or circumstances a mentality of fanaticism. And it should be no surprise to anybody that Eisenhower was raised with this mentality of fanaticism, for as recently as 1942 his mother was arrested for participating in a forbidden parade of Jehovah's Witnesses. . . . Everything Eisenhower has done for the past 18 years can be fitted into the explanation based on that type of mentality. And I do not believe that the events of his personal story during those 18 years can be satisfactorily explained in any other way.

When such unrealistic thoughts grow out of free-floating anxiety and fear, the person harboring them feels secure in his accusations, however monstrous they may be.

The Birch Society's organ, *The Bulletin,* advocates members' support of other hate movements that are clearly anti-Catholic or segregationist, such as the ultraconservative Christian Crusade led by Billy James Hargis.[17]

The membership is secret, but judging from the millions of dollars donated to the large staff at the headquarters in Belmont, Massachusetts, and the network of

libraries and sales outlets throughout the United States, we must assume that it is large and represents money and influence.

Birchers are against the United Nations, foreign aid, and our "loose" immigration laws. They are against labor unions or any social reforms designed to benefit the people, terming them "handouts." They are opposed to civil rights in general and specifically to integration in the schools and elsewhere. They consider most textbooks now in use "obscene or radical," and complain that the public schools are dominated by leftists. They refer to the American newspapers as the "Communist press," and are quick to recommend use of force, particularly the atom bomb, against any foreign power they consider guilty of "Communist aggression." Most oppose a strong Federal government and favor the abolition of any income tax, although they do not say how they expect to fight Communism without money.

Ironically, the Birchers seem unconsciously to project their own needs to dominate just as much as do the Communists they are accusing. In the face of a threatening and complex world, they fear being overwhelmed and controlled. Deep within themselves they desire to bring back the "good old days" of masters and servants, bosses and workers—when nobody talked of equality, when everyone "knew his place," and when the masses were controlled by the few. Most of them yearn for a past that resembles a fantasy childhood. Like children dependent upon their mothers, they endear themselves to those who love sentimentality and are wrapped in a dream of wishful thinking.

On the other side of the coin are the Communists and

other extreme leftist groups who disturbed the American scene in the twenties and thirties. The paranoid-tinged fears aroused by their subversive or espionage activities led to the establishment in 1944 of the Martin Dies' Un-American Activities Committee, which recommended that 3,800 government employees be discharged for Communist activities. The Department of Justice found that only 36 cases actually required such action.[18]

Truly, the advent of the Federal Government Loyalty Order in 1947 eventually resulted in the 1949 conviction of a number of people for espionage activities, among them eleven top leaders of the United States Communist Party. But the exaggeration and enormity of the accusations reveal a frightening degree of hidden fear and hate.

Prejudice against individuals or groups for religious or ethnic reasons begins as hidden hostility but often ends in open violence. Such discrimination is characteristic of a number of subcultures across the United States. A recent study by Charles Y. Glock and Rodney Stark [19] reveals that anti-Semitism is particularly strong among regular churchgoers and is most prevalent in the South and Midwest. Rising in economic or educational status or moving to the city apparently does not alter the religious basis of anti-Semitism. The study finds that conservative Christians show especially strong anti-Semitic feelings. Among sects, the lead is taken by the Southern Baptists, of whom 24 percent are avowedly anti-Semitic; they are followed by the Missouri Lutherans with 23 percent, the Disciples of Christ with 21 percent, the American Lutherans with 19 percent, and the Presbyterians with 18 percent. The American Baptists and Episcopalians each show 12 percent with anti-Semitic feelings, while the

Roman Catholics show 11 percent and the Methodists 9 percent. Lowest of all are the Congregationalists with 7 percent. Prejudice against Negroes will be discussed fully in the next chapter.

Another form of hidden violence is the often conscious anti-intellectualism that has played such a prominent role in our history.* It represents a hidden hostile aggression against those people who prefer to use their minds for inquiring into life and its uncertainties, raising questions where there were none. Henrik Ibsen described this activity: "My task is not to answer; rather it is to raise problems."

In the words of Hofstadter, "The intellectual is engagé—he is pledged, committed, enlisted. What everyone else is willing to admit, namely that ideas and abstractions are of signal importance in human life, he imperatively feels." [21] Using his observation and conscience in his search for creating a meaningful life, he is basically concerned with problems that he conceives of as issues of his time. Today the intellectual is concerned with Vietnam, the black man, and the atomic bomb.

Let it be said in passing that when we talk of the intellectual we do not necessarly mean the professionally trained man, who might well be called an intellectual although most often he is a technician. But if he is an intellectual, he is able to inject new creative concepts into his work because his doubting mind is searching for new horizons. In psychoanalytical terms, an intellectual is a man who transforms vague, unconscious feelings and ideas into consciously integrated concepts.

Anti-intellectualism, which flourishes in a fear- and

* For a full account of this phenomenon, readers should study Richard Hofstadter's admirable *Anti-Intellectualism in American Life.*[20]

anxiety-filled climate, expresses itself in destructive criticism of the man with an inquiring mind, belittling the
value of his search for new answers to steadily emerging
questions.

What better name could anti-intellectuals in America
put upon their targets, particularly in Governor Adlai
Stevenson's time, than "eggheads"? The hostile and
contemptuous attitude of anti-intellectuals is a defense for
their own inadequacy. They unconsciously think of themselves as "emptyheads."

One reason for this hostility is that throughout our history we have by and large admired doers rather than
thinkers, practical people easily led to impulsive acting
out rather than men of ideas and vision. The first Americans' struggle was with nature, not with building an
organized society similar to that from which they had
fled. Life was a continual inroad on the frontier. The man
who succeeded was the man of action with few words
and maybe fewer thoughts. People became wary of the
intellectual, and this suspicion has survived to this day.

But what is the emotional need of the contemporary
anti-intellectual? Since he undoubtedly feels threatened
and uncertain about his own values and his place in society, he desires desperately to maintain a status quo
position on all levels. He therefore directs his anger
against all those who menace his security through intellectual inquiry. He actively resists the constructive
changes proposed by the intellectual, who constantly
questions society's beliefs and attitudes. He wants people to conform to the "average," to stereotypes, to that
which is fixed, to that which once was. What he really
unconsciously seeks is childish gratification, and he aligns

himself with others seeking that same gratification. This is the reason for his rumination on the past, his sentimentality for that which once was: he wants to return to the real or imagined pleasures of his childhood. Unconsciously he seeks a paradise—the life the American Dream promised him.

A classic example of the anti-intellectual is the late Senator Joseph McCarthy. Although his avowed enemies were Communists, he squarely attacked any person who dared to oppose his views. Intellectuals, therefore, became a particular thorn in his flesh. Raging against Communists in particular and intellectuals in general, he instituted a witch hunt that not only shattered careers and spread misery and tragedy among the guiltless, but brought about such agitated unrest that in his reign of terror, short-lived as it was, he himself became the incarnation of much of the hidden violence in America. His characteristic earmark became one of violence and recklessness carried out with a singular combination of naïveté and aggression.

He never did understand the hidden and manifest violence he inflicted upon the minds and lives of so many people. Having studied his life from available biographies, I have come to the conclusion that he was the prototype of a frustrated, dissatisfied man who could not identify with his father since he desired unconsciously to be the favorite of his overprotective mother. Wanting to take care of her, to replace his father in her affections (the classic Oedipal situation), he also desired to take care of what she symbolically stood for— country and patriotism. His need to uproot or at least silence anyone who threatened his desire, be he Communist, intellectual, or merely dissident, hearkened back to his childhood fear of his father. I am inclined to believe that his dream about America as a pure and innocent country free from Communism and conspiracy represented the innocent bliss of being alone with his mother. Seeking that Paradise of America that was part of his own dream and part of the American Dream, his mental condition transformed the dream into a nightmare.

How could one person for several years keep important segments of America trembling and fearful? Undoubtedly, the many followers who flocked around McCarthy shared his hidden aggression and reveled in his apparently guiltless acting out of their own fear and anger. They admired him, as they admired Wild Bill Hickok, for taking the law into his own hands.

Anti-intellectualism in general, then, and McCarthyism in particular, reflect the "man-of-action" syndrome we have already seen as a paramount example of hidden violence.

Another facet of this syndrome is our fascination with the American robber barons. Commodore Vanderbilt wrote to Charles Morgan and C. C. Garrison of Accessory Transit Company, who had sold his interest in the company down the river, "You have undertaken to cheat me. I won't sue you, for the law is too slow. I will ruin you." [22] Although he did not succeed in ruining them, he crippled and humiliated them, again obtaining control of the company. Fed by a sense of his own power, his egocentricity and his omnipotent fantasies became so immense that he believed himself to be the law. "The public be damned," he said.

Other would-be kings in railroads, iron, oil, mining,

real estate, banking, or the stock market have become
part of our mythology. There was Jay Cooke, who sold
shares of the projected Northern Pacific Railroad to the
public just as he had sold government bonds during the
Civil War. His was a magnificent dream, truly American,
but it came to an unhappy end when his house of finance
closed its doors in September, 1873, thus precipitating the
great panic of that year. And there were Daniel Drew and
John Jacob Astor with their famous "watered stock." It
may of course be debated whether such manipulations
lead to violence, but it would be difficult to believe that
during this tremendous industrial upsurge stimulated by
the powerful robber barons no killing or wanton property
destruction occurred. By taking the law into their own
hands they became lawless.

Rugged individualism, that potentially constructive
quality on which much of America was founded, can, in
a setting of hidden hostility, manifest itself as violent acting out.

Hidden aggression is not only harbored by the individual American; it exists on all levels of our society including our state and Federal government. While our
government has been more than generous toward other
nations, what has been its attitude toward its own people? Strange as it may sound, the first department of
welfare was not established in the United States until
1929 (in the State of New York); whereas in Europe such
departments had existed for a long time.

For us to acknowledge the magnitude of our poverty
was difficult, for it meant we had to admit we had failed
our national heritage as embodied in the American
Dream. Since the poor had forced the admission upon us,

they deserved little more than to be left to their punishment.

Poor people have always felt violated against, and in return, have violated the senses of those more fortunate. There is hidden and open aggression against the poor, against the worker, and against the employee (and now also against the employer for the aggression has come to a full circle). Only recently have we developed some insurance against illness, but only a small portion of the population is insured. During the Depression, companies employed detective agencies to combat unions—as a weapon to keep workers in line. In December, 1929, three million people were out of work; the next winter, four to five million; the winter of 1931–32, eight million. In the fall of 1932, thirty-four million men, women, and children, better than one-fourth of the population, were members of families that had no full-time breadwinner. By 1933, there were fifteen million people unemployed.[23] I do not mean to indicate that the Great Depression came about because of hostile feelings (although there were plenty of them; remember the stock answer "Get lost"), but does not this staggering total of unemployed, deprived human beings indicate that our government, for three long despairing years, was indifferent to the point of outright hostility toward our people? Of course our tradition of hands-off government inhibited active help, but in view of the facts, it is not unreasonable to ask what attitudes lay behind this tradition.

On the surface these attitudes might seem rather subtle, but in fact, they are not. Hostility has been expressed in the form of hidden violence, and as we have seen, hidden violence frequently leads to manifest aggression. In

1931, under the orders of President Hoover, General Douglas MacArthur and his troops of cavalry marched on the Bonus Expeditionary Force—thousands of World War I veterans who had come to Washington in the hope of influencing Congress to issue their bonuses earlier than promised so that they might survive the Depression. The shacks and tents they had been living in were burned, several lives were lost—among them children's—and the force was driven out of Washington. Washington claimed that the Force was Communist infiltrated, but that claim was never substantiated.

Throughout history governments have evinced a lack of awareness, a lack of conscience regarding the welfare of their people. But that we, the foremost land of bounty, could go through three years of a degrading and agonizing depression without much help forthcoming from our Federal government indicates a specific national brand of hidden violence.

We might well raise the question: Are these phenomena of hidden aggression more specific to the United States than to any other country? It is difficult to prove this point directly. The effects of hidden violence can be felt indirectly in the way a state takes care of its citizens by protecting them through public insurance against sickness, unemployment, and old age. European countries such as Austria, Holland, Germany, Norway, Sweden, Denmark, and recently England, have made extensive use of public insurance, while the United States's tradition has been that the individual should take care of himself. Only recently, and partly supported by the private sector, have we responded in kind to the urgent needs of our people, and our response is still far from adequate. Also, one cannot help but wonder, in view of our current history of social and racial turbulence, whether our government's tardy response to the needs of the people is in reality a fear reaction to a growing hostility that is potentially more powerful than its own.

Hidden violence, I therefore must conclude, seems to be more specific to our country than to many others. Only here are violence and lawlessness condoned to a large extent: The Ku Klux Klan, for example, could not have become so powerful unless there were enough Americans in whom feelings of violence and hate could be easily evoked. It could not operate so widely and for so long unless enough of us were willing to close an eye to its lawless activities. Our indifference, although an act of omission rather than commission, is still a condoning of such brutal behavior, and therefore, a sign of dormant violent impulses.

It is time for us to examine and to ferret out the hidden violent impulses in and around us.

Racial
Violence

Racial violence erupted in Negro neighborhoods in New York and New Jersey in July of 1964, and reached a temporary climax in the Negro ghetto of Watts, Los Angeles, in 1965, when 34 people were killed, the injured numbered 1,032, and some 3,592 persons were arrested.[1] More violence followed in Chicago and in Springfield, Illinois. In 1966 and 1967 there was considerable violence in San Francisco and in Newark, culminating in Detroit, where 43 people were killed, 2,250 injured, 4,000 arrested, and property damage amounted to over $60 million. The fires and rioting presaged more serious disorder which, in fact, followed in 1968. These events are as significant to American history as was John Brown's raid on Harpers Ferry, Virginia, in 1859, when he tried in vain to arm the slaves for rebellion and was hanged.

Why is most of our citizenry surprised and numbed by this unprecedented mass violence? Can we expect anything else when one hundred eighty million white people keep over twenty million of their Negro fellow citizens outside the mainstream of American life?

This exclusion did not start yesterday or today. It began when our country was founded. The sins of our forefathers have come back to haunt us. And we must fully understand now that Negro violence cannot be ordered stopped; law and order cannot be enforced until we change our basic feelings.

Many white people believe that by God-given right they are better than the Negro and thus justified in oppressing him. For generations we have used the Negro as something like a human beast of burden, allowing him only enough livelihood to insure his ability to work for us. This hidden violence has been part of our cultural heritage for so long that it has rarely been questioned.

Most of us have failed to understand the agony of the Negro because we do not want or need to. We have emotionally resisted looking at his point of view. Many thought that the passage of the School Desegregation Law in 1954 and the new Civil Rights Law in 1964, creating more opportunities for education and work, would abolish discrimination and eliminate Negro slums and unemployment. After the Newark riots in 1967, a number of white people professed to be surprised and shocked because, they believed, "the Negroes had it so good." When racial violence began to mount in Detroit, where more had been done for the Negroes than in any other city, many were at a loss to understand why. The motivation for racial disorder seemed to become still more of an enigma when in the same year New Haven, Connecticut, considered to be the American city foremost in its understanding of the Negroes' problems, became a pinpoint of racial violence. To FBI Director J. Edgar Hoover there was one common characteristic in the 1964 race riots. "Each incident," he said, "was a senseless attack on all constituted authority without purpose or object." [2]

There is, however, "purpose or object" to the Negro riots. They are an expression of a protracted and deep-seated frustration over a situation that the white community has refused to admit. Since many Negroes are only beginning consciously to acknowledge how they feel about their degradation, much of the rioting can be attributed to an almost instinctive acting out of feelings long repressed.

Negroes today are angry and bitter, much more so than only two or three years ago when they still were living in the hope that equality and integration were "just around the corner." Finding that this prediction was as unrealistic as President Hoover's hopeful dictum about prosperity, they have felt betrayed.

Their reactions have ranged from quiet despair to violence. "Legislation," one Negro told me recently, "hasn't brought any change at all: the same ghetto, more unemployment, utter despair." Another Negro, a professional man, said to me, "Having lived here for forty years, I'm quitting. I'm going to live in Europe." He was quiet, but beneath this quietness were controlled anger and bitterness. Feeling trapped in his own country, he believed he had found one way out of his hopeless existence.

A great many Negroes have felt emasculated, robbed of all strength and power by a life that permitted them to be only servile. This conditon is a direct continuation of their forefathers' lives as slaves.

That dark phase of our history has had traumatic

influence upon the minds of black and white men. Most whites have *unconsciously* accepted the fact that the blacks are still slaves. They still automatically expect the Negroes to behave in a docile and passive manner like Uncle Tom, to respond to their white superiors with "Yas suh, Massah."

How well I remember the first Negro I treated over twenty years ago. As would be natural, I addressed him as "mister." When I later on said "sir" to him, he could not hold back any longer. "You say 'sir' to me?" he asked, his eyes gleaming. "Why not?" I answered. Recently he called me, referring a patient to me. Giving his surname, he asked me whether I remembered him. I remembered his name very well. He was surprised. He had migrated from the South, where, although he was a professional man, white people had addressed him as "boy" or merely by his first name, and he had been forced to respond, "Yas suh."

What we see here is a sado-masochistic relationship that has developed over the years between white and black. The latter, regardless of his age or station, was reduced to a "boy"; by infantalizing him, his white master kept him in a position of dependency.

Paternal despotism—a kindly form of sado-masochism —prevents the victimizer from consciously realizing that he is harming his victim. How can he when he loves him? Many a parent cannot understand a son's rebellion. He is only concerned with the son's "good," his protection, his care. The right of a child to his own individuality is hard for such a parent to understand, for underlying his confusion is his unconscious competitiveness with the child. In the same way, many well-meaning Southerners cannot understand the present delinquency of their long-time dependents, the Negroes. In fact, they often blame their intransigence on the "bad boys next door," the Northern whites.

The result of this sado-masochistic relationship was the obliteration of the Negro's individuality. He was forced to dehumanize himself as a defense against the white man's threats. But threat and defense can become ways of life, and the relationship developed over the generations into one of symbiosis, fulfilling emotional needs on both sides.

Of major importance to our understanding of the relationship between black and white is the large number of white children who have been brought up lovingly by Negro women. Since the Negro was considered inferior, this necessarily produced in the white child an ambivalence directed not only toward the black mammy but also toward other black women. Identity confusion resulted from his having been raised by a representative of an unrespected race. Hypocrisy and smugness often resulted, thinly disguising strong hostility and intolerance. While trying to identify himself with the black woman, the white child must have experienced both revulsion and a feeling of forbidden desire for her, giving rise to hatred of himself as a white man.

It is not unlikely that many of those today who wish to maintain the black/white relationship on its old terms are unconsciously oriented toward sado-masochism. Their hidden aggression has to a large extent determined the Negro behavior pattern that has brought in its wake a "social paranoia" in the form of suspiciousness and defensiveness. This social paranoia, fundamentally emotional in nature, has often pushed the black man into the realm of emotional or mental disorders. Now, however, he has begun to break through his complex set of defenses and express his long-repressed anger. The excellent book *Black Rage* by Drs. William H. Grier and Price M. Cobbs [3] contains a fascinating study of his necessarily defensive life style.

How ironic is our moral indignation at the Negro revolt when we recall the many acts carried out by white people in the name of patriotism! The Founding Fathers looted, burned, even hanged some of their Tory opponents. In 1773 in Massachusetts Sam Adams set up several "local committees of correspondence" for the purpose of active rebellion, and Thomas Jefferson and Patrick Henry organized similar committees in Virginia and other colonies. We are proud of our forefathers' rebellious acts, and yet we unconsciously expect the Negro to accept his inequality as if he were still the downtrodden slave of bygone days.

It will take more than legislation to remove discrimination. The white man's prejudice goes into the core of his mind, into his whole being, and governs his whole attitude and behavior toward black people.

The human mind with its powerful unseen emotions has a stranglehold on our behavior. We believe we are the masters of our feelings, while more correctly they— in particular the unconscious ones—master our behavior and actions. They make us live in the past, conditioned by habits we accept and take for granted. While today the Negro is considered a free citizen, the stigma of slavery is attached to him still. And if he has emancipated himself from the chains of slavery, nevertheless unseen emotional chains are still with him. Our prejudiced minds have seen to that.

The past is not easily wiped out. As a matter of fact it can rarely be completely erased. A wound, even if it heals, leaves a scar on the body. It may be unseen, but it is still there. And if the wound has been big enough, in spite of the body's healing power, a weakness may remain.

This also applies to the fabric of a society. Slavery was a trauma, a deep and festering wound on the body of our nation. Not yet healed, constantly irritated by prejudice and discrimination, it continues to fester.

Not too long ago, slavery was an essential ingredient of our society, particularly in the South. Almost all non-English immigrants prior to the 1730s secured their passage to this country under a form of "white servitude." While the servitude usually lasted four to seven years, often servants tied themselves for life. George Washington himself ordered purchase of servants for his Virginia plantation in 1784. And at the end of the eighteenth century the general opinion was that "tampering with the indenture system would bring severe social and economic dislocations." [4]

Until 1660 no particular difference was made between white and Negro indentured servants. [5] The first Negroes —twenty of them—came to Virginia as bond servants in 1619. As early as in the 1630s Maryland planters began to use Negroes as laborers. But the importation was slow, since most of the farm labor was carried out by whites. It is estimated that in 1681 in Virginia there were only 3,000 Negroes. But then the slave trade began routinely and brutally, spurred by the "selling and sailing triangle, molasses, rum, slaves—slaves, rum, molasses." By 1708

Virginia had 12,000 Negroes. By 1756 the number had
risen to 120,156,[6] and the Negro slaves made up over 40
percent of the population.[7] "By the eve of the American
Revolution Virginia's population was nearly evenly divided between Negroes and whites; in South Carolina
the Negroes outnumbered the whites by two to one."[8]
By 1782 there were in Virginia alone 259,230 Negro
slaves.[9] Including all other states in 1790, out of a white
population of about 3.1 million, there were almost 700,000
slaves and almost 60,000 free Negroes. By 1860 there were
5 million slaves.

This slave system, although on a much smaller scale,
extended also to the North: to Newport, Providence, Boston, and Salem. In a Boston newsletter in the 1770s ad-
vertisements appeared for "every new importation of
fripperies and lace," followed by the notice of cargoes
altogether different—but cargoes that paid for the luxuries
advertised: "To be sold, a parcel of likely Negroes, from
ten to twenty years, imported last week from Africa. . . .
Just imported from Africa, a number of prime young
Slaves, from the Windward Coast."[10] It was later hard for
Southerners to forget that "the ancestors of the abolitionists had helped to keep them well supplied with
slaves."[11]

Carol N. Degler asserts that lack of recognition of the
Negro as a human being with human rights—that is,
prejudice and intolerance against him—preceded the
system of slavery.[12] The white man's subjugation of the
Negro through hostility is vividly shown by his methods.
By mixing members of various tribes on the same ship,
slave traders diabolically prevented them from commu-
nicating because of language difficulties. The second step

in breaking their spirit was the passage itself, the horrors of which defy any description. The third was that the Negroes, uprooted from their African homes to become slaves in America, were deprived of their native culture. The fourth was intentional breakdown of their individual respect. And the fifth was the systematic breakdown of their family structure. Through these and other insidious means the Negro came to be an outcast, without rights, responsibilities, or privileges. Living in fear of the white man, he realized that he must defer to his master and agree with him in every respect. Every Negro slave was made aware from his early childhood that he was only a piece of property, a piece of merchandise, and that the white people considered him inferior, without morality or character.

In the 1660s Maryland and Virginia introduced various statutes providing that Negroes were to be slaves for life, that Christian baptism did not change their status, and that a child of a Negro mother inherited her status as a slave.[13] They became the legal property of the whites, who could handle them according to their whims. Interracial marriage was forbidden by law. (It was not until a few years ago that Maryland was compelled to permit a Negro man and a white woman to marry and live together as husband and wife.) By the end of the seventeenth century, dark skin had become a stigma, not only of slavery but of inferiority. Color prejudice and chattel slavery had been written into the customs and laws of our country long before there was any appreciable Negro population.[14]

This type of prejudice also engulfed New England. The use of Negroes as slaves was neither unknown nor undesirable to the Puritans. "One correspondent of John Winthrop, in 1645, for instance, talked of the desirability of war against the Indians, so that captives might be taken who could be exchanged 'for Moores (Negroes), which will be more gayneful pilladge for us than we conceive, for I doe not see how wee can thrive untill wee get into a stock of slaves sufficient to doe all our business, for our children's children will hardly see this great Continent filled with people. . . .' " [15] Even in Connecticut, where there were few Negroes, they were forbidden in 1690 to be outside the limits of the town, and forbidden in 1717 to own land.

It is clear that prejudice and hate against the Negroes was essential to maintaining the slavery system. Not only had slavery, particularly in the South, become an essential part of the labor system, but also the law of the land recognized and accepted the idea that Negroes were inferior.

This feeling of inferiority is described succinctly by William Styron in *The Confessions of Nat Turner*, a document of human misery:

This feeling Hark called "black-assed," and it comes as close to summing up the numbness and dread which dwells in every Negro's heart as any word I have ever known. "Don' matter who dey is, Nat, good or bad, even ol' Marse Joe, dey white folks dey gwine to make you feel *black-assed*. Never seed a white man smile at me yet 'thoug't I didn't feel just about twice as black-assed as I was befo'. How come dat 'plies, Nat? Figger a white man treat you right you gwine feel *black-assed* th'ough an' th'ough. Figger when I gets to heaven like you say I is, de good Lord hisself even *He* gwine make old Hark feel black-assed, standin' befo' de golden throne. Dere he is, white as snow givin' me a lot of sweet talk and me feelin' like a *black-assed* angel. 'Cause pretty soon I know His line, yas suh! Yas *suh*, pretty soon I can hear Him holler out: 'Hark! You dere, boy! Need some spick and span roun' de throne room. Hop to, you black-assed scoundrel! Hop to wid de mop and de broom.' " [16]

Depriving the Negroes of their character and soul was mental cruelty, hidden and manifest aggression that was instrumental in eliciting behavior forms of politeness, smugness, fear, anger, rebelliousness, revenge, or violence. In this respect the traumatic effects of slavery on the black people are not unlike those suffered by victims of the Nazi concentration camps during World War II and found later in many of their children. In many cases, even when the parents *seem* to have overcome the effects of the fundamental traumatic concentration camp experiences, these effects are still being transmitted to their child. They unconsciously expect him to replace their beloved dead ones in the family, and this puts a burden on him. Feeling guilty about his parents' sufferings, he cannot rebel or express any normal adolescent resentment against them; he feels that he has no right to. The parents are lenient toward their child, unable to discipline him, in part because they have put too many of their own demands and needs upon him. In fact, in one case I had in treatment, the boy "forced" his parents to move to a suburb where he could have "peace," a move they were unable to oppose, although it put them in a hardship situation. The effects of concentration camp trauma that the parents had experienced had been transmitted to their child, making him frightened and anxious, to which he overreacted with panic.

In much the same way, the traumatic and damaging effects of slavery have been transferred to later generations of black Americans.

Financial motivations were also instrumental in building the Negro slavery system, and they became more pronounced in maintaining it as the white people reaped their profits. "According to the computations of Thomas Govan, for instance, the value of real and personal estate in the Southern states between 1850 and 1860 jumped from $2.8 billion to $6.2 billion—an increment of over 100 percent." [17] Slavery as a profitable system of labor became a defense for the South, but it also sapped their morality and distorted their values. The master-slave relationship resulted in the white man's moral degradation. How long can anyone, in the face of all evidence to the contrary, and just for economic reasons, continue to dehumanize a fellow citizen without dehumanizing himself? The triad "molasses, rum, slaves," became on the psychological level "fear, rationalization, guilt."

Slavery became an almost irresistible force, which Southern whites embraced with passion and fervor. It survived the Revolution with its Constitution and the waves from the French Revolution with the promising sentiments of freedom and equality expressed in the Jeffersonian and Jacksonian democracies. It not only withstood with unashamed force all the severe and constant criticism from the Northern abolitionists and some Southern emancipators; it grew more and became more and more entrenched while white Southerners became influential and rich.

We have heard much about how well the Negroes took

to slavery, as evidenced by their deference and servility, and how well the owners cared for their slaves. While this is substantiated by some records, it was far from the complete picture. Deep down owners and slaves feared and hated each other. While the owners exploited the slaves, the slaves stole from them whenever the possibility arose.[18] The most common slave crime, constantly feared by the slaveholders, was arson.[19] Setting fire to their owners' houses or barns served as a release for the slaves' pent-up, long-standing anger and frustration. This proclivity reveals a revenge attitude on the most basic level—the same attitude present in today's lootings and burnings.

Self-mutilation or suicide were other means of revenge. "[Another] Negro, after being punished by his owner, retaliated by cutting off his right hand; still another cut off the fingers of one hand to avoid being sold to the Deep South. . . . A Texas planter bewailed the loss of a slave woman who hanged herself after two unsuccessful breaks for freedom: 'I had been offered $900.00 for her not two months ago, but damn her . . . I would not have had it happen for twice her value. *The fates pursue me.*'" [20]

Thus the white people were caught in their own web of fear and guilt brought about by the slavery system—and consequently, defended it ferociously. In order to cope with their emotions, they rationalized their attitude, claiming that it was morally right to have slaves. As long as they persisted in their belief that the Negro was biologically inferior, they were able to avoid confronting their guilt. In other words, they repressed it. But it is in the nature of repression that emotions cannot always stay submerged: they are apt to surface when circumstances

dictate—as they did when Southern slavery was attacked. The prejudice and hate exerted against the Negro
today are conscious or unconscious manifestations of
these lingering yet fierce emotions. The power they gen-
erate when they emerge to the surface, breaking the
bonds of their repression, maintains to a large extent the
firm basis and the compelling nature of today's prejudice
against Negroes.

Southern prejudice and discrimination came to be explicitly expressed through the growth of the Ku Klux
Klan. Founded at Pulaski, Tennessee, in 1866, it was a
secret society of young Southern white men whose osten-
sible purpose was the protection of community values.
Although it originally operated as a separate group, other
secret Southern societies of that era, the Knights of the
White Camelia and the Invisible Circle among them,
eventually banded together under the name "Ku Klux
Klan" with a common purpose: to combat the "threat"
presented by the newly emancipated Negroes.

Having accidentally discovered that their hooded cos-
tumes and weird cross-burning rituals frightened the
Negroes, the Klansmen quickly exploited these weapons
of fear to prevent them from exercising their newly won
freedom and right to vote. With open or concealed support from almost all Southern whites, they were eventually
able to subdue the Negroes and maintain their "white
supremacy." Despite the Force Laws of 1871 and 1872,
aimed at disbanding the movement and instituting fair
elections in the South, they circumvented all the Northern Reconstructionists' efforts, successfully ousting the

new Negro-supported political party and substituting government officials of their own choosing.

It is psychologically interesting to note that although the Ku Klux Klan structured its organization after the pattern of the Federal Union, it completely excluded the North, as if reverting to the original Confederate plan of secession. The "Invisible Empire" took in all of the South and came under the control of one central leader, the "Imperial Wizard." Each state was labeled a Realm, directed by a Grand Dragon. Several counties constituted a Dominion, under the jurisdiction of a Grand Titan; a single county, a Province, under a Grand Giant; and any smaller unit, a Den, under a Grand Cyclops. Individual members were called Ghouls.

These names, very much like the gang names selected by juvenile delinquents today, reveal the Klansmen's wish to inspire fear and create the impression that they not only had mysterious attributes but were omnipotent. Their full dress regalia and burning of crosses before their own flag, the Rebel Stars and Bars, was also intended to instill fear and awe in the hearts of their followers. In much of their ritual they resemble primitive tribes who use masks, drums, and fire to conjure evil spirits and frighten off their enemies.

To punish Negroes for the slightest "insubordination" or to subdue any whites who opposed the Klan view, they employed a variety of brutal methods, many of which they continue to use today. They would burn a cross on the offender's lawn as a warning, or they would abduct him and subject him to torture or lashing, or they would even lynch him before a mass meeting of Klansmen to make certain that no one underestimated their power.

The first Ku Klux Klan reached the height of its reign from 1868 to 1870 and continued to operate thereafter, although there was no longer any central organization. "By 1871, the invisible empire had a membership of over half a million, and a congressional investigation that year uncovered hangings, shootings, whippings, and mutilations in the thousands. In Louisiana alone, two thousand persons had been killed, wounded, or injured in a short few weeks before the election of 1868. The commanding general of Federal forces in Texas reported: 'Murders of Negroes are so common as to render it impossible to keep accurate accounts of them.'" [21] It is reported that "from 1878 to 1915 over 3,000 Negroes were lynched in the South" [22]—a necessary protection, it was said, against Negro rapists. Yet most lynchings were either for no specified offense or for such causes as "insult," "bad reputation," "running quarantine," "frightening children," "shooting at rabbits," or "mistaken identity" —the same reasons for killing that were used during slavery. Another report covering the period from 1885 to 1923 states that 4,487 people were lynched, 1,038 of them whites and 3,449 Negroes. [23]

The second Ku Klux Klan was organized by a traveling preacher on Thanksgiving night of 1915 at Stone Mountain, near Atlanta, Georgia. It came into being with the sanction of a charter from the State of Georgia, which granted it lawful existence. Among its chief aims were to "protect womanhood," promote the concept of the "Fatherhood of God and Brotherhood of Man," preserve "white supremacy," and in general observe "real patriotism," and "pure Americanism." In other words, it sought to protect the "innocent" against the "dark forces."

This group was not confined to the South alone but extended itself throughout the United States. In 1920, when the movement seemed about to collapse for want of funds, its fire was fanned by 1) a last-ditch effort to revive it through an advertising campaign, and 2) the aftereffects of World War I. Its ranks were reinforced by overzealous anti-German patriots, excessively puritanical moralists, and people who felt that the law was much too lax or slow moving. Before long the Klan was estimated to have a membership of five million,[24] its greatest strength lying in the South and Midwest among descendants of the first Protestant English and Scotch-Irish Americans who had founded this country.

In the ensuing years, the Klan again gained both political and ideological power, becoming powerful enough to insure the election of a number of United States congressmen and senators, as well as state government officials. Within one single year—October, 1920 to October, 1921—the following brutality occurred:

Four killings, one mutilation, one branding with acid, forty-two floggings, twenty-seven tar-and-feather parties, five kidnappings, forty-three persons warned to leave town or otherwise threatened, fourteen communities threatened.[25]

In 1928, however, the power of the Klan declined sharply as it came into disrepute because of corruption and political bribery that led the Alabama State Attorney General to relinquish his membership, stating that the Klan was a menace to decent government.

Nevertheless, the Ku Klux Klan has always kept itself alive, pouncing upon opportunities such as the 1954 Supreme Court ruling on public school desegregation to renew the spread of its poisonous hate and terror. In recent years, in addition to persecuting Negroes and Catholics, it has intensified its hostility toward Jews, pointing them out as Negro sympathizers and blaming them for the Supreme Court's decision. To estimate the actual Klan membership is difficult because the members are anonymous and figures are not disclosed. Louisiana, for example, claims to have 18,000 to 19,000 members.[26] We do know, however, that there are numerous individual units, that the Klan is particularly powerful in Mississippi, Alabama, Georgia, and Florida, and that the present Imperial Wizard is Robert M. Shelton, Jr.

Typical of the Klan's contradictory attitude toward violence is Shelton's declaration: "We don't advocate violence. If someone steps on our toes we are going to knock their heads off their shoulders." [27] The Klan denied having participated in the 1963 bombing of a Baptist Church in Birmingham, Alabama, during which four small Negro girls were killed. Yet in St. Augustine, Florida, Klansmen were told by a speaker:

If they can find those fellows, they ought to pin medals on them. It wasn't no shame they was killed. . . . Why? Because when I go out to kill rattlesnakes, I don't make no difference between big and little rattlesnakes. . . . I say good for whoever planted the bomb.[28]

We can distinctly see in these people the same ferocious hate and contempt for the Negro that their slaveholding forefathers had one hundred years ago.

Although it might be supposed that the investigation by the House Un-American Activities Committee in 1966 would discredit the Klan and hamper its growth, recent

FBI reports indicate that the membership and activity continue to grow.[29] FBI investigations have revealed Klan participation in incidents involving beatings, killings, and the general denial of civil rights to Negroes and other minority groups. It has been proven in court that the Klan was an active participant in such crimes as the murders of Viola Liuzzo, Colonel Lemuel Penn, and the three civil rights workers in Mississippi.[30] Indeed, the terrorist practices of the Ku Klux Klan have by no means abated; they have increased during the racial conflicts of the past several years, reflecting the Klan's desire to keep the fires of race violence burning.[31]

Recently, moreover, Negro difficulties have been intensified in the North through the formation of the "white backlash." Over the last thirty years more than four million Negroes have migrated from the South to the North and West. While the South a generation ago contained more than three-quarters of the Negro population, today only one-half of them live there.

The lines of combat between Negroes and whites have become more tightly drawn than before, particularly since the School Desegregation Law of 1954 and the new Civil Rights Law of 1964 created targets for destructive and disruptive hate groups. Such a group is the Coordinating Committee for Fundamental American Freedoms, which became the main instrument of the "Sovereignty Commissions" established by eight Southern states, whose purpose it was to agitate against the acceptance of the new Civil Rights Bill.[32]

This emotional spectrum of fear and hate has now brought about the necessary consequence of mobilizing

Negroes against whites. One of the first well-organized movements of "Black Power" was the Black Muslims, who since 1932 have spread into more than eighty cities, with an estimated following of anywhere between 70,000 and 250,000.

Although such verbal aggression as "We are told by the white man to bury the hatchet. We'll bury the hatchet in his head" [33] has come forth from the Muslims in the past, thir activity has been for the most part peaceful. This is really why Malcolm X left the movement, convinced as he was that more direct action was necessary.

Most of the Negroes attracted to this group, which originated in Detroit, were poverty-stricken *émigrés* from the South, with limited education and no future. The Black Muslims offered them hope of bettering themselves, while no doubt also appealing to their feelings of bitterness and hate, which, having been conditioned to servility, they had previously been too fearful to express.

The originator of this cult was an ex-convict who changed his name to "F. Muhammad Ali," inventing a fantastic tale of his royal ancestry, which gave him the right to take the title of "Supreme Ruler of the Universe." He disappeared after a scandal involving the murder of a man by one of the Muslims during a human sacrifice ceremony in 1952, and Elijah Poole, posing as the "Messenger of Allah" and changing his name to Elijah Muhammad, assumed leadership. Under Elijah Muhammad's tutelage, the Muslims amassed tremendous wealth and influence, cowing the Negro press into silence about their provoking activities. Within this militant organization strict observance, severe discipline, and fear keep the followers in line.[34]

Unlike members of the Father Divine and Sweet Daddy Grace cults, some of the Black Muslims have strongly asserted that praying or turning the other cheek will not accomplish their aims. Openly advocating "an eye for an eye, a tooth for a tooth," they have challenged the white society, confident of their ultimate victory.

Best known of the Black Muslims was the leader known as Malcolm X, who, convinced more direct action was necessary, split from them, forming his own group, The Organization of Afro-American Unity, in New York City. An excellent orator, unconcerned with religious practices, he convincingly debated the racial conflict with people of far greater education than his own and attracted followers among Negro intellectuals and professionals who believed with him that the races should be separated if the United States problems were to be solved. In a message to delegates of African nations he asserted the "right of maximum retaliation against our racist oppressors." [35] He was shot to death in 1965.

While the Black Muslims and Malcolm X's followers do not represent the majority of the Negro people, they have spearheaded the black revolution and have adopted an aggressive attitude—a living illustration of hate breeding hate.[36] The violent emotions underlying our society have been absorbed by the Negro through osmosis. The origins of hate begin in fear. What people fear, they hate and, if necessary, will try to destroy. The fear of other people keeps the prejudiced person from controlling his own aggressions. Unable to hold back his anger, he rationalizes it, and hides the prejudice it engenders behind a mask. Thus the Klan and other extremist organizations on both sides loudly proclaim their intention to save America from the "reds," Jews, "niggers," foreigners, and other "seditious" folk while preying on the fears and insecurities of their fellows. Their behavior recalls Dr. Johnson's much-quoted observation that "patriotism is the last refuge of the scoundrel."

While the ideal of protecting the country from its enemies is praiseworthy, the practice by which these groups implement that ideal—labeling as an enemy everyone who does not subscribe to their own narrow, rigid beliefs and relentlessly hounding him, often with violence—is clearly paranoid. In effect, these people behave like the two-year-old who tries to keep everyone else out of "his" yard the only way he knows—by biting, kicking, and punching intruders or throwing things at them.

Fortunately, some people grow up and learn to enjoy sharing their possessions; they are not unduly afraid that their belongings will be taken from them, since they feel quite capable of getting them back. But the prejudiced person, like the two-year-old, finds the world filled with frightening strangers beyond his competence to deal with. He feels safe only with what is familiar, and consequently rejects anyone who is "different."

This is particularly obvious in most white people's prejudice toward Negroes. Our country condoned discrimination and segregation from the start. Indeed, the practice of exploiting Negroes and Indians began virtually with the establishment of the first settlements on the soil of what was much later to become the United States.

The first American settlers were motivated by insecurity and fear strong enough to make them leave their familiar surroundings and migrate to a distant, unknown land. Consequently, they were concerned, once they had arrived in the new land, not only with physical and cultural survival but also with ideals of political democracy that were ultimately to be crystallized in the American credo. This distinctly American idea came to symbolize a new security, a new and freer way of life than they had known before.

The American credo can be defined as the ego-ideal of the American—exemplified by the white, Anglo-Saxon Protestant. Actually, it was an expression of the WASP's need for security and status. By denying the same security and status to other immigrants on ethnic and/or religious grounds—and on grounds of color in particular—he could reinforce his own feeling of having attained it. Thus we see that the American ideal of egalitarian democracy and the American practice of racial, religious, and ethnic discrimination arise from the same motivation: an intense desire for status. Even though they are eminently contradictory, the high ideal and the base reality have all along been complementary aspects of the American struggle for status; they are, indeed, the warp and woof of the very fabric of our society.

But still another reason for the continuing violence and discrimination shown by whites against blacks is centered in the psychosexual sphere of their unconscious emotions. The white man is afraid, as Gunnar Myrdal has written, that Negroes want to rape his women.[37] What has not been sufficiently understood, however, is that in every fear *an unconscious wish is present*: the white man unconsciously wants to rape the white woman, and fears that he may act out this repressed wish. To neutralize this fear, he projects his hostile aggression onto the black man, accusing him of the very same sexual desire he himself harbors.

He may also have designs on black women. If so, he exculpates himself in the same way for this forbidden desire by asserting that the Negro wants *all* women.

Leslie was a thirty-five-year-old Southerner who had lived in the North for fifteen years as an executive in an engineering firm. Though he professed to be open-minded on the subject of race, he worried about Negroes entering his business world, and felt especially threatened when his firm began to integrate.

He was the youngest of three children, ten years younger than his next oldest brother. His closest childhood relationship was with a Negro maid who looked after him while mother worked to supplement her husband's meager earnings. At the age of twenty he tried to make love to a Negro girl, but panicked and ran away from her. Later, when he again tried to have sexual relations, he found to his surprise that he was impotent, and thereafter began to engage in homosexual practices. But as this gave rise to strong guilt feelings, he resumed dating girls, among them a white girl whom he married after a three-month courtship.

He had been, he said, "reasonably happy" with her, and had had two children. He had been a successful young executive and family man for some time when his wife, "like a bolt from the blue," asked for a divorce. This was why he had come to me for psychiatric help.

Leslie was a strapping six-footer. During his first interview he admitted the existence of sexual difficulties in his marriage, "but not more than usual," he thought. Then he added, "I never cheated on my wife."

Important to our understanding of Leslie's disturbance is that he secretly admired Betty, a young Negro girl in his office. He never made any overtures to her; on the contrary, he took to task any co-workers who expressed desire for her. For half a year he had had a recurrent dream in which he had sexual intercourse with a Negro girl, whom he finally identified after much hesitation as Betty. On waking, he would become moody and irritable; he would lie in bed all day and quarrel with his wife.

During periods of free association, Leslie confessed that he resented his "workhouse" mother for having let him down by neglecting him. He scarcely mentioned his father, who apparently might just as well never have existed as far as he was concerned. When he did talk about him he ended up by excusing him for his failure as a father. Nevertheless, one sensed a strong resentment against him; he blamed him for letting his mother "wear the pants." Feeling rejected by his strong mother, he reacted by becoming drawn to black girls, unconsciously looking for the Negro woman who had taken care of him in his childhood.

Though Leslie thought that the Negroes "hadn't gotten an even break," he firmly believed that they were too aggressive in their demands. "They are all masculine," he added. When asked what he meant by that, he answered, "They are always potent, with lots of sex in them, ready to attack."

At the bottom, Leslie felt powerless and anxious, exaggerating the Negro's aggressive sexual tendencies and at the same time minimizing or denying his own sexual inclinations. By projecting his sexual aggressions onto the black man, he could remain pure and innocent, the little child he imagined his mother wanted him to be. His lack of masculine identity—his inability to see himself as virile, as a man—was reinforced by his belief that his penis was small. This wholly imaginary idea, in turn, reinforced his belief in the old myth that Negroes have larger penises than whites, and are therefore dangerous sexually.

This myth, along with its implication that the Negro has no sexual problems, is utter nonsense. Every boy, regardless of his color, goes through a period, particularly in his Oedipal and latency stages, when he contrasts "his own tiny nozzle with his father's mighty hose," [38] and this feeling of sexual inadequacy may carry over, if neurosis develops, into adult life. But the matter does not end there. Psychoanalytical studies have shown that adolescent and adult Negro males, in addition to the usual sexual conflicts, are subject to an overriding—and not, as history shows, unsupported—fear that white men will rape *their* women.

On the other hand, Negroes are often provoked—by the humiliations visited on them and the pent-up hatred thus engendered—to rape white women. The emotions involved in such an act of violence have been vividly described by Eldridge Cleaver in *Soul On Ice:*

I did this consciously, deliberately, willfully, methodically— though looking back I see that I was in a frantic, wild and completely abandoned frame of mind. Rape was an insurrectionary act. It delighted me that I was defying and trampling on the white man's law, upon his system of values, and that I was defiling his women—and this point, I believe, was one of the most satisfying to me because I was very resentful over the historical fact of how the white man had abused the black woman. I felt I was getting revenge.[39]

The violation of a person's sensibilities can provoke him to violent aggression. Although affronts of this kind occur to almost all Americans, the fact that they do so most frequently and conspicuously, and with most vehemence, between whites and Negroes is a consequence of the peculiar affinity that binds the two races together. A white man who, consciously or unconsciously, hates Negroes must feel guilty about it, since hostility always produces guilt. And guilt feelings are a key factor in sustaining any emotional relationship, whether it be in a marriage, in a family, or in society at large. So long as unresolved feelings exist, a relationship, however flawed, will continue to last. The nagging guilt feelings never leave one at peace. And so it has always been with the white man toward the black man.

The Negro's skin color has been of tremendous importance in the white-black relationship. If it repels many white people, it also attracts them: remembering that every fear contains a concealed wish, we may infer that the dread, or at least the discomfort, the white man feels in the presence of the black man also draws him to him. The black man's strangeness unquestionably has sexual overtones. And because sex is thought of as sinful and dirty, it is inevitably associated with the Negro, who, being black, epitomizes in the white man's unconscious mind all that is evil, strange, and dangerous.

But why should blackness, or darkness, connote evil? That which goes on "after dark" has from earliest times aroused fear and suspicion of evil in men's hearts. The night, in which nameless terrors lurk and creep, is opposed to the day, in which everything is clear to sight and nothing mysterious can happen. When darkness falls, the fantasy of sinister men performing dreadful deeds begins to take hold. And since the Negro is dark in color, it is assumed by extension that he alone is capable of committing truly evil actions.

Think of our verbal associations with blackness: blackmail, blacklist, black death, black countenance, black deed, black heart. These and other related expressions (dark day, darkest hour) have always reinforced—albeit on the unconscious level—the white man's fear and hatred of the black man. At the same time, they have had a near-fatal effect on the black man's image of himself. The experience of being kept in poverty and ignorance, subjected to prejudice and discrimination, has nourished his feelings of inferiority, perpetuated his superstitiousness, and depressed still further his already low self-esteem.

The pejorative associations with "black" and "dark" are, of course, directly opposed to the notions of purity, goodness, and cleanness associated with "white" and "fair." Unconsciously, many white Americans call on the latter associations to support their own characterization of themselves; unconsciously again, or even consciously, they tell themselves and others—and sometimes actually manage to believe—that they themselves are without sin or stain, harboring no evil thoughts or desires. For them, the fact that they are white is proof enough of this. Some people, however—particularly in the South, where covert miscegenation has been widely practiced since long before the Civil War—are not so sure they are completely white and pure; naturally, their insecurity on this score makes them all the more anxious to prove that they are.

Like Leslie, many white men strive to sustain the belief that they are better than black men without being able to blank out the myth of the black man's superior vitality.

Behind race prejudice and violence is a struggle for power that has been and still is rooted in the Negro's imagined sexual superiority. Conceiving of the Negro as a stranger, the white man imputes to him everything that is taboo, especially lust.* In other words, he projects his own unconsciously directed sexual aggression onto the Negro—but this projection expresses his *own* wish to gratify his *own* forbidden cravings.

Race violence is thus intimately linked to the *white man's sexual fantasies*. Pitted against them are the black man's sexual fantasies, inflamed by his fear of the white man and his longing for revenge upon him. So white and black are locked in a bitter, continuous, and many-leveled struggle for power. Feeling threatened with the loss of his superiority, the white man redoubles his accusations against the Negro, thereby justifying the prejudices and violence that arise from his unconscious motivations.

Some writers, belittling these psychological motivations, attribute anti-Negro prejudice and violence largely to fears bred by economic rivalry. It is true that many, if not most members of the Ku Klux Klan and similar hate groups come from the poorer and less educated class of whites—those most directly involved in competition with Negroes for jobs. But it is also true that the John Birch Society, the Minutemen of America, and numerous other extreme-right-wing organizations that are hardly less virulently anti-Negro than the Klan include members conspicuous for their wealth and influence. It would seem, then, that the economic explanation is at best an argument after the fact, and that the fundamental sources of such

---

* This reaction is not, to be sure, peculiar to the United States. Virtually every society conceives of strangers as dangerous.

prejudice are, as we have said, emotional insecurity and immaturity which, abetted by anxiety inspired by the black man's supposedly superior sexual power, produced a warped, hate-filled identification for the individual and the group. All people involved with racial prejudice are polarized around this threat. Unable to achieve an identification based on love, they construct one out of fear and hatred. But this negative hostility cannot help them to accept themselves as they are; on the contrary, it accentuates their need for identification and intensifies their lust for power. Driven by the fears that spark their hostile aggressions, they are bound to overcompensate at times by acting out these aggressions in violence.

Typically, a person who joins a hate group is emotionally rootless, in search of his identity. Joining the group gives him a sense of purpose and serves to justify his hatred for those outside the group who represent the imagined danger. But far from helping him achieve his identity, this alienates him still further from his real self. Ignorant of himself, he cannot know the people who, as he thinks, threaten him; he is like the self-satisfied Nazi-era Germans in Katherine Ann Porter's *Ship of Fools* at whom a fellow-German, married to a Jewish woman, shouts in a sudden fury, "You don't even know who you are!"

Ignorance of oneself, of one's strengths and weaknesses, is a salient motivation for seeking power. And this conscious and unconscious quest for power on the basis of a distorted identification is, as we shall see later, the alpha and omega of all hostile aggression, whether on the part of whites or blacks. H. Rap Brown has said that "violence is as American as cherry pie." I disagree. Violence, I think, is as American as *apple* pie: we love violence, we love to fight. The blood from our frontier days still runs through our veins. Racial violence is but one aspect of our aggressively oriented society. Racial violence has become part of our violence.

IV

Sex–An Instrument of Violence

The reason for our fascination with violence lies deeper than we think. Behind every type of violence are hidden wishes and fears that one time possessed us and are now gone, seemingly, to rest. The violent act, finding its climax in murder, carries with it, therefore, a sense of mystery.

Death, ever mysterious, is always beyond our experience. We are simultaneously attracted and frightened by it. Our unconscious does not accept it as a final matter. Yet fascinated and frightened as we are by Death, we continue to be curious about it. But despite our curiosity, Death keeps its secrets.

A deliberate murder, the most enigmatic form of death, is also the most fascinating, since we all harbor unconscious murderous impulses. Many who to all intents and purposes are law-abiding citizens secretly admire the killer because he dares to do what they have only fantasized. Their denunciations of him and cries for his punishment indicate their guilt about their own homicidal wishes. Not all people, however, are aware of their guilty feelings or their murderous impulses.

When the unconscious part of our mind wants to kill someone, it does not necessarily mean for all time. It also has desires to bring the dead one back to life. By killing, therefore, the unconscious means to get the person out of the way and to recall him to life when appropriate. This is what happens when a child (or adult) has death wishes against his parents or brothers or sisters; he need not feel guilty about his wishes since he thinks he can restore his victims to life when he want to.

Our fascination with murder is shown through our avid interest in the mystery story. While the plot varies unendingly, fundamentally it is the same. The central focus of the mystery is: Who is the killer and what is his motivation? All this has to be discovered, by the reader as well as the fictional detective. Many readers involved in the enigma of a mystery story exhibit a curiosity similar to that of the child who attempts to find out about the secret things that go on in his parents' bedroom. Every healthy child has a desire to know what his parents are doing at night in the same bedroom, in the same bed. One evening he may "accidentally" bump into the door, which through some "magic" opens up, or make his way into their bedroom on some other pretense.

Parents often are not aware that their child is curious about sex, that he wants to see what goes on between them. Somehow—and for him the reasons are unexplained —he wants to observe sexual intimacy (the primal scene) between his parents. His interpretation of the sex act, whether it is based on other children's stories or his own

observation of animals, is that it is a struggle, a violent
fight between the man and the woman in which the man,
being on the top, is hurting (a sadist) the woman, who
suffers (a masochist). She is injured and may be killed.

To the child's mind sexual intercourse—the primal
scene—is a bloody crime which, because it is secret, he is
forbidden to watch. Yet he still wants to find out the details about this crime, particularly since (as will be
mentioned later) he is at an age when he is emotionally
involved—attracted to his mother and hateful or resentful
of his father. Even though his parents' crime is a secret,
no one can forbid him to use whatever is in his power to
find out about it. This is just what happens to the adult,
particularly the mystery reader. This fascination with the
murder mystery is in reality a reactivation of the forgotten
(repressed) childhood fantasies he had about pregnancy
and menstruation, defloration and birth, life and death.
Above all, it is a reactivation of the observation of the
primal scene, where the secret crime was sexual intercourse, violent and bloody.*

Believing that the primal scene is a sado-masochistic
act, some children become frightened and anxious, and
their emotional development and outlook are impaired.
In the throes of their distorted belief they are unable to
change their childish idea that the primal scene was a
bloody deed. As they grow up they cannot see facts of
life as they are. In the same way that the mystery fan
needs to indulge in his mystery story to reassure himself
that a murder has been committed in secret (in other

---

* After writing this I became aware of Martin Grotjahn's lucid account of the relationship between the mystery fan and his repressed
sexual impulses.[1]

words, that the sexual act is brutal instead of tender and loving), so also any adult with this distorted view will confuse sex with violence or conceal his violence behind his sexual behavior.

At times sex even displaces our interest in murder, as evidenced in our puritanically colored culture, in which, for instance, adultery is believed to be a much more serious crime than murder, since the former is much more enjoyable. The often unconscious reaction of people to adultery is that they too would like to do it but don't dare, and if they cannot do it, then no one else is going to do it either.

There is a strong sexual element in what we call senseless or aimless violence. No action, whatever its type, is carried out without any motivation. While a violent act on the surface may seem senseless, to the murderer it has meaning, even if that meaning is hidden from him.

The story of a young man I shall call Tom demonstrates how unconscious sexual emotions can affect violent behavior. In the company of his brother, Tom killed a shopkeeper, was arrested, tried, found guilty of first degree murder, and sentenced to death. When it was found that his brother, on whose testimony he was convicted, was psychotic, the testimony was declared void, the verdict was reversed, and Tom was set free after having spent over four years in prison waiting to be executed. Some time after his release he went on a killing spree, shooting seven people in a short period.

When I examined him in the jail, he was thin and unshaven, and his jacket and pants were dirty. "I've been locked up a great deal of my life," he burst out. "At least twelve years in reformatories, jails, and prisons. I've played hookey, stolen bikes, broken into stores. When I was seven years old, I wanted to run away from home." He suddenly stopped and looked at me.

"Did you?" I asked.

"Later on," he answered.

Tom's life was made up of a series of flights from and returns to his home and the repressed sexuality it represented.

His father had immigrated from Central Europe when he was twenty years old and had found himself a job as a carpenter, but since he was sickly, he became depressed for long periods of time, took to drinking, and was unable to keep his job. When Tom was five years old, his father attempted suicide several times. That same year he was hospitalized because of suspected tuberculosis. Later he was again placed in a hospital for about two years for a complicated "nervous" condition. Because of his prolonged illness the family became a charity case, and was compelled to move around a great deal. In the course of five years they lived in seven or eight different apartments. Moved from one school to another, Tom developed a pattern of truancy. He began to steal, and after repeated thefts of money and bicycles, was placed in an institution for two years. He came home to intense conflict with his father. They often fought brutally with bare fists, the mother standing by and encouraging Tom, which pleased him immensely. These fights aroused his subconscious desire for his mother, who, although she cheered him on, remained with his father. Frustrated, angry, and confused, Tom left home.

He went hitchhiking all over the country. When he was seventeen years old, he was picked up twice in the

South for vagrancy. Later he was arrested for robbing a store, a tavern, and a gas station. He joined the National Guard, but after stealing an automatic gun he went AWOL and was ultimately discharged.

He returned home and became a truck driver but bored with this job, and still a wanted man, he left his hometown and hitchhiked to the Midwest, where he gave himself up because "it was cold." Upon his ultimate return to the East he burglarized several stores and was sent to prison. Paroled after several years, he went to live with his mother again, but again he left her and took up residence in California, where he was a prize fighter. There he was caught stealing and returned to prison. When released, he took up boxing and truck driving once more. It was shortly thereafter, in the company of his older brother, that he committed his first murder, for which, as mentioned earlier, he was gven a death sentence that was later commuted.

When I asked him what he felt while he was in prison waiting to die, he answered promptly, "After a while it didn't bother me. But sitting in prison became rather monotonous. I never intended to shoot him, but I was scared when he came after me. I never felt too much about it except when I came back in the evening. Then suddenly I got the shakes and it lasted about half an hour. But after that it didn't bother me at all."

As I talked with Tom he would become jovial, joking that his cell "wasn't exactly a living room," and making remarks similar to what the Negro said when he was going to be lynched: "This sure is going to be a lesson to me." Below his grim attitude were expressions of *Galgenhumor*—gallows humor—obviously an attempt to incite my pity. At other times he would give quite a frank account of his explosive experiences and his encounters with the police. But then he would become cautious, waiting for me to talk.

Never in his life had he had any interest. The only thing he had wanted to do was to travel. Unconsciously he wished to run from himself—to find his mother.

Through a lonely hearts' club he met a girl, fell in love with her (so he thought), and married her a few months later. Up to that time he had kept company with a woman nine years his senior, but he had left her. His marriage was constantly stormy; his in-laws interfered, he said, and his wife would not have sex relations the way he wanted her to. He told me, "She thought sex was dirty. She wanted to read rather than make love. She was afraid of sex."

While married, Tom paid a series of visits to his mother, and it was in the course of robberies committed during these visits that he shot seven people. The reason he gave for shooting the people was "I didn't want to be recognized." Behind these shootings were frustration because he felt his mother had rejected him and a wish to get rid of the man who in his eyes was the cause of his rejection—his father. Interestingly enough, when I asked if he shot the people because he was afraid of being identified, he answered, "No, I never was afraid."

What he really meant was that he did not allow himself to be afraid. Before his fear could surface, he had killed. Getting himself out of a dangerous situation by acting out his violent impulses seemed to free him from his anxieties; he was able to obliterate the menace, and his fear along with it.

Asked why he robbed and killed, he stated frankly, "When society kills another human being, they don't think it's wrong. They wanted to kill me. They look on killing me as if they enjoy it. Even the taxpayers enjoy the killing of other people, and the ministers enjoy it, they watch the execution. If the majority thinks it is all right to kill, why shouldn't I do it? If the majority thought it was all right to go around without pants, they would think it was right to do it."

What did he think the trial would bring? I asked. He answered flatly, "I'd rather be dead instead of going to prison."

"You have a spotty work record," I said. "Why?"

"I could never get a job because of my record."

"Do you think people are against you?"

While denying this, he repeated that he never could get a good job.

Tom had no insight into his actions, nor did he have any feelings of guilt. "If it hadn't been for my mother," he said, "I wouldn't have admitted it."

Asked about his dreams, he answered, "I am a spiritualist. I don't believe in my religion."

He stated freely that he used to daydream about having a beautiful house and a large car so he could drive fast. Most of all he dreamed about pretty girls—all considerably older than he. While boasting that he had had much sexual experience, he showed great hostility toward his wife.

"Is there anything wrong with you?" I asked.

"There must be something wrong with me," he replied. "Maybe I have no conscience. It's funny, though. These things don't bother me. I never was afraid."

"Do you have any feelings for your family?"

"I have feelings only for my mother. Mother is the only one who can make me cry. She takes it very badly. I want to die instead of doing life in prison. My wife didn't want to move to the town where my mother lives, and I wanted to see my mother."

"Why did you return to your hometown in order to carry out your crimes?" I asked.

"It was exciting," he said. "But I really wanted to see my mother."

It was because Tom had never resolved his relationship with his mother that his marriage was a failure. His killings occurred when he was visiting her. Like many other robbers, he was unaware that his conflict about his mother and not money was the primary cause of his breaking into stores: deeper than his yearning for her was a desire to rob her. Unable to bring himself to do this, which would symbolize a sexually based act of violence, whenever he went to see her he deflected this drive into a pattern of robberies culminating in the discharge of a gun. In this way long-repressed sexual yearnings were expressed in violent acts.

He wanted to die for his crimes. "I remember," he told me, "that they were trying to pass a bill here against capital punishment. I was sitting in prison at that time and I prayed that they wouldn't pass it."

Tom showed considerable general knowledge, which indicated a better than average intelligence. In spite of this his judgement was poor and distorted. He had no motivation, either for gainful employment or for being a constructive participant in society. His emotional life was shallow; defiant and bitter, he put up a superficial front of compliance. Unable to warm up to anyone, he could not get along with anyone. He displayed a pronounced callousness, as evidenced by the fact that he did not feel any remorse about the many people he had killed. One of his sayings was: "Most people are honest mainly because they are afraid of being caught."

As I talked with Tom, I could feel the hatred within him which he somehow tried to control but could not master. Because he had been brought up in an environment of violence and fear, he reciprocated with violent acting out by inducing fear in others.

The driving power behind Tom's murders was his frustration at not being prevented from staying close to his mother so that he could show her that he was not insignificant as she thought, but powerful. Most of his murders were carried out when he was on his way to or from his mother; they were acts of revenge because he felt that she had rejected him. The shooting of his victims was a symbolical substitute for ejaculation.

Sexual overstimulation always brings fantasy into play which may trigger violence. It nourishes fantasies of omnipotence to an exaggerated degree in the child, particularly when he has no healthy male figure with whom to identify. Out of his omnipotent fantasies arise feelings of vengefulness because he feels rejected by his mother and believes himself, therefore, to be insignificant.

In studying the life experiences of murderers, we find considerable evidence that they have been sexually overstimulated, particularly through having observed sexual intimacy between their parents (primal scene). This overstimulation can result in profound psychosexual disturbance and feelings of helplessness from which a child often tries to defend himself through hostile acting out, which gives him a feeling of power or omnipotence.

An extreme case of vengefulness, narcissistic withdrawal with helplessness and fantasies of grandiose accomplishments is that of the twenty-seven-year-old man Charles, who on three separate occasions during a single week, killed three people, ostensibly to rob them.

When Charles was asked, "Do you consider yourself a criminal?" he answered, "From society's standpoint, Yes! A rebel against modern times." This distortion is also reflected in his fantasies of revenge against the District Attorney. He told me, "I want to have my sweet revenge." Despite his state of helplessness—he was confined behind bars in a maximum security prison—he imagined himself as having the power to strike back. We will have more to say about Charles in Chapter IX.

When a man commits a violent crime, it is invariably founded on his unconscious feeling that *he must show his mother that he is not insignificant and is able to take revenge upon her for rejecting him.* The feeling of helplessness behind his acting out is most striking. The self-betrayal that the criminal frequently exhibits by revisiting the scene of his crime stems not only from his unconscious need for punishment, but also from his unconscious need to *proclaim that he is not helpless to strike back.* He must show that he is powerful, that this act of revenge belongs to him *alone.* These feelings are grouped around his Oedipal helplessness—"The struggle against passivity," as Freud termed it [2]—and his attempt to restore his self-esteem.

The phenomenon of helplessness, or impotence, is present in extreme cases of violence; it is also present to a

lesser degree in all people who act out their violent impulses. As a reaction to this helpless dependency, they
have to strike out with force to show everyone—particularly their mothers—that they are not such weak people.
If these assumptions are correct, and since there is such
a high degree of violence here, it is possible that our
country has a higher percentage of weak people than
other countries. If so, we must raise the question of
whether there is something particular in the American
environment that stimulates the mother's feelings about
her son, effecting a more dependent attitude. We shall
return to this point later when we discuss in detail the
unconscious social elements in American life.

In contrast to the openly hostile murderer, we see the
murderer in whom all hostility is disguised—often termed
the "model child" type. There is often an overwhelming
emotional involvement between this murderer and his
victim. While the sexual elements here are in the background, they still exert a fatal effect. Interesting in this
respect is Margaret, a fifty-seven-year-old unmarried woman who killed her ninety-five-year-old mother. When I
was called in to examine her at the prison ward of the
psychiatric hospital, I learned that for thirty years she
had held the same job, living with and supporting her
aging mother and masochistically sacrificing her own desires in favor of her mother's demands. Only in the last
few years had she openly exhibited her angry feelings by
becoming suspicious and critical toward her co-workers.

Four months prior to the murder, her mother had
suffered a broken hip and become bedridden. With the
staggering prospect of increased emotional, physical, and

financial strain, Margaret became depressed and suicidal and sought the help of a physician, though in vain. Early one morning as she watched her mother sleeping, she was overcome by confusion and helplessness. Using a hammer she had covered with cloth to soften the blows to the skull, she clubbed the old woman to death.

After receiving a suspended sentence, she came to me for treatment. One day she related a dream:

"I was in a big spiderweb which covered the length of the bed. I must have moved to get out, but I woke up."

In her free associations about this dream she said, "I think of my mother, the good times we had, of Christmas time, what we would have been doing. . . . I have not gotten rid of Mother, which is not the way things should be. I was caught in a web. I must have felt I was in a web."

This dream with its image of her own flylike insignificance and helplessness was her first realization of having been ensnared by a devouring mother. The web covering the bed suggests feelings of being seduced into submission, of a need for embryonic protection, of growing awareness of her dependency, and perhaps most important, of being forcibly prevented from having a sexual life of her own.

Despite the fact that she had remained a virgin and had no romances because, in her own words, "I never had the time," the major part of her sessions centered around remembrances of how good her mother was, revealing her inability to recognize and assert her hostile feelings, which, of course, only increased her dependency on her mother. While her superego retained only the image of her overwhelmingly demanding mother, she created the picture of a good mother who deserved her obedience and love—the ego ideal being made up of imaginary positive maternal components. Having pushed away from her mind her sexual libido for the good of her mother, she had put herself in a situation of helpless dependency. This dependency eventually led to murder—Margaret's revenge on her mother for denying her an identity of her own.

Since revenge is originally family-bound, there is in the violent act often a strange affinity—a symbiosis—between the attacker and the attacked that is sexual in nature. The sexual element, almost unconscious, is present to an overwhelming degree in the families of men who assault or beat their wives. (This sexual factor is often overlooked in the scant literature that exists on wife-beating.[3]) This symbiosis between attacker and victim is seen most clearly in sexual assaults. These are usually sado-masochistic situations in which the victim's role can be summed up as "being seduced in order to be attacked." The attacker often creates the circumstances (of which he too becomes a victim), but the victim herself, unconsciously desiring to be punished, may provoke him.

One case that despite its seriousness had an element of humor is that of a young man who, while burglarizing an apartment, entered a bedroom where a woman was sleeping. He was leaving the room after having ransacked it for jewelry and other valuables when the woman woke up. Seeing the stranger, she became frightened and exclaimed, "Don't rape me! Don't rape me!" The man stopped at the door, turned around surprised, and thought for a second, If I don't rape her, she will believe

I'm queer. "You give me an idea," he answered, proceeding to rape her. The following day he called her to find out how she was and asked to meet her again. She met him one day later—with two detectives. He was arrested, tried, and sentenced to prison for several years. What the court didn't consider was that a woman often unconsciously wishes to be taken by force.

Flirtatious young girls place themselves in dangerous or unusual situations, exposing themselves to sexual assault. The attacker's sadistic drives usually find a target in the masochistic feelings of the victim, who through an unconscious tendency to expose herself to attack, invites punishment for her real or imagined wrongdoings.

Many murders are interwoven with homosexuality, a prevalent form of sexually deviated feelings. Most famous of these, perhaps, was the 1924 murder of Robert Frank, a child, by Richard Loeb and Nathan Leopold, where homosexual elements hidden in the maze of the case played a decisive role.

When we look into the young men's backgrounds, we understand that their meeting was not only a matter of chance. They were deeply attracted to each other. Both of them had been brought up by strict governesses to whom they had been attached. Lacking in self-esteem because of distorted sexual identification, they overcompensated for it by excelling in school. But this did not satisfy Richard Loeb. His high intelligence, coupled with his vivid imagination, set him on the course to crime and violence. His choice was in no small measure due to his homosexual tendencies. As an early adolescent he often daydreamed of himself as the greatest criminal of the century.

Nathan Leopold, whose mother had died when he was a child, was also highly gifted. He too developed a vivid fantasy: from the time he was five years old, he would alternately imagine himself as a king or a slave, usually preferring the role of slave. He adored the memory of his mother, his aunt, and the Madonna, indicating strong identification with the female and his own lack of masculinity. Being unable to conceive of himself as a man, and therefore unable to establish a relationship with a girl, he became obsessed with intellectual pursuits, in which he excelled.

Because of the many emotional and mental similarities between them, these young men were drawn together. Loeb was the aggressor, the stronger one, and he took the lead. Leopold on his side idolized him, becoming in time the slave of his own fantasy. A firm love relationship developed between them during which homosexual practices were reported to have taken place, even in the presence of a fraternity brother. Loeb's desires, however, could not be gratified by these activities alone. His twisted sexual drive had to find another outlet.

After they had robbed their fraternity house in 1923 without being detected, Loeb became depressed because of his homosexual tendencies and guilt feelings and wanted to commit suicide. This was in part a forewarning of their contemplated crime, since every suicide is an indirect form of homicide.

The manner in which they killed and buried Robert Frank shows the unconscious sexual character of their violence. Following the roles they had played in their own relationship, Loeb selected the tool, Leopold the receptacle. They poured acid over the victim's penis, testicles, and face, reflecting their own guilt and confusion about their own sexual identification. Then they dragged the body through the swamps, pushed it into a dark tube (a cistern), and buried it under a railway track. Each act symbolized their own hidden desires.

The pervasive presence of conscious sexual elements in violence has always been feared. Therefore there are two crimes, murder and incest, that have been almost universally condemned. It is interesting to note that while the criminal code adopted in the early seventeenth century by the Pilgrims listed seven capital offenses—treason, murder, witchcraft, adultery, rape, sodomy, and arson—they actually took life for only two, murder and sodomy.[4]

Aggression is a normal part of sex. When because of fear an individual is unable to establish a sexual relationship, the aggressive element present in love turns into hatred. A person who resorts to violence is, in the last analysis, attempting to achieve power whereby he may enhance his self-esteem. Self-esteem is fundamentally rooted in sexual identity. Those who lack a genuine sexual role try to compensate for it by becoming competitive. This is what motivates the unceasing struggle for power between two homosexuals or between a poorly adjusted man and woman: their sexual identity is inadequate or lacking. Many try to compensate for a distorted identity by compulsively seeking status in whatever field they can excel. If they are talented, they may when they are rejected in love sometimes be able to sublimate their sexual drives in the creative arts and sciences. Most people, however, lacking in ability to love genuinely and therefore feeling unloved and insecure, react explosively to sexual failure or rejection. The result may be murder.

V

Instinctive and Learned Aggression

History has shown that most events occur in repetitive patterns. But while the historian presents the picture of an era by describing the leading national figures, the mood of the people, and the temper of the time, he does not explore the great part unconscious motivation plays in the lives and actions of individuals and nations. In order to do so he would need appropriate tools and special knowledge.

We have always had war and poverty because these and other social ills are intimately associated with human emotions. Therefore our social disorganization will be with us until we understand its origins and learn to deal with the feelings that keep it alive.

Psychoanalysis has equipped us with new tools to probe into the deepest recesses of the human mind. These same instruments may be employed in delving into the causes and meaning of historical and sociological occurrences. Some relationship between individual personalities and particular historical events has always been recognized. But it was not history that made George Washington or Thomas Jefferson; it was the men, with their manifold and obscure motivations, that made history.

We have already observed the repetitive patterns of violence and prejudice against Negroes, going back to the time of slavery. And we have seen the expression of individual and collective violence—manifest and hidden.

Through psychoanalysis we have learned a basic truth about human beings: that every pattern of behavior, however obscure, is linked to the unconscious mind.

It was Freud who gave us a plausible working concept of our unconscious mental life and changed our orientation toward human behavior. For the understanding of violence, Freud's map of the unconscious is indispensable. What I will say in this chapter may be elementary and already familiar to the reader. Nevertheless, within the framework of our subject it is necessary to elucidate briefly the workings of the human mind and the fundamentals of psychoanalytic theory so we can establish a comprehensive concept of violent behavior.

We like to believe that our inner life is orderly and that our actions are always logical, but even our most trivial actions are connected with unconscious emotions. Our everyday slips of the tongue or pen, our mixing up or forgetting dates and names, our misplacing objects, all indicate that our unconscious wishes interfere with our conscious ones. To be sure, these mistakes, which on the surface seem only thoughtless, happen to the healthy as well as the disturbed person.

Our behavior while being loving can also be erratic, impulsive, destructive, directed either against others or against ourselves. Unable to control the unconscious, and hence to a large extent human behavior, we are left with a rather pessimistic outlook for the human race. And it becomes more pessimistic when our lives, our property, or what we consider to be the values of our society are threatened.

As human beings, we are equipped to create symbols that express our feelings and ideas. As a matter of fact, we live by symbols. Our flag, our Constitution, even our own dreams and hopes crystallized in the Promise of America reflect our individual and national feelings of self-esteem. If they are threatened, we react emotionally —often irrationally. Our charged emotions rise to the surface to defend our ideals, if necessary by violent action.

One unique situation that underlies our tendency to violent impulses is that the human being as an infant and child has to go through a long period of biological and emotional development during which he is helpless. Of all mammals, the human is the most helpless at birth. This particular circumstance is instrumental in mobilizing fear and aggression, for every infant consists of bundles of emotions rooted in his instinctual drives, known as the id. (From other parts of the unconscious develop, as we shall see later, the ego and superego—in lay terms, the personality and conscience.) The id is the reservoir of instinctual drives and makes up the deepest level of the unconscious. It is the most obscure part of the personality; consisting of chaotic, untamed forces, it is in contact with the somatic and chemical-physiological processes of the body and furnishes the emotional expression of their needs. These instinctual drives contain energy that has erroneously been termed libido. (Freud reserved the term libido for only that energy which stems from the sexual instinct.)

Instinctual drives are physiological cravings or needs necessary for the preservation and continuation of life. These needs are more complex in humans than in lower animals—and also more obvious in that we are aware of them within ourselves and therefore can study them. They are felt as thrusts, motivations, directed toward particular goals. Instinctive behavior in man is specific only in the goal, but is not specific in the activity necessary to reach that goal. This is in contrast to reflex action, which involves specific response to stimulus.

Instinct is expressed in behavior reaction that aims at the fulfillment and satisfaction of a need and its inhibition. When an instinct has been satisfied, it tends to return to its earlier state of inactivity. Our physiological and biological needs are intimately related to our emotional needs in social and love relationships.

The earmark of an instinct is that it requires immediate gratification. Its frustration interferes with our normal functioning, resulting in emotional upsets or disturbances.

Constituting a force within us, whether awake or asleep, the instincts make themselves felt as a need, an impulse that has to be satisfied.

This is most clearly seen in the human infant. If his hunger is not stilled, he becomes frustrated and angry, behaves restlessly and cries, until he is fed. Frustration of his need brings tension, while satisfaction creates relaxation.

All our lives center around satisfaction and dissatisfaction, or as Freud put it, around the pleasure-and-pain principle. The newborn baby tries to protect himself against the daylight when he is taken up from his crib to be shown to admirers. The unpleasant light causes tension in his body, and he becomes fearful and anxious. Instinctively trying to protect himself, he cringes, squints his eyes against the painful light. Then he relaxes. The baby's state of *tension-relaxation* is a forerunner of the dissatisfaction-satisfaction that later is perceived through his budding ego and crystallized into various degrees of hate and love. The first sensation an infant has is that of fear; his first reaction is one of self-protection. We may thus agree with the saying that hate is older than love.

The child's mind with its cravings and fantasies develops much faster than his body. Because he cannot satisfy his own wishes, he has to depend on somebody else; and when his desires are not satisfied, he will feel frustrated and react with anger.

But anger does not arise only out of frustration. It also stems from intrinsic destructive aggression rooted in the death instinct. Our existence fundamentally centers around two poles—life and death. In the final analysis, all our conflicts between man and man, man and society, or father and son are matters of life and death. Human instincts follow the same rules. We are all acquainted with men who become excited or fascinated when there is a brawl. Impelled by some inner drive, they have to get into the act. It reminds me of the man who, when taken before the police sergeant, was asked why he had joined the fracas: "Sir," he answered, "it was Saturday; it was my day to fight!" Blatant aggression is admired as a form of masculinity—sexual power—in street gangs of adolescents ("The tougher I am, the more they like me"), in many subcultures, and in some cultures. It is very easy to make people fight: witness the universal enthusiasm for war. We have, along with our constructive tendencies, *destructive* ones, which, as Freud pointed out, are an expression of the *death* instinct.

A great deal of confusion has risen around Freud's concept of the death instinct. He sees it not as a person's wish or longing for death, but as an inherent tendency in human beings and animals—animate matter—to die, to return to an inanimate state, to "try to bring living matter back into an inorganic condition." [1]

We know that living or animate matter evolved out of inanimate matter. When we remember that instinct tends to return to an inactive earlier state, we can understand the functioning of the death instinct. Whether an individual wishes death or not, the manifestation of the instinct is beyond his power of choice.

We differentiate between two instincts—one for life and one for death. The first consists of the sexual instinct (in the sense given by Plato to Eros in *The Symposium*) and the instinct for self-preservation, the aim of which is to establish greater units and to bind them together to maintain life. Opposed to this, the death instinct (Thanatos) seeks to dissolve the units and destroy matter. From this instinct arise our destructive impulses, either directed outward toward the world or inward toward the self.

These two fundamental drives follow the universal love-and-hate constellation, and are necessary for the functioning of life; they co-exist, attempting to keep a state of balanced conflict. While the act of eating is a destruction of food, digestion and assimilation, which incorporate the food, are constructive activities. And while aggression is displayed in sexual intercourse, its aim is procreation and pleasure. It is this interaction between the life and death instincts, the one modifying the other, that gives life its great variety.

All human actions are directed by a combination of instinctual impulses; therefore all human actions contain elements of aggression. Generally speaking, we think of aggression as destructive, but it can also be constructive, fundamental to the survival and maintaining of the race. Constructive aggression exists in whatever we do—reading a book, moving a chair, painting a picture, or building a house. This type of aggression is delineated as activity.

Although Thomas Hobbes said three hundred years ago that man is by nature a selfish animal, always at war with other men, it has taken us a long time to admit that destructive aggressive tendencies, instinctual in nature, exist in us. We would like man to be "good"; therefore we consider his anger, his violence, and his brutality to be reactions to social conditions (forgetting that he himself established these very conditions).[2] This viewpoint is still being advocated; one of the latest protagonists is Konrad Lorenz, who in his otherwise highly interesting book *On Aggression* has fallen victim to it.

But history has shown us that believing in man's good nature is a delusion. We are justified in applying and comparing animal instinctive aggressions to man, as Lorenz, Storr, and Ardrey have done recently,[3] but this comparison would seem to be correct only insofar as attack-and-defense reactions are concerned. We have to agree with Freud, that man is equipped with instinctive tendencies of aggression and destructiveness that are rooted in the death instinct.

In sadism and masochism we have the fusion of the two types of instincts—the sexual element being part of the life instinct and the destructive, aggressive element part of the death instinct. Masochism, which has as its aim self-destruction, and sadism its aim in hostile aggression against and destruction of others, are the two conditions under which the death instinct exists.

We know from clinical experience that when a man's aggressive tendencies cannot be satisfied because of environmental frustrations, his self-destructiveness will increase with the result that, in order to prevent himself from self-destruction, he has to destroy others through violent acting out. Or if he is unable to exert himself against the encroaching environment, he may turn his self-destructive aggressive inclinations toward himself in the form of self-humiliation, psychosomatic illness, or suicide. Under normal circumstances aggressive energy neutralizes itself, but if it is internalized without being neutralized, it leads to some kind of self-destruction, just as libidinal energy when internalized results in neurosis.[4]

Every child goes through a long emotional development characterized by three stages—oral, anal, and Oedipal—during which fear, aggression, and violent impulses that shape his attitudes in adult life are mobilized. Within certain limits, these manifestations are normal.

During the oral stage, so termed because the baby's interests in the first year are centered around his mouth, he sucks the breast, the bottle, and his thumb and puts whatever is given him in his mouth. The satisfaction produced by this oral activity can be characterized as sexual in nature. Since the baby's oral preoccupation gives him pleasure and gratification, he feels loved. At the same time, however, his oral attachment makes him dependent upon his mother or whoever cares for him. If his feeding time is postponed and irregular, or if the parents wean him too soon, for instance, he will feel rejected, become fearful, frustrated, and angry. As a result of his oral frustrations, he will, as an acting out, cry or even bite. His sadistic impulses will come to the fore even before his teeth begin to appear. Because of his hostile feelings he may, at one and the same time, want to be fed and rebel against it. He is of two minds—ambivalent—toward his mother.

On the other hand, if this oral period lasts longer than one year, he will develop the habit of wanting predominantly oral satisfaction. As a result of not being weaned in time, he will become more and more dependent on his mother, and this will continue through his adult years. Because of his oral orientation, stemming in particular from the cannibalistic part of the oral stage, during which he wants to devour everything, he will become talkative, or smoke or drink to excess. Such individuals are dependent, fearful, passive, and frustrated to such an extent that their frustrations can sometimes mobilize their oral-sadistic fantasies into violent aggressions, particularly criminal sexual acts.

The oral stage is followed by the anal stage, during which the child's sadistic impulses are highly intensified. This stage, which lasts until the child is about two-and-a-half years old, is often termed the anal-sadistic because he finds great satisfaction and pleasure in being aggressive and in his bowel movements. During this time he is toilet trained—made aware that he cannot soil himself as he used to. Because he feels that his mother is infringing upon his freedom, he believes she doesn't accept or love him any more, and he becomes fearful and anxious. He feels on the one hand, guilty of not pleasing her, and on the other hand angry and rebellious. Motivated by his unconscious hostile feelings, he may simultaneously want and not want to "produce," again an ambivalence that becomes intensified during the following Oedipal stage and often lasts throughout life.

In many instances where the toilet training is strict, the parents insist that the child sit until he "produces." He resents having to give away something that is part of him —feces—and he holds back in order to defy them. His enjoyment at their resultant anger is his secret way of taking revenge upon them because he feels that they have invaded his rights. During this period he may become stubborn, compulsive, defiant, and hostile. He may pull another child's hair, bite him, tear his toy car or airplane to pieces, or in the case of a girl, tear the head or arms off her doll.

During these first two phases the child's ego, which stems from his id, begins to develop. It is through his growing ego that he expresses his desires and learns to test his reality situation. Also beginning to emerge is his superego or conscience, which in part takes its start when the parents try to train him: "Don't touch this," "Don't do that," "Keep clean." Gradually he begins to unconsciously incorporate their imposed rules and restrictions into his behavior and adopts them as his own. Whether or not he follows these dictates depends upon his relationship with his parents. If he wants to be like them, he unconsciously identifies with them; if not, he rebels.

Significant to our study of violence is the fact that

aggressive traits and sadistic fantasies may originate during the oral and anal stages of development. Whether or not these traits appear depends in part on the parents' handling of these two stages and in part on the child's reaction to it and his inborn instinctual drives.

The anally fixated individual enjoys acting out his sadistic impulses on others. He may become a stern disciplinarian, cruel, suspicious, and sadistic. All of us experience such regression at times, but these traits are permanent components of the anal character.

Both orally and anally fixated individuals exhibit childish traits of dependency and helplessness that make them less able to tolerate disappointments than other people. They demand immediate gratification, a need present particularly in children and criminals, who, when frustrated, have to act out their impulses in order to relieve their inner tensions. This acting out, which is triggered by the least provocation, often takes a dramatic and violent turn.

Hostile fantasies may become intensified during the third stage of development, the Oedipal stage, in which a boy is attracted to his mother and hates his father and a girl is attracted to her father and resents her mother. It usually lasts from two-and-a-half to five or six years of age.

At this age the child's ego has developed so that he is capable of directing his feelings of love toward his mother and his emotions of rage and fear, guilt and jealousy toward his father, who looms as a rival. Freud introduced the term "Oedipus complex" to depict the child's emotional and ambivalent turmoil, his violent wishes and stormy fantasies, his anger, fear, and guilt at this phase of the development because his drama is similar to that of Oedipus, who unwittingly killed his father and married his mother.

In the throes of this emotional upheaval, the child is on the one hand hostile, frightened, and guilty, and on the other hand kind and cooperative in order to be loved and accepted. These ambivalent feelings are at first typical and normal of the Oedipal phase and lead to an ambivalent identification where emotions can turn into anger as easily as affection. The ambivalence is intensified during the later phallic phase of the Oedipal stage, during which every child has a strongly developed bisexual predisposition, a dual orientation toward both masculine and feminine, active and passive tendencies. The boy fights for his manhood, the girl for her womanhood. Feeling his masculinity is threatened, partly because of his fear of being punished by his father for his desires and partly because of his fear of his own feminine tendencies, the boy becomes afraid of losing his penis. This is known as castration fear. The fears and anxieties accompanying the Oedipal conflict in girls develop into jealousy and shame—called penis envy.

If the Oedipus complex is unresolved and remains active, the child continues to be tied to his parents, and therefore dependent on them. Normally, though, during his latency stage (from six to twelve years of age), he overcomes his ambivalent and angry Oedipal feelings by identifying with and emulating the parent of the same sex. At the same time, he makes an effort to be on good terms with the parent of the opposite sex. These attitudes give him a feeling of acceptance and belonging and make him part of the family.

If, however, he is unable to identify with the appropriate parent, his hostile feelings and fantasies will stay with
him and be revived during puberty and later in life. A
revival of these wishful and angry fantasies can be seen
in the passively inclined adult with homosexual leanings,
who, stimulated by his environment, will be preoccupied
with seeking power in order to make up either for the
power he failed to gain over his father or for that he feels
he lost as a child. His passivity will lead him impulsively
to act out his aggressive urges. We always find a higher
degree of inner passivity in violent persons than in the
average law-abiding citizen. This passivity is associated
with the helplessness mentioned in Chapter IV, which
we pointed out was connected with the violent acting out
of the individual desiring to show his mother that he is
strong.

Imperative to the healthy repression of violent impulses
is the formation of the superego and morality. This takes
place when the Oedipal situation is abandoned, when the
unconscious incestuous feelings between the child and
his parents are eliminated, when society, in fact, wins
over the individual's sexual impulses. The Oedipus
complex, therefore, stimulates the creation and growth
of the superego, and its resolution is essential to the
healthy emotional and sexual development of every
person.

When parents deprive their child of love and affection,
he feels rejected, thinks there is something wrong with
him. Combined with his own desires, this makes him feel
guilty and afraid, and he is unable to identify with his
parents. His image, the impression he has of himself,
becomes blurred, and he has little or no sense of inner

direction. Without a sense of belonging, he feels alone, alienated from his parents and shut out of family life. This disturbed identity stays with him throughout life. While the following case is extreme, it illustrates clearly the role identification plays in human behavior.

Bill, an eighteen-year-old, had never gotten along with his father. Ever since he could remember they had argued and fought, his mother sometimes taking his part. Whenever he tried to become close to his mother, however, she sternly rejected him. Feeling ambivalent toward Bill since he was an unwanted child, she tacitly condoned her husband when he spanked him. While agreeing on the surface about their son's "bad" behavior, the parents fought tumultuously, particular since the husband, unable to tolerate his wife, spent most of his time at work.

When Bill graduated from high school, his father wanted him to work in his store. The boy, however, felt that this was below his dignity, and after a bitter argument he left the house and stayed out the whole night. When he returned the next morning, he was given the "silent treatment," which alienated him still more from his family. Having no sense of belonging in his home, he sought company with other boys. So angry and vengeful was he against his father than he planned with them to rob his store. Through some miscalculation the plan went awry. One week later, during a violent argument with his father, Bill shot him to death.

This acting out of violent, hostile aggressions came about because of Bill's inability to find any tie with or any humanity in his own father. He felt unwanted, and therefore had no sense of identity. As he said to me, "I might as well have been born on the moon." His blurred identification and his weak ego, results of the poor family relationship, made him vulnerable to violent rages and unable to express his impulses in a rational way. Periodically he lost control and acted out his repressed impulses.

Unconsciously he wanted to possess his mother, but his desire was blocked by her hostile attitude and his much stronger father. Fighting for his manhood, he was, because of his repressed Oedipus complex, living with the emotions of a child, much in the same way as described by the French philosopher Diderot two hundred years ago: "If the little savage were left to himself, keeping all his foolishness and adding to the small sense of a babe in the cradle the violent passions of a man of thirty, he would strangle his father and lie with his mother." [5]

To summarize, then, during the first five or six years of life the child goes through an emotional and biological revolution during which he suffers three *traumatizing experiences*—weaning from breast to bottle, toilet training, and rejection by his parents—all accompanied by fear, anger, and guilt. These traumatic experiences, which are effected partly by his instinctual drives and partly by environmental influence, produce frustrations that have a tremendous bearing upon all behavior, including violence.

Unlike other animals, man must go through a social adaptation (or maladaptation) in which he learns to use language, to develop sympathy and cooperation, to create and participate in cultural, religious, and social institutions. In other words, he must learn to postpone immediate gratification.

Those individuals who cannot do this become abnor-

mally hostile and aggressive, acting out their violent impulses against others or themselves. We see this pattern
of behavior in rapists and killers—also in those automobile drivers who habitually cause collisions.

The need to obtain power is ingrained in everyone and
is the *learned* part of aggression. Man's aggression, thus,
is in part instinctive and in part learned. In the animal,
the aggressive action is carried out in an instinctive pattern until it has run its course and is terminated. In man,
however, the basic action and reaction—attack and defense—is instinctual, but the manner in which the aggressive action is carried out is learned. The degree of
aggression differs from person to person, depending upon
how the instinctive impulses and the ego and conscience
have been conditioned by the environment. Whether
we employ hostile aggression or violence openly or imper-
ceptibly, we use it unconsciously to achieve power,
expressing our essential emotional need.

If we are afraid of being overcome by what is going to
happen to us, we instinctively counteract our fear by
becoming defensive, aggressive, or violent. This native
fear is mobilized in our childhood, generated from our
home environment through reactions and impressions
associated predominantly with Mother, and later spurred
on by the social environment. What we fear we learn to
hate. Eventually we begin to feel an impelling desire to
destroy the object of our fear and hate, leading to the
release of hostile aggressions.

In the same way the home situation exerts a strain
upon the child, so society exerts a strain upon the individual. The process of healthy adjustment is the same
in society as in the family—we have to learn to renounce

our instinctual gratifications, to curb our aggressions. Freud felt such limitation of aggression to be the first and perhaps the hardest sacrifice that society demands from each individual. In order to obtain a reward tomorrow, we have to postpone satisfaction today.

Postponement of gratification in the long run is the foundation for an emotionally satisfying life in society. As we grow up, we are constantly exposed to forces that infringe upon our personal wishes, which, when unfulfilled, frustrate us. These forces are felt as stress and strain. We have, in part, inherited the animal environment—witness the jungles of our cities and the crimes of the suburbs—and have attempted to transform it into a human one. Our environment mobilizes our instinctual impulses from which love and hate grow so that either tendency is weakened or intensified depending upon our family environment and our personality reactions to situations. Some of us love greatly while others hate bitterly in the same society; some of us cheerfully accept what is socially approved while others rebel aggressively.

We live in a society where frightening and frustrating forces threaten most of us and intensify our ambivalence. Since fear leads to hate, any stress and strain situation where fear is involved always makes us ambivalent and aggravates our dual tendencies. Ambivalence is the simultaneous existence of opposite feelings toward a person or object. When we are ambivalent, our love and hate are directed toward the same person at the same time. Our emotions fluctuate constantly between the two poles, following the pattern of the life and death instincts. Up to a point feelings of ambivalence seem to be normal, but when they are intensified and lasting, they signify emo-

tional disturbance—neurosis or psychosis or character disorder. The unconscious hostile feelings that underlie all
ambivalence can, under sufficient pressure, erupt in violent action.

Personal ambivalence is reflected on a larger scale in
our political and social ambiguity. Just as contradictory
feelings exist side by side in the unconscious mind of the
individual, opposite ideas exist simultaneously in group
situations without conflict from the logical contradiction
between them. The ambivalence in our political system
is most conspicuously present in our two great political
parties, both of which contain conservative and liberal
factions. They approve, condone, and condemn the same
issues at the same time.

Our record of social ambivalence is unenviable. We
take pride in helping to free even the smallest oppressed
nation; yet when the American Negro attempts to gain
equal status and opportunity, many of us rigorously oppose his strivings.

During World War II we proclaimed the Nazi concentration camps where millions were killed evil, yet saw no
parallel with our own. To compare this manslaughter with
our putting Japanese-Americans in detention camps is
of course invalid, since we didn't kill any of them. We for-
got, however, to condemn these detention camps.

We have given away millions of dollars worth of food
and clothing to the needy all over the world, but until
President Johnson's 1964 Anti-Poverty Bill, we did not
have, even in prosperous times, a comprehensive program
to help the needy in our own country, except in some
instances in the form of relief.

While we preach religious freedom, our own religious

prejudice is too frequently seen. In 1924, for example, the bigoted Ku Klux Klan was so influential as to prevent the Presidential nomination of Alfred E. Smith, the Catholic Governor of New York.

We loudly proclaim our deep concern for our fellow citizens, and the concern is reflected to some extent by the work of our numerous charitable organizations and the fringe benefits and profit-sharing and pension plans provided by some business firms; advanced social reforms, however, which could benefit every American and have long existed in other democracies, have in this country, if they exist at all, been unusually slow in coming. Despite our stress on learning, many of our schools and educational facilities are totally inadequate. Despite our emphasis on the importance of good health, a great majority of our people lack sufficient medical care because we resist taking steps to make those services available within the limits of their income.

We pride ourselves on being open-minded, liberal, and advanced in our attitudes—and certainly we have the greatest opportunity in the world for freedom of thought and speech. Yet when we scratch the surface of many an American's views, we often find the narrow, puritanical beliefs of a century ago. Our attitude toward sex is conspicuous in its contradictions: we permit and relish every public sexual titillation while criticizing, condemning, and even punishing sexual indulgence.

We want to give and yet to take. We grant freedom, yet we still want to control and take it back. In other words, we are an ambivalent society.

We find, then, that one origin of violent impulses lies in the already existing emotional conflict during our formative years, and becomes intensified by our family environment, which may traumatize our identification and outlook and disturb our object relations. One particular outgrowth of this traumatization is the search for power—the unconscious mastery of sexual potency—in adult life to compensate for a real or imagined loss of power in childhood. This need for power is transposed to society where the struggle for the supremacy of power is ubiquitous.

The roots of our violence thus lie in unresolved hostile aggression, the sign of which is our personal and social ambivalence. The bounty and vastness of our country, while creating opportunity on the one hand, on the other hand have aroused our aggression. With all this richness around us, there is more to be violent about. Much more is at stake when there is more to gain. Consequently, our fears and frustrations become intensified through our specific environmental conditions.

VI

Lee Harvey Oswald: Psychological Capacity for Violence and Murder*

This is a portrait of a failure, of a mentally disturbed young man who felt powerless and insignificant, who clung to the hope of stunning accomplishments and nurtured deep fantasies of revenge. . . .

The assassination of President John F. Kennedy in Dallas on that grim day in history November 22, 1963,

* Part of this material was presented at the meeting of the Association for the Advancement of Psychotherapy at the New York Academy of Medicine, March 31, 1967, and published in *The Bulletin of the New York Academy of Medicine* (Second Series, Vol. 43, No. 10, October, 1967).

was only an hour and a half old when Lee Harvey Oswald was captured. Some hours later he was charged with the murder of the President and of police officer J. D. Tippit, and in the next twenty-four hours he was tried and convicted by the news media and the public. His execution was equally swift, at the hands of his self-appointed executioner, Jack Ruby, in an unexpected, split-second shooting.

Throughout Lee Harvey Oswald's two-day imprisonment he relentlessly professed his innocence. During visits from his wife, his mother, and his brother Robert, his story remained unchanged. Even under intensive interrogation by the police—which lasted intermittently for twelve hours, although there is no trace of its having been recorded—he steadfastly denied that he had shot President Kennedy or Officer Tippit.

Oswald wanted to—and did—take his secret to the grave. Such was his nature. If he was the murderer, nobody was going to learn it from him, despite the overwhelming accumulative evidence. This does not conform to the behavior patterns of previous assassins of American Presidents—Lincoln, Garfield, and McKinley—who not only readily admitted their guilt, but publicized it. (Most well known in this respect is John Wilkes Booth, who after having shot President Lincoln, leaped to the stage and exclaimed: *"Sic semper tyrannis!"*)

But not Lee Harvey Oswald. His behavior after the assassination differed markedly in one respect from that of the other assassins. No confession, no written statement was forthcoming from him to testify to any motive or responsibility on his part in killing President Kennedy. The absence of a confession may seem strange, but it is not, if one considers the possibility that this was not a political murder.

The absence of a confession, along with the unusual emotional reaction to the assassination, has thrown a shroud of mystery around President Kennedy's murder and raised doubts as to whether or not Oswald committed the violent crime—despite the Warren Commission's findings that he *was* the assassin, acting without assistance.

Although strong circumstantial evidence does seem to indicate Oswald's guilt, our understanding of human behavior through psychoanalytical knowledge can further substantiate it by evidence of his psychological motivation and capability of murder. If we can uncover a person's early psychological motivations and their influence upon his character and personality structure, we are able not only to construct a meaningful picture of the forces shaping his past and present behavior, but also to predict some significant trends of his possible future behavior. Bearing in mind Freud's reminder that we must "fix the limits of what psychoanalysis can accomplish in biography in order that every omitted explanation should not be held up to us as a failure," [1] we will concentrate this study upon Lee Harvey Oswald's instinctual and emotional development, his behavior and experiences, and in the light of what we already know of murderers in general and of Oswald in particular, study specifically his psychological capability for violence and murder. Lee Harvey Oswald is typical of the violent man in our society, and a study of his background and personality will shed more light on the subject of violence in America.

As early as 1906 Freud pointed out one of the differ-

ences between a criminal and a hysteric: "In the case of
the criminal it is a secret which he knows and hides from
you, but in the case of a hysteric it is a secret hidden from
him, a secret he himself does not know." [2] Freud more
than anyone, however, was aware that both the criminal
and the neurotic may unconsciously withhold information as a form of resistance against awareness of the true
meaning of the aggressive impulse and the object, as for
example, the murder of a person who represents unconscious homosexual attachment to a parent.

Ascertaining the tie-in between a criminal's personality
structure and his deed is often further complicated by
conscious elements. As I pointed out in my 1944 paper
"The Psycho-Dynamic Connection Between Personality
and Crime," [3] when a criminal repudiates his deed, his
ego defenses are repudiating his own id desires, as they
do in all conflict situations. In addition, even when he is
not psychotic, a criminal often feels his deed is so justified
that he denies it because he believes the punishment
resulting from his admission will be totally undeserved.

The murderer is unaware of the intense inner conflict
between his sexual and aggressive impulses and his environment. This conflict, as mentioned earlier, is due to
serious childhood traumatic situations—often the primal
scene—and to a fixation at or regression to the latter part
of the oral or the anal phase. Unable to withstand frustrations because of his emotional stunting, the criminal is
led to impulsive hostile acting out.

Many criminals are deliberately acting out murderous
rages when they have been disappointed because a superior or an equal has let them down, although these let-
downs are often more fantasy than fact.

We often find in murderers visual hypersensitivity and

speech and spelling difficulties that have been developed as a result of a distorted relationship between speech and the related thought processes in early childhood.[4]

For purposes of orientation, here are some distinguishing characteristics of the murderer.

TABLE I
SOME DISTINGUISHING CHARACTERISTICS OF THE MURDERER

1. Intense vengefulness and withdrawal due to feelings of helplessness, insignificance, and distrust related to pre-Oedipal and also Oedipal fixations
2. Primal scene experiences and sexually overstimulating situations
3. Extreme regressive fantasy life, such as fantasies of grandiose accomplishments, which may facilitate acting out of hostile impulses
4. Speech or spelling errors related to possible disturbances during the pre-Oedipal period
5. Tendency toward plasticity in identification
6. Inability to withstand frustration and to find sufficient gratification for the discharge of hostile, aggressive drives through constructive outlets
7. Inability to transform primitive narcissism into healthy ego-ideal and superego elements, with dependency expressed in subservience to or contempt for authority
8. Suicidal tendencies with wide mood swings
9. Victim often constitutes composite picture of murderer's self-image
10. Previous antisocial, delinquent, or criminal acts accompanied by actual or threatened violence

Do Lee Harvey Oswald's personality structure and behavior, so far as we can determine, follow this pattern? As the basis for my study of Oswald I have researched his "Historic Diary," his letters to his mother, wife, and brother, extensive magazine and newspaper reports, the records of the Warren Commission Hearings with the psychiatric examination of him at age thirteen, and material received through personal communication with others who have studied him and his family's background and life. However, I will cover only the most salient aspects of his life experience which, to my mind, have had a crucial bearing upon his early development.

The twenty-six volumes put out by the Warren Commission, containing 352 witnesses' testimony related to President Kennedy's death, include an exhaustive inquiry into Lee Harvey Oswald's life, behavior, and family background. Unfortunately, little of his early development was probed, and there are a great many contradictions, especially in the testimony of his mother, Marguerite Claverie Oswald, who had the most sustained contact with him. But although the information disclosed is spotty,* a picture of a personality with definite character traits emerges.

A trait that stands out consistently in the memories of those who knew Lee Harvey Oswald is that he was withdrawn and lonely. Mrs. Murret, the aunt with whom he lived on and off as a small child, states, "He would just rather stay in the house and read or something. . . . He

---

* A great deal of material about Oswald's early childhood is also given by, among others, his maternal aunt, Mrs. Lillian Murret; his mother's friend of some twenty-five years, Mrs. Myrtle Evans; his half-brother, John Pic; his brother, Robert Oswald; his wife, Marina Oswald; and many of his former schoolmates, teachers, and neighbors. Information about his adolescence and early adulthood is given by the aforementioned as well as by men who served with him in the Marines, and by Mrs. Ruth Paine and others who befriended Lee and Marina Oswald.

wouldn't go out and play, and he just wanted to be in that room all the time, and he wouldn't even talk to the other children. . . ." [5] His mother says, "Lee was a very quiet and studious boy. . . . The children were always more or less home. And particularly Lee. . . . He was a normal boy. . . . He could keep himself occupied. . . ."[6] Mrs. Evans, close friend and landlady of Marguerite Oswald, says that "he didn't bring boys in the house . . . he would always seem to prefer being by himself . . . the way he kept to himself just wasn't normal, I think. . . ." [7] And Edward Voebel, a former junior-high-school classmate of Lee Oswald's, states, "He didn't make friends. . . . People and things just didn't interest him generally. He was just living in his own world. . . . Lee didn't go out and look for friends. He didn't seem to care about having friends. . . ." [8]

Although his brother, Robert, states that he considered Lee to be normal in every way,[9] the impression of him as lonely, uncommunicative, and unfriendly or even hostile is confirmed by almost everyone who knew him, including his wife and his fellow Marines.

The details of Lee's infancy and early childhood indicate that he was predisposed to becoming severely emotionally disturbed. His problems began early—in a sense before he was born. His father's sudden death two months before Lee's birth in New Orleans on October 18, 1939, and his mother's subsequent financial difficulties were the beginnings of a disrupted infancy and childhood that were to have far-reaching consequences. His inability to understand his father's death may have made him imagine, as do many children faced with the same circumstance, that his father had not cared about him, that he had thought of him as a burden or deserted him for being "bad."

His father's death and his own uprooting deprived Lee of a home and family life with constant parental figures. He stayed in his aunt's house with his mother, his five-year-old brother, Robert, and his eight-year-old half-brother, John Pic, for one or two months until Mrs. Oswald began to go to work.[10] The family was then split up. Mrs. Oswald went back to her home with Lee, while his two brothers were put in a Lutheran boarding home. The neglect in his early childhood is shown inadvertently by his mother's own testimony: "I let a couple have my home, plus $15 a month in order to care for Lee while I worked, and this couple after about two months' time had neglected Lee and so I had to put them out of the house and there again I had to quit a job, and take care of Lee until I could make arrangements and my sister could help me with it." [11] Myrtle Evans says that neighbors told Marguerite Oswald that "when Lee was in the high chair . . . he used to cry a lot, and they thought they were whipping little Lee, so she came home unexpectedly one night, and the child had welts on his legs, and she told them to get out and get out now." [12]

There were many different people who took care of Lee—aunt, maids, couples, baby sitters. It is reported that one baby sitter who lived with the Oswalds for fourteen days in the middle of 1942, when Lee was two-and-a-half years old, had said that "she couldn't take it any longer . . . he wouldn't listen and he was bad. He had a littly toy gun, and he threw it after her and broke the chandelier in the bedroom. . . . He threw it at her when he got mad, and she had an awful time with him. . . ." [13]

The many difficulties his mother had are again shown by her own testimony: "So when Lee was three years old, I was having it very difficult with Lee, because of the different people to take care of Lee, and the different jobs I had to give up." [14]

Unable to cope with her situation, she put him in the same boarding home as his two brothers—on the day after Christmas in 1942. But this place too was a transitory one, since she took him out from time to time for varying periods. Thus it became difficult for Lee to be close to anyone, not only because of the great age difference between him and his brothers but also because his mother, whenever in the mood, insisted upon having him stay with her, an impression we find confirmed in various testimony.

Lee's father's death prevented Lee's being able to form an adequate male identification and a healthy ego and superego. Also, according to various reports, his mother had wanted a girl when he was born. Mrs. Myrtle Evans thought she remembered Marguerite telling her, either during her pregnancy with Lee or after Lee's birth, that she wanted a girl. [15] Such a wish, no doubt, aroused guilt feelings in Marguerite for which she tried to compensate by smothering her son with love. We may also assume, on the basis of the data, that her intermittent overindulgence of him could be related to her guilt feelings over boarding him out and her identification with him as an orphan, she herself having been a semi-orphan. Her mother had died in 1911, when Marguerite was four or five years old, [16] and like Lee, she had been raised by relatives and housekeepers. [17]

Marguerite is described in her youth as having been a

"very beautiful girl," [18] gregarious, talented, and "money conscious." [19] In making a living for herself she was ingenious. Her tongue was sharp; "she was a person that kept to herself." [20] Proud and independent, wanting the best for her children, in a moment of anger she was quick to pretend she needed no one; yet her ambivalence is evident in the fact that she showed strong dependency and self-pity in accepting money and other favors from her sister. Because of her narcissistic self-esteem she used terms such as "people of our caliber" and took it for granted that help should be given her, although she resented any inference that she would accept charity.

Mrs. Murret, Marguerite's eldest sister, relates that "if you disagreed with her or if you expressed an opinion that she didn't agree with, then she would insist that you were wrong. . . . She would do things at the spur of the minute," and was impulsive. "She would just act right now regardless of the consequences once she made up her mind." She was also unforgiving. Easily offended, she would walk off in a huff and not talk to the offender for months. Then when she needed something, she would come back as if nothing had ever happened.[21]

Three months pregnant, she left her first husband, Edward John Pic, Jr.; then she married Robert Edward Lee Oswald who died; and in July, 1943, she met Edwin A. Ekdahl, whom she married in 1945 after an intermittent courtship. After three years of arguments, separations, reconciliations, and new arguments, they were divorced in 1948, the jury finding that Marguerite was "guilty of excesses, cruel treatment or outrages" unprovoked by Ekdahl's conduct.[22]

In Marguerite Oswald's emotional makeup we find

many of Lee's traits, in particular her rigidity, unrealistic and narcissistic self-idolatry and attention-seeking, withdrawal, hypersensitivity, possessiveness, disrespect for authority, false pride, exploitation of people, cruelty, impulsiveness, and acting out regardless of consequences. In Lee, however, these traits were more sharply delineated, in particular his acting out tendency, withdrawal, sadism, desire to be in the limelight, and contempt for authority.

We have relatively little information about the first eighteen months of Lee's life. Indirectly, though, we can surmise that there was considerable disturbance during this phase, since as we have seen, he was unmanageable. His oral phase was obviously a difficult time for him, leading to intense frustration later in life. In his early teens, according to Mrs. Evans, "he would come home, and he would get his books and his music, and then when he wanted supper, or something to eat, he would scream like a bull. He would holler 'Maw, where's my supper?' . . . Her whole life was wrapped up in that boy, and she spoiled him to death. Lee was about thirteen about that time. . . . [23] The main thing that seems to stand out in his conduct was the way he demanded to be fed when he would come from school. Margie would be downstairs maybe, talking to me or something, and he would come to the head of the stairs and yell for her to come up and fix him something to eat. He would just stand up there and yell, 'Maw, how about fixing me something to eat?' and she would jump up right away and go running upstairs to get something for him. . . . [24] Lee had gotten to the point where he was noisier and more determined with his mother, and it was getting a little unbearable.

. . . It seemed to be a situation that was getting worse all the time. . . ." [25]

Lee's later parsimony and cruelty are suggestive of problems and fixations related to his anal phase. Although we have no specific information about his development from eighteen months to three years of age, his half-brother John Pic's impressions from the years in the children's boarding home are interesting: "Robert and I enjoyed Bethelehem. . . . Things for myself became worse when Lee came there. . . . They had a ruling that if you had a younger brother or sister there and they had bowel movements in their pants the older brothers would clean them up, and they would yank me out of classes in school to go do this and, of course, this peeved me very much. . . ." [26]

Of special significance also is the fact that throughout most of his childhood Lee slept in the same bed with his mother, as revealed in his half-brother's testimony: "Lee slept with my mother until I joined the service in 1950. This would make him approximately ten, well almost eleven years old . . . in the same bed." [27] This kind of intimacy frequently elicits feelings of guilt, revulsion, and fear of being devoured.

Mrs. Evans' testimony further reveals Marguerite Oswald's excessive attachment to Lee: "She dumped all her love on Lee. . . . [28] She kept Lee with her all the time [during her marriage to Edwin Ekdahl and possibly for a period preceding it] so that they would all be together on these business trips he had to take. . . . He was her baby, and she loved him to death . . . and she spoiled him to death. . . . I don't think that she ever parted with Lee for a minute. . . . She just poured out all her love on him, it seemed. . . ." [29]

Under these conditions Lee may well have been exposed to his mother's intimate sexual experiences and to sexual overstimulation during his Oedipal stage; this would have reinforced his affection for his mother and hatred for the intruding stepfather, and stirred up considerable fear in him, making him feel helpless and overcome with anxiety—castration anxiety. His strong ties to his mother, which may have reinforced his "femininity" as well as his castration fears, showed up later in his pronounced shyness with girls, his attempts to belittle other men, his interest in uniforms and guns, and his loss of sexual interest, ending in impotence, during his marriage. Only for a short time, while in the Marines and in Russia, did he exhibit interest in girls, apparently because he was outside his mother's domain. But once back in the United States, his maternal dependency need came through again in his relationships both with his mother and with his wife.

Most important however, for our probing of his disturbed psychosexual development is that having slept with his mother for so many years, Lee was probably exposed to her sexual intimacy with his stepfather—primal scene—further stimulating his infantile anger and increasing his already severe frustrations. Such sexual overstimulation, in combination with his heightened orality, narcissism, and decreased tolerance for frustration, may well have elicited acting-out tendencies in the form of a desire to see and watch—scoptophilia. These tendencies he partially gratified through incessant reading, through watching television all day, and later through observing and investigating. For example, in a letter he sent from Russia to his brother, Robert, November 26, 1959, he wrote, "I have been a pro-communist for years and yet I have never met a communist, instead I kept silent and observed." [30] A former Marine acquaintance felt that his going to Russia to investigate Communism personally rather than simply joining the American Communist Party "seemed to fit his personality." [31] Scoptophiliac acting out was later transformed into exhibitionistic acting out. His identification with a figure like Castro, for instance, is an example of this. He was beginning to see himself as an aggressor. The ultimate of this exhibitionistic acting out is to become an arch aggressor through a criminal act.

Exhibitionism associated with childhood disturbances may manifest itself in a variety of ways, among them delayed speech and poor spelling. We have no information about possible speech impediments, but we do know that Lee's ability to spell was greatly impaired. In the third grade he received A's in all subjects but spelling, in which he received a D. His fourth grade "IQ was recorded at 103; on achievement tests in each of the three years, fourth, fifth, and sixth, he twice did best in reading and twice did worst in spelling." [32] In 1952 his IQ on the Wechsler Intelligence Scale for Children was 118, indicating, the psychologist noted, "a present intellectual functioning in the upper range of bright normal intelligence." [33]

The number of spelling errors in his "Historic Diary," letters, and notes is striking. These errors express onomatopoesis—the making of a name or word from a sound.

Lee's extensive writing as well as his continual need to expound his political views verbally was a means of exhibiting himself rather than of communication. Listening to a recording of his 1963 New Orleans radio interview

TABLE II

EXAMPLES OF SPELLING ERRORS
IN LEE HARVEY OSWALD'S WRITINGS

complusery	compulsory	opions	opinions
kicten	kitchen	esspicialy	especially
yonuge	young	jelous	jealous
exalant	excellent	conservorie	conservatory
tehniction	technician	aquiataces	acquaintance
sptacular	spectacular	domatory	dormitory
divocied	divorced	cimima	cinema
oppossition	opposition	arrestled	arrested
enviorments	environs	disire	desire
permonet	permanent	reture	return
admiriers	admirers	understade	understand
habituatated	habituated	admirares	admirers
quiality	quality	freiend	friend
patrioct	patriotic	marraige beaure	marriage bureau

about Castro, I had the distinct impression that he was merely talking without giving any real meaning to what he was saying—exhibiting himself. His words came automatically, without much feeling behind them.

His misspellings originated from the same root as his craving to be in the limelight. His desire was to call attention to himself, to pose and display himself, to appear more than he was. The manifestations of the childhood disturbances in association with this hysterical form of exhibitionism is a common attribute of schizophrenic conditions.[34]

His need to call attention to himself was vividly manifested in other areas of his short life. In his earlier years he tried to amuse people by clowning. For example, he made a joke of an ill-fitting shirt by saying, "Ma bought 'em big. She thought they'd shrink."[35] A photograph of Lee in the classroom at age fifteen shows the entire class paying serious attention to the teacher, except for Lee, who is facing the photographer in the rear of the room, pointing to himself and mugging for the camera.[36] His clowning, we may assume, was also a defense against his feelings of insignificance.

Lee went to Moscow secretly, thus increasing the element of shock in his defection. There he walked into the American Embassy and threw his passport on the desk, declaring he was through with America. Later, according to his "Historic Diary," he went to the Russian Embassy and offered to reveal everything he knew of Marine Corps operations, certain that this would impress the Russians and coerce them into accepting his citizenship application.[37] When he returned to the United States in 1962, he was disappointed because "there were no photographers present when he arrived."[38]

Connected with Lee's need to show off and shock people, which turned his neurotic tendencies into acting out, we see his antisocial, delinquent, and criminal activities before he was accused of assassinating President Kennedy.

TABLE III

DELINQUENCY AND VIOLENCE IN LEE HARVEY OSWALD

1) 1948   Chased half-brother John Pic with a knife and threw it at him[39]

2) 1952   Threatened John Pic's wife with pocket knife during a quarrel[40]

3) 1952   Struck his mother during same quarrel (second reported incident of his having hit her)

4) 1952   Extensive truancy. Of 64 school days, he was "present on fifteen full and two half days"[41]

5) 1953   Remanded to Youth House for three weeks (April 16 to May 7, 1953) and then put on probation

6) 1955   Wrote and signed note to his school, under his mother's name, falsely stating he must leave school because they were moving out of town, although his plan was to join Marine Corps

7) 1957–59   Court-martialed twice in Marine Corps (once for insubordination, once for illegal possession of a gun)

8) 1956–59   Shot himself in the hand "accidentally" while in Marines

9) 1959   Attempted suicide in Russia

10) 1962–63   Used aliases and falsified his identification card

11) 1962–63   Struck his wife on a number of occasions[42]

12) 1963   Shot at General Walker

It would be wrong, in this connection, not to include the minor delinquencies displayed by Marguerite Oswald, who may have unwittingly reinforced her son's own criminal propensities.

TABLE IV
DELINQUENCY IN MOTHER, MRS. MARGUERITE OSWALD

1) 1945   Changed Lee Harvey Oswald's birth date from October 18, 1939, to July 9, 1939, to get him into elementary school earlier[43]

2) 1947   Exposed sixteen-year-old son, John Pic, to stepfather's infidelity by having him and his young friend accompany her to the other woman's home,

where the friend posed as Western Union messenger so that Mrs. Oswald could force her way into the apartment

3) 1948   Falsely swore John Pic was seventeen so that he could join Marine Corps Reserves to supplement family income. Disapproved of his going back to finish school, which compelled him to sign her name to report cards and excuse notes [44]

4) 1953   Without notifying authorities, when Lee was on probation as a truant, left New York City with him and moved back to New Orleans

5) 1955   Arranged with lawyer for papers showing Lee's age as seventeen instead of sixteen so that he could join Marine Corps, although authorities discovered his true age and refused the application

In Lee's case, his acting-out impulses reflected an organized activity which was rooted in inability to withstand frustrations. Lee's wish to show off was ambivalently tinged, counterbalanced by withdrawal and his desire for revenge against parental figures, which he wanted simultaneously to proclaim and to keep secret. His fantasies indicate the intensity of this desire.

A report by the psychiatric social worker at New York City's Youth House for Boys, to which Lee was remanded from April 13 to May 7, 1953, because of truancy, states that "he admitted to fantasies about being powerful and sometimes hitting and killing people, but refused to elaborate on them." [45] He was then thirteen years old.

The psychiatrist's report from the same institution says of his fantasies, "Lee has a vivid fantasy life turning around the topics of omnipotence and power through which he tries to compensate for his present shortcomings and frustrations." [46] This same report also states that "Lee has to be diagnosed as a personality pattern disturbance with schizoid features and passive-aggressive tendencies." [47] Nowhere does the report state, as reported in news media, that Lee was considered potentially dangerous and suffering from schizophrenia. However, as we can see from his later fantasies and behavior, in all probability he was already at least borderline paranoid.

At age sixteen he worked out a plan to steal a pistol displayed in a store window by using a glass cutter to cut the window and a plastic pistol to threaten any intruders. A classmate to whom he divulged the plan says, "It was just a fantastic thing he got in his mind." [48] He never carried out the plan.

His wife, Marina, describes Lee in one respect as different from average people: ". . . at least his imagination, his fantasy, which was quite unfounded, as to the fact that he was an outstanding man. . . . He was very much interested . . . in autobiographical works of outstanding statesmen of the United States and others. . . . I think he compared himself to those people." [49] Indicating that the prospect of helping Cuba seemed to quicken his hopes of fame, she further testified, "He was even interested in the airplane schedules, with the idea of kidnapping a plane. I talked him out of it." [50] And in another segment: "He very much wanted to go to Cuba and have the newspapers write that somebody had kidnapped an aircraft. . . . He said that after twenty years he would be prime minister. I think that he had a sick imagination —at least at that time I already considered him to be not quite normal—not always, but at times. . . ." [51]

The lack of a permanent father and the trauma of Ekdahl's all-too-short-lived presence constituted Lee's greatest personal (narcissistic) emotional injury. This lack of a father/law-authority figure, in addition to the many substitute parent figures in his childhood, made the boundaries of his ego fluid, at the same time giving him an identification plasticity such as we find in the schizophrenic, the homosexual, or the criminal. The weakness of Lee's ego due to his narcissistic disposition also resulted in clinging yet fluctuating relationships built on infantile dependency or on his selfish object choice—which led to a dread of emotional involvement.

One striking example of his inability to be emotionally involved occurred in 1959 as he was nearing the end of his duty with the Marines in California. His mother, ill and apparently unable to work because of a nose injury, persuaded him to obtain a hardship release so that he could return home to support her. But after barely three days at home he insisted upon leaving again. According to his mother, "He wanted to work on a ship in the import and export business" because he felt that was the only way he could earn enough money with his lack of skills and training. Despite her pleading with him to remain, on the third day "He came with his suitcase in the room and said, 'Mother, I am off.' So since his mind was made up, I told him goodbye." [52]

Although apparently he had saved $1,600 while in the service, his mother states that all he gave her was $100 to tide her over until her insurance claim was settled. Obviously he had used her illness as a means to his own selfish ends, to hasten his long-planned defection to Russia. He had in fact obtained his Russian visa in Los Angeles shortly before returning home. So obsessed was he with his own immediate gratification that he could not postpone his desires even when his mother seemed to need him most.

On September 19, 1959, two weeks after leaving his mother, he wrote her the following brief letter from New Orleans:

Dear Mother:

Well, I have booked passage on a ship to Europe. I would of had to sooner or later and I think Its best to go now. Just remember above all else that my values are very different from Roberts or your's. It is difficult to tell you how I feel. Just remember this is what I must do. I did not tell you my plans because you could harly be expected to understand.

I did not see Aunt Lillian while I was here.

I will write again as soon as I land.

Lee [53]

On the surface, the letter seems no more than a cryptic apology. But reading between the lines reveals a great deal more. The entire tone is accusing yet wistful, almost resigned; determined, yet pleading for acceptance. He intimates that his mother approves more of Robert because his brother shares her attitudes. He has despaired of making her understand his feelings and must therefore keep them to himself—in order to be free of her control, he must be secretive.

The letter gives us an inkling of his jealousy, his sense of isolation, his intense narcissism, and his fear of involvement with her.

Significant also in these brief lines is his unexpressed hostility toward his mother. He is saying in effect, "You never loved me, so I may as well do what's good for me!"

There is not so much as perfunctory concern for her health or finances. He left her to discover his true intentions from newspaper reporters some weeks later, hung up on her in November when she phoned him in Moscow, sent her a note in December asking for money without even knowing whether she could afford it, and then wrote her and Robert in January, 1960, "I do not wish to ever contact you again. I am beginning a new life and I don't want any part of the old." [54] He did not write her again until some two years later, when all his attempts to get out of Russia had been unsuccessful and he obviously needed her help once more. We see here the hostile behavior of a dependent individual. As long as his mother could do anything for him, he was good to her. But if she was unable to help him, he lost all interest in her. He only valued people in proportion to their usefulness to him.

His desire for revenge was directed not only against his depriving mother but also unconsciously against the father who had deserted him and whom he had wished, at the same time, to replace. His images of father and mother intertwined, with a confusion of giving and withholding that he projected onto others. The world became nothing but an endless procession of people tantalizing him, holding things out to him on a string—giving and punishing.

Nowhere more than in Lee's attitude toward the United States and Russia did he express so symbolically his fantasy wish for the all-giving father-mother, and his desire to lash out and punish them both. When America failed to fulfill his expectations, he deserted her, pinning all his hopes on finding his Utopia in Russia. But there also was disillusionment.

Lee's feeling of personal rejection first hit a low point when, five days after he had arrived in Moscow, the police telephoned to say that his visa had expired and he must leave the country within two hours. This was a crushing blow. For years he had lived in a fantasy of Russia's welcoming him with open arms, like a good parent, and instead she was rejecting him outright, as if he were an orphan. His reaction was immediate and violent: he slashed his wrist.

Again the manifestation of secret exhibitionism had come to the fore. His suicide attempt suggests a violent acting out of a rejection fantasy. The wish to be dead signifies an unconscious identification with his dead father, of the sort so well demonstrated by Freud in "Dostoyevsky and Parricide." [55] But Lee's attempt also served to put him in the limelight.

Only the quick action of a girl who had befriended him saved his life. Waking up in the hospital ward for the insane was a shock to Lee. Seeing mentally ill patients frightened and upset him. It was like looking in a mirror, no doubt, and he cringed from his own reflection. After much insistence and complaining, he was after a few days moved to the regular ward. In his "Historic Diary" he comments that the nurses there were suspicious of him. He did not recognize the extent of his own emotional sickness—the threatening disintegration of his personality structure.

His despondency was soon offset, however, by the attention he gained. Not only was he released from the hospital and his visa extended, but Russia gave him financial subsidy, an apartment in Minsk, and a job at which he earned a good salary. Women flocked around him, and for a while he could feel superior to other men. He was in high spirits.

But soon everything changed. He grew disenchanted with the Russian system, its discipline, its party rules and restrictions. His dissatisfaction reached a peak, it would seem, when the girl with whom he had fallen in love refused his marriage proposal. Now, when Russia offered him citizenship, he turned it down, reverting to his old pattern of rejecting whoever he felt rejected him. He applied at the United States Embassy for return to America. In the meantime he met Marina.

In the light of his past withdrawal from close emotional relationships, Lee Oswald's marrying Russian-born Marina Nicolaevna Pruskova and having two children with her is surprising. But this, too, was part of his need for revenge. He married her on the rebound, to hurt the girl who had turned him down. Although he eventually felt he loved Marina and did bring her to the States with him, his narcissistic pattern nevertheless ran true to form: she and the children were primarily sources of self-gratification, his own needs taking precedence over theirs. He would leave home and return according to the pressure of his own compulsive drives. Although he could seldom provide them with even the barest of necessities because of his difficulty in finding and holding jobs, he nevertheless indulged himself with such personal extravagances as having his notes on Russia typed professionally, buying a rifle, and having circulars printed for his Fair Play for Cuba Committee activities. All too often his family's comfort depended upon the kindness of Marina's Russian-speaking friends, whose efforts were usually rewarded with Lee's jealous resentment.

Although sometimes affectionate toward his wife, for the most part he was domineering, possessive, and punishing. Marina admitted that he struck her on a number of occasions and was quick to rebuke her harshly for such trifles as being five minutes late with dinner or forgetting to serve the butter.[56] Although she was a stranger in a foreign country, he refused to help her learn English because *he* wanted practice in speaking Russian. He seemed determined to keep her from having friends; in fact he drove away any except those who could overlook his arrogance and sullenness.

Once rejected, Lee never forgave. In his paranoid-tinged obsession, anyone who opposed him loomed as an authority and a threat to his masculinity. This feeling may also have derived from an unconscious homosexual conflict that became heightened by his impotence. In the past, his defense had been withdrawal, which had served a dual purpose: he could ward off rejections and inflict them simultaneously. Thus self-preservation and revenge had been interlocked. No one could hurt him, but he could hurt them. He was in control—superior and safe.

This defense, however, no longer brought him gratification. One by one his refuges were disappearing, and with them went his self-regard. He was left frustrated and alienated.

But loneliness and alienation were not in themselves enough to turn Lee into a potential murderer. It was the accumulation and relentlessness of the rejections he experienced and the way he reacted to them. It was his inability to appraise himself and others realistically, and the degree to which he felt unjustly persecuted. It was the feeling that he must refrain from making any demands and that he dared not express any anger over his frustration. Above all, it was the hopelessness that resulted from his still unexpressed anger, and consequently, the extent to which he had to withdraw into his fantasies to find satisfaction.

Because of his primitive narcissism, it became impossible to deflect gratification into personal, social, or altruistic values.

His egocentricity having remained on a childish pregenital level, he had failed to develop a mature ego-ideal. Instead, he pursued the narcissistic gratification he had lost in his childhood. His relations with men remained principally, although latently, homosexual, as evidenced by his ambivalence toward strong masculine figures and his attempt to act out their strength by imitation. In his relationships with his mother and wife, he took on the role of dictator, but on a childish, pre-Oedipal level. On the Oedipal level he had to act out the unconscious impulse to kill the strong person.

By early autumn of 1963, his feelings of rejection and frustration reached a crisis. Russia had disappointed him, he had failed to reverse the undesirable discharge issued by the Marines, and he was losing job after job in America. He was in a fury, obsessed with vengefulness and proving his own power. He would show the Russians what a mistake they had made in waiting so long to accept him. He would show everyone that he could not be humiliated, pushed around like an insignificant child. His feelings of persecution became magnified. He saw all men as wielders of power, always standing in his way, a constant threat to his having whatever he wanted. They were authorities he had to combat.

Although Lee Oswald had great hostility toward women, his hatred for men was far deeper and more consuming. He felt both rejected and overwhelmed by them. They stimulated his feelings of helplessness and doubts about his own masculinity, which he had to conceal in order to maintain his own sexual identity. He had learned to assuage these fears—by showing contempt for men and remaining aloof from them. He dared not come close to them for fear of being exposed and rejected. Thus self-preservation and revenge were interlocked: no one could hurt him, but he could hurt them.

Now, however, this defense no longer brought enough satisfaction. He had to show his power more directly. But, as in childhood, he was biding his time. He kept his every move secret. That way he could look down on them as he felt they had looked down on him. He could enjoy the feeling of knowing something they did not know— that he was as powerful as they. And one day he would shock them all by proving it.

Secretly, and under a false name, A. Hiddell, he bought a rifle and practiced at a firing range. His use of the name Hiddell is interesting, since it starts with the same letter as his real middle name, indicating that for narcissistic reasons he could not give up the first letter of his real name even in falsification—he could not completely give up his own identity.*

The gun, a symbol of masculinity, bolstered and reinforced his feeling of manliness and power. One night he took a shot at General Edwin A. Walker, a man who

---

* In this connection it is worth mentioning that the main reason Heinrich Himmler, Chief of the Nazi Gestapo, was caught by the British Intelligence Service at the end of the Second World War was that he had taken on a pseudonym beginning with the same letter, H, as his real name. He too could not completely give up his own self.[57]

was against all social progress that gave the "fair share" Lee felt entitled to. He missed his target, and it no doubt redoubled his need to make himself felt.

In his paranoid-schizophrenic state of mind and exalted opinion of himself, he was indignant and enraged at the world that refused him the recognition he felt was his due. Although he concealed it, he was in a state of frantic desperation. He must prove his worth and power!

On or about September 23, 1963, he deceived his wife by telling her that he was going to Houston to look for a job. He sent her from New Orleans to Dallas with a friend, and he himself disappeared the following day from his cheap lodging without paying the bill. Instead of looking for a job, he went to Mexico City on September 24, conspiring to obtain a visa back to Russia via Cuba. His request was for himself only. When the Cuban Consulate told him he needed a visa from the country of destination before they could do anything for him, he flew into a rage and slammed out of the place. Adding insult to injury, the Soviet Embassy told him it would take four months before they could act on his application. Again men in authority stood in his way. But now there was no holding him back; he was determined to win out over them. In a mood of rejection and defiance he returned to Texas on October 3, 1963.

What his motive was in wanting to go back to Russia is not clear, but conjecture offers a number of possibilities. It may have been his old pattern of rejecting America because he had again been rejected by her. We might venture the thought that it was a way of insuring his escape once he had murdered someone who opposed all that Russia represented; he could then return in triumph

to Russia, where they would acclaim him as the hero of
their country.

The night before President Kennedy's assassination
was a tumultuous one for Oswald. He had been living
in a room in Dallas, to be closer to his new job at the
Texas School Book Depository, and now spent only weekends with his wife and children, who were staying with
a friend in nearby Irving. But that Thursday he returned
unexpectedly, ostensibly to patch up a quarrel with
Marina. She had been angry with him after discovering
he had rented his room under an assumed name, and
hardly talked to him. He tried to placate her, but she
remained cool and aloof, although she testified later that
she had not been as angry as she had pretended. She
stated that Lee was upset and went to bed before her;
she doesn't think he slept much that night. When she
awoke the next morning he was gone, and she later discovered he had left his ring and $170 in a dish on a
dresser—possibly as a symbolic goodbye, since he had
taken his rifle with him.

Marina's seemingly inconsistent, submissive-rejecting
behavior merits attention here because it appears to be
similar to that of the wives of many sex offenders. As disclosed in a research project I conducted a number of years
ago, these women are often basically masculine types who
compete with men; frequently they unconsciously provoke
their husbands' attacks on other women by being seductive and then rejecting.[58] In Marina's case, her masochistic
submissiveness covered masculine and aggressive attitudes. Her ability to control Lee was perhaps a threat to
his masculinity and revived the Oedipal helplessness he
had felt toward his mother. It may be that a rejecting and

hostile attitude on the part of Marina that evening contributed to his determination to carry out any secret plans
he might have had.

On November 22, 1963, Lee was in a paranoid-
schizoid state of mind, and his opinion of himself was at
an all-time low. The time was ripe for his childish fantasies of proving his power by taking revenge to become
operative. Obviously, if he were a killer he would not be
an ordinary one. He would not have chosen his victim at
random unless faced with an emergency situation; in
that sense he was special. He would have chosen a victim
who represented all he had ever wanted in vain to have
and to be—someone who could command attention and
control others as he himself wished so desperately to do.
President John F. Kennedy fitted well within that frame.
He was the composite of all Lee's yearnings and frustrations. He belonged to a close family, and he had a father
who protected him, and he had power and authority.
He was Commander-in-Chief of the Armed Forces, including the Marines. As President he represented all
America—the America Lee now hated more than ever for
belittling and degrading him as long as he could remember. Perhaps most significant, President Kennedy was a
father, the father of his country and the father of two
children toward whom he showed great love.

Lee's old narcissistic hurt—abandonment by his father
and deprivation by his mother—was being revived. His
disrupted family life had made him turn to the Marines,
where he had hoped to find masculine identification,
gratification for his dependency needs, and yet an escape
from the greatest menace, his mother. But not only were
these unrealistic expectations not fulfilled during his ser-

vice in the Marines, but later they had even refused to rescind his undesirable discharge, all of which led him to see the Marines as a frustrating object. His anger at this frustrating object underwent a change—a displacement toward the United States government, with particular focus on the President, who was the embodiment of the government. His desperate need to identify with Marxism was an unconscious rejection of his own parents —as represented by the United States government.

President Kennedy was the composite of Lee's parental images, fundamentally a mother figure with a superimposed father figure from whom, as we have seen, he expected either total help or punishment—or both. His murder would have been for Lee the sublime act of revenge—the fulfillment of his death wish against a hated mother and father, as, by obliteration of the man who represented ultimate power, a proclamation to his mother that he was strong—a man. But in the wish to kill, he also unconsciously expressed his deep longing for death. His homicide can be seen as an unconscious suicide—signifying his identification with his dead father—a death wish that was quickly and ironically fulfilled.

Was Lee Oswald's personality that of a murderer? Beyond a reasonable doubt. Taking the circumstances as they are, his personality fits the makeup of a murderer like a key in the lock. In view of his highly disturbed early childhood emotional development, his inability to withstand frustration and his hostile acting out, his character distortion resulting in the lack of superego and ego-ideal formation, his displaced anger toward men and his lack of masculine identification, his withdrawal, his narcissistic core leading him to feelings of insignificance and impotence, his revenge wishes and fantasies of grandiose accomplishments, his previous delinquent violent acts representing desires to seriously harm a person, we find an intimate connection between his personality structure and a motivation and capacity for homicide. He was moving toward violence and revenge as inexorably as a character in a Greek drama, where fate—the unconscious —dictates the events.

During his last months Lee Oswald moved into a make-believe world where fantasy and reality were intertwined. He was functioning in accordance with what he wished the situation to be, not what it actually was. If he desired that President Kennedy, the most important man in the United States, should die, he most certainly, following his wish fulfillment, could wish that he be innocent of the crime. Protesting his innocence would have increased his sense of power, intensifying the gratification he derived from his revenge. Further, by denying the murder of the President-father, he would also be denying that he had ever had any sexual designs on his mother. Like the secret of her sexuality, he would now have a secret of his own.

VII

The Political
Assassin in
America*

Is political assassination, a recent and dramatic outgrowth of our national violence, becoming an American habit? Judging in particular from the increasing threats to the President and other government officials, the answer would seem to be Yes.

This report, which in some respects is preliminary, is based upon my study of 1) people charged with or suspected of having threatened to kill the President of the United States or other government officials, 2) people suspected of being capable of such a violent act, and 3) people who actually have killed a President of the United States. My assumptions are based on my studies in hospitals, clinics, state and Federal courts, at Sing Sing Prison, at the New York State Psychiatric Institute, Colum-

* Part of this material was presented before the National Commission on the Causes and Prevention of Violence.

bia University, and in private practice—studies of several hundred adults, children, and adolescents who threatened to kill, murdered, or committed other violent criminal acts.

Threatening the life of the President of the United States is a punishable offense under Title 18, 1958, of the United States Code, Chapter 41. Following the assassination of President Kennedy, the murder of the President was also made a punishable Federal offense.

While it is difficult to estimate the number of people who threaten the President or other government officials, there has been a definite increase of such threats. The number of threat cases investigated for the years 1960–63 averaged approximately 200 per year—or 17 every month. Prior to November, 1963, there were no more than 22 threats in any one month. Following the murder of President Kennedy, however, a sharp increase in the number of threat cases investigated took place. In November, 1963, there were 121; in December, 158; in January, 1964, 153. In the six months subsequent to January, 1964, approximately 90 cases were investigated each month. During the years 1964–68 approximately 1,100 persons—about 90 each month—were investigated. It should be noted that these figures pertain only to threats against persons worthy of investigation and protected by one government law enforcement agency, and do not cover threats to other government persons. We may therefore assume that the actual number of threat cases per year is much higher.

In interpreting this increase from 200 threats to about 1,100 per year—an increase of over 450 percent—it must be remembered that, following the recommendations of the Warren Commission, law enforcement agencies of the

United States government, through liaisons with other government and police agencies and through expansion of their own criteria, were able to increase their resources for locating some of the people who had threatened the President. Thus, after the assassination of President Kennedy, the agencies were able to pick up more information about people who were believed to constitute a threat to the President or other government officials. The increase of threat cases worthy of investigation may be due, therefore, not only to a rise in actual numbers but also to intensified investigative processes. However, since there has been an assumed increase of letter and telephone threats against the President, a factual increase may be presumed.

This rising tendency is reflected in the sudden increase of threat cases seen in the U.S. District Court, Southern District of New York, during an eight-month period in 1968. While previously cases of this type were few and far between, in this period the Federal Court had eleven defendants charged with threatening the President or other government officials. I examined eight of the nine defendants referred for psychiatric examination. The ninth was examined by another psychiatrist, and the remaining two had personal evaluations, the records of which I have studied.[2] Some of the cases are still under judicial consideration.

While the number of these cases seems statistically small and unimportant at first glance, they reveal under examination a significant pattern.

All those examined—ranging in age from twenty to the middle forties, except one who was past sixty—had either telephoned on one or several occasions or written letters threatening to kill President Johnson, Vice President Humphrey, or Attorney General Ramsey Clark.

They all showed personality traits in common. They either denied their threats or minimized them (except one individual, who finally admitted to threatening the President). In general, they could not seem to understand why they had been arrested. One man mentioned that he only called up the operator and said something about President Johnson—"Then they picked me up"—when, in fact, he had threatened President Johnson and planted a bomb. Another defendant who had threatened the President twice within six months said that it was a "misunderstanding" and that he had been too drunk to remember it. A third person had sent a letter to the Vice President, stating that he had become "disillusioned to all world problems." He did not consider his letter threatening, but "Before I knew it they were there and picked me up."

This denial of having threatened government officials is significant. It is similar to the denial of the child who is caught stealing but convinces himself he didn't do it. Such a child creates a feeling of omnipotence by acting in accordance with the way he wishes the situation to be. While there are exceptions to this pattern—John Wilkes Booth, whom I shall discuss later, is a case in point—the actual or would-be assassin often denies his guilt. Lee Harvey Oswald, as we know, throughout his two-day imprisonment denied having shot President Kennedy or Officer Tippit, in spite of intense police interrogation. This denial was consistent with his strong omnipotent feelings: if he could wish that President Kennedy die, he also could wish that he be innocent of his murder. In his fantasy world he gave himself the right to believe what he wanted to when he denied the crime. And this belief increased his sense of power, intensifying the gratification he derived from his revenge.

In actual or would-be assassins we find predominant intense and recurrent fantasies of revenge and omnipotence that may stimulate the acting out of violent impulses. The man who wrote the threatening letter to Vice President Humphrey explained to me that there was no threat in the letter. "It was only a reminder that things had to be taken care of." Asked what he meant, he said "I expect the wholesale extermination of the government and its top personnel." Asked whether he believed in his own plan, he answered, "It is down in black and white." Complaining about having had to work all his life, he said, "They had taken advantage of me. They were going to brainwash me." He was certain the government agents who had arrested him had kidnapped him, and he accused them of a "criminal-political" conspiracy. He believed in "the science of God" and averred that his master plan was the creation of all sciences. Throughout the interviews he expressed glorious thoughts about himself and a high opinion of his accomplishments. He talked about important jobs when in reality he was a low-salaried employee. His childhood home situation had been chaotic, and ten years prior to his arrest he had left his wife and children to seek his own fortune.

Behind his desire for revenge against the President and the government was his hatred of himself, his feeling of having been left alone to fight against the whole world.

Another defendant examined was Frank, a divorced

man in his twenties who was charged with threatening to assassinate the President. Early one morning he telephoned the FBI office in Washington, D.C., and, refusing to identify himself, said that he was on his way to Washington to "assassinate one of your big wheels." He called again later to say that he was wanted for robbery and to describe himself—down to the hat he was wearing and the fact that he was carrying a gun. He said that he had done many bad things during his life. Asked who he was thinking of killing, he answered, "The President." When he was picked up on the train and arrested by the law enforcement agency he told them that he had been in the Marine Corps and was not responsible for his actions when he was angry. He told the agents to keep a close watch on him because he would try to escape. He then asked them to handcuff him, as he was subject to fits of violence and would not be responsible for their personal safety. While en route to Washington he admitted that he was not a Marine veteran. He said that he had called the FBI because he had met two Cubans or Puerto Ricans who had offered him $200 to assassinate the President. This was proven to be untrue. On the spur of the moment, he said, he had decided to go to Washington. When interviewed later, he admitted that he had made the phone call but, since he was drinking heavily, could not remember why he did it, "I do crazy things when I drink." * He drank to get away from his troubles and to escape responsibility.

* Alcohol often serves as an excuse for the would-be assassin. Those who claim to be intoxicated or who really are intoxicated at the time of their threat use alcohol as an unconscious preparatory step in their desire to carry out their threat.

Frank's father came from Central Europe and settled in this country. Frank was the only issue of his second marriage. When he was about two-and-one-half years old his father bought a restaurant. The father and mother worked there eighteen hours a day, leaving Frank in the care of neighbors and pretty much on his own. In spite of this, he believes that his childhood was happy and that he had a good relationship with his parents. Both Frank and his mother stated on various occasions that the father drank moderately, but rarely got drunk. The public records indicate, however, that he was arrested twice, once for disorderly conduct, and some years later for assault and battery. Frank's mother, born in this country, was the dominating force at home. A heavyset, talkative woman, she blamed her son's problems on his period of military service. When he began to drink, she said, he became "nervous" and argumentative.

Frank began to attend school when he was six years old and left when he was in the third year of high school in order to enter the Armed Forces. While he stated that he got along quite well with his classmates, public records indicate that his attendance was poor and that he had to repeat a grade. He admitted that he occasionally played truant. In the service he began to drink in excess; he went AWOL on three different occasions, and he was discharged under other than honorable conditions.

According to his mother, Frank often did strange things. On one occasion he sent himself a telegram saying that he had won a large prize in a contest. On another occasion he showed people a telegram that he later admitted having sent to himself.

He was married to a woman two years his senior. They

are now divorced and their two children live with the
wife.

After his discharge from the service he got a job, which
he quit nine months later after an argument with his
wife about money. He left her at this time and went back
home. On his next job he stole some money and was
arrested; however, the charges against him were dropped
after he made restitution. About six months earlier he
had been involved in a fight, but no charges were made
against him. After he left his second job he began to
drink quite heavily and was hospitalized for about three
months. He then went to the West Coast and was admitted
to a psychiatric hospital there, telling them that he was
very impulsive and had suicidal tendencies. He returned
East, and being afraid that he might kill himself or have a
nervous breakdown, he went to a clinic there. According
to hospital records, he said that he was afraid of people
and that he stammered. He said that his mother was nervous and excitable, and that she frequently babied him
and needled him with stupid questions. He said that he
was always impulsive, that his wife angered him as his
mother had, and that he discharged his tension by getting into fights, drinking, or stealing. He claimed that
prior to episodes of acting out he suffered from nervous
headaches. Since he was thought to be suicidal, he was
given medication and group therapy. About one year
after he was discharged from the psychiatric hospital he
got himself admitted to another under an assumed name.
He claimed that he had been brought up in an orphanage
and that he suffered from severe headaches resulting from
head injury sustained while he was in the Marines.

After he was arrested for threatening the President, he

was admitted to a psychiatric hospital for examination. It was found that he had been drinking, especially on weekends, for a long period of time. The report said, "Patient is frightened, tense, but totally appropriate and relevant. He has a vague memory of claiming that he was intoxicated." It concluded that he was a chronic liar and an excessive drinker. There were no signs of psychosis, and he was well aware of the charges against him.

Characteristic of his whole behavior is the fact that most of his actions were attempts to attract attention to himself. It was reported that he used to tell pointless tales; he was especially fond of one in which he alleged to have seen a person who had at that time been reported missing and later was found dead. Because of his low frustration tolerance he would readily resort to acting out his impulses by way of either drinking or aggression. On one occasion he assaulted his father. Of particular interest is the fact that his name is similar to that of persons who were involved in the assassination of President Kennedy; he may well have identified with this act of violence.

He became passive, remorseful, and depressed when asked about his threats against the President. He had no animosity toward the President, he said; in fact, he cried when President Kennedy, "the greatest President we have ever had," was assassinated. His intelligence was about average; his personality makeup, inadequate. He was a passive and dependent individual who felt threatened by everyone, particularly women, and feared, therefore, that he would be unable to live up to his aspirations. Several times during his life he had started psychiatric treatment, but had always resorted to alcohol to escape from his own shortcomings. In order to make his mark, he tried to excel, and this brought about disastrous results. Frank showed strong self-destructive tendencies that were turned both inward against himself in the form of alcoholism and outward in the form of hostile aggression and threats. His bravado and his escapades were to Frank an unconscious way of showing his mother that he was not as inadequate as she thought he was, that he was able to act like a man. But at the same time as he felt strong, he also felt weak. His fantasy of omnipotence, in turn, counteracted his weakness, resulting in an inner battle in which he was looking for revenge, ready to attack.

Although Frank was seriously disturbed emotionally, he was not found to be insane. The real or would-be assassin is not necessarily insane, although many prove to be. There is an aura of mystery about these men who flash for an instant before the public, create nationwide chaos —then disappear behind a barrage of newspaper editorials, the cautious sentimentalizing of their families, personal reminiscence based on casual acquaintance, and official reports.

Of the eleven threat cases examined, four were considered to be psychotic, suffering from schizophrenia of which they had exhibited symptoms for a long time and which made it imperative that they be kept in a mental hospital. The other seven showed varying symptoms of either neurotic conditions or character disorders. They were considered able to stand trial in that they understood the charges against them, and were able to confer with lawyers and aid in their own defenses. They were considered responsible for their threats because at the time of their conduct they did not lack substantial capacity to know or appreciate the wrongfulness of their conduct or to conform their conduct to the requirements of law.*

All of the persons examined had either an antisocial or criminal record or a history of some mental disturbance, often both. One defendant had been arrested and imprisoned because he had turned in five false alarms. All had poor school records in which truancy had played a great role.

Would-be assassins in general seem more concerned about world events than other criminals. Many of these examined read a great many newspapers and books, and evinced strong interest in things happening around them. They looked at the world as a place of chaos and unrest that they themselves were somehow ordained to "clean up." Of course, their assertions that their "right" values were being threatened, that the world was chaotic, reflected in part their own feelings of being threatened. Threatening governmental leaders was in one way a cry for help: they felt that their government should take care of them, help them out of their misery—in other words, meet their dependency needs.

There is a remarkable similarity in the family constellations of real and would-be assassins. In the backgrounds of most of the defendants examined, the father was found to be weak, unassuming, or absent from home. Not having any manly, stable figure with whom to identify, the defendants often identified with strong and

* The data given here differs substantially from the findings of Dr. David A. Rothstein, who examined eleven similar prisoners at the U.S. Medical Center for Federal Prisoners and found them all psychotic. The reason for this difference is that he examined patients who in order to be committed to the mental hospital are all psychotic, while my investigation dealt with individuals whose cases were pending trial in court.[3]

dominant mothers, bringing about a distorted identification.* Consequently, being unable to drain off their childhood omnipotent fantasies, they became engrossed in them to such an extent that they believed they could do more than the average person, they could change the world. Their threats and attacks against governmental officials, therefore, seemed justified in their fantasies—in a desire to be in the limelight, a reflection of their own importance.

A need for revenge was perhaps the most significant motivation underlying their threats, an outgrowth of their intense desire to have what they once were denied. And even when reality was against this fulfillment, they tried to achieve it, regardless of obstacles.

Unconscious sexual elements underlay and permeated the revenge motivation. The mother was often described as kind and nice, although records indicated that this was far from the case. This indicated a tendency on the part of the would-be assassin to "protect" his mother, at the same time, of course, protecting his own feelings toward her. To him the mother was forbidden—and forbidding—territory. Being unable to sublimate his sexual feelings, he would rather deny any closer feeling to her. But being at the same time unable to accept his own sexual aggression, he had to find another outlet for it. Ten of the eleven defendants had married, but they had very poor marital relationships, resulting often in divorce.

We have found the same crippling maladjustment in rapists and other violent sexual offenders. Unconsciously

* It is noteworthy that some of the mothers of the would-be assassins expressed to their children angry or vengeful threats against the husbands who had deserted them.

inviting sexual aggression, the wives of these rapists responded only with coolness and rejection. This stimulated the husbands into trying to prove themselves, but all these attempts ended in frustration and magnified their doubts about their masculinity. In creating this pattern the wives unwittingly related to the sex offenders as their mothers had.[4]

While most threats were serious, two of the defendants had been anxious to be caught, prevented from committing these violent acts. They both called the FBI and all but blueprinted their own arrests.

The would-be assassins examined all experienced intense hatred; feelings of helplessness, dependency, and frustration; fearfulness; extreme fantasies of omnipotence; and gory death wishes. They were sadistic and exceedingly sensitive to criticism; during the interviews they frequently became suddenly angry, indicating their low frustration level. Some of them had grown up in families where the parents were brutal, thus experiencing violence at an early age. Those who threatened to kill or were suspected of doing so were found to have been stimulated sexually and then frustrated by their mothers, producing the same psychological mechanisms seen in sex offenders. The mother was seductive toward the child, alternating with cruelty and harshness. The real or imagined violent act was thus a displaced attempt to force the seductive and yet rejecting mother into giving.

Is there any difference between the would-be political assassin and the man who threatens someone in his family or his environment? What is the difference between the murderer who, for instance, kills his unfaithful wife or someone who interrupts him during a robbery, and the one who kills a governmental official because he "stands in the way of world order"? Under what circumstances does violence spill over from the family into society, directing itself against the leaders of a government? These questions are particularly important to us because our country has suffered the grievous loss by the hands of an assassin of four presidents: Lincoln, Garfield, McKinley, and Kennedy. In addition, serious threats of assassination have been made against Presidents Andrew Johnson, Franklin Delano Roosevelt, and Harry S. Truman.

Looking broadly at the political assassin in our history, we see that he was always a personal failure, an isolated human being, incapable of exhibiting genuine human relationships and possessing extraordinary ambitions that were out of proportion to his intellectual and emotional assets. Most significantly, the American assassin—with the possible exception of Lincoln's slayer, John Wilkes Booth—never acted in a plot together with others to overthrow the government.

The assassin may justify his act by grandiose declarations of political motivation, as did Leon P. Czolgosz, who shot President McKinley to death on September 6, 1901.

I don't believe in the republican form of government and I don't believe we should have any ruler. It is right to kill them. I had that idea when I shot the President, and that is why I was there. . . . After I shot twice they knocked me down and trampled on me. Somebody hit me in the face. I said to the officer that brought me down "I done my duty." I don't believe in voting, it is against my principles. I am an anarchist. I don't believe in marriage. I believe in free love. I fully understand what I was doing when I shot the President. I realized that I was sacrificing my life. I am willing to take the consequences.[5]

The underlying emotional motivations, however, are always consistent with the pattern we have seen. American political assassins have never killed a President who was a dictator or a tyrant, as has so often happened in Europe. Our Presidents, I believe, have been benevolent. Although some of them were mediocre, none was a dictator. Our Constitution with its checks and balances has seen to that.

The fact, then, that we have nevertheless had our share of assassinations indicates that the emotional climate here may have had more to do with it than would be discernible from the social factors alone.

The assassin sees the world around him as ugly because his own inner world is ugly. He would like to rationalize his violent act—give it some moral-political cause. This was the case with Czolgosz, and this is also what we find in the case of President Lincoln's killer.

John Wilkes Booth's murder of Lincoln is often attributed to his fanatical belief that the President, having abolished slavery, had become an enemy of the people and therefore had to die. His personality structure and his life, however, tell a different story.

Looking into Booth's childhood, we find intense fantasies of power and revenge. As a youth he confided to a schoolmate that he fantasized of toppling the Colossus at Rhodes, one of the seven wonders of the world. He also asserted that "he would do something that would hand his name down to posterity never to be forgotten, even after he had been dead a thousand years." [6]

The assassin, unlike the nonpolitical murderer, is motivated by grandiose ideas, usually of revenge, to the point of "derangement," as they said a century ago—or as we would say today, "displacement," the displacement of a deep uncontainable hatred for a family figure to an authority figure in public life.

The grandiosity of Booth's fantasies were heightened by his mother. His birth was preceded by a series of deaths and family misfortunes that no doubt affected her sanity. When he was an infant she had an hallucination: in the fire on the hearth she saw an arm in the flames, bent and menacing, which signified to her a magnificent destiny for her son. She often spoke of this "vision," no doubt prompting him to fantasize around it.

A failure as an actor in comparison to his famous father and older brothers—particularly Edwin, who was idolized by the public—Booth felt slighted by the world as well as within the family. When he was fourteen, his father, who consciously wanted none of his sons to be actors but nevertheless shaped the careers of his two older sons, split the family in half, taking the two older brothers to San Francisco and leaving John behind on a Maryland farm with his mother, sisters, and younger brother. Bitterly resenting this, John began to plan defiantly for his own acting career.

His acting developed a stealthy, surreptitious, aggressive quality. His youthful, fanatical espousal of the cause of the Confederacy (at twenty-one he joined the militia that assisted in the capture of John Brown) was in direct variance with the politics of his most successful brother, Edwin, who voted for Lincoln. His decisive and final plot—to assassinate Lincoln, Seward, and Johnson—was formulated at the time of Edwin's greatest period of success, when, no doubt, his thwarted ambition and repressed anger against Edwin were particularly virulent, and when the close of the Civil War and the defeat of the South served as the rationalization for his act.

On the night of the assassination, before entering Ford's Theatre he went to Taltavel's Tavern for a drink, where he was accosted by an intoxicated man who belittled him with "You'll never be the actor your father was." He replied with calm certainty, "When I leave the stage, I will be the most famous man in America."

His plan for multiple assassination of three government figures suggests that his victims as a group represented his father and two older brothers. He had left the deaths of the minor figures to two accomplices—it is perhaps noteworthy that one of them was a woman.

There was great distance between John Wilkes Booth and his father, not only physically but emotionally. Therefore he grew close to his mother, who with her husband often away on tour, exerted a tremendous influence upon his early development. There was almost a symbiosis between the mentally deranged mother and her son, to whom she undoubtedly transmitted some of her own distorted ideas. Feeling deprived of a father and unable to find any male figure with whom to identify, John formed a distorted identification in which threats against his masculinity were prominent. As he matured, the struggle grew to compete with his father and his successful older brothers, particularly Edwin. Somehow he had to out-do them.

Nurtured by these feelings of revenge and dominated by a strong mother from whom he ambiguously tried to liberate himself, he set upon his fatal course.

From clinical experience we know that acts directed against one particular person are unconsciously directed against someone else. The hatred John Wilkes Booth focused on President Lincoln was a displacement of his hatred for his father and Edwin, which stemmed from his early childhood. This hatred, combined with a distorted identification that left him in limbo, resulted in his murder of the President.

The assassin or would-be assassin unconsciously selects a victim who represents what he himself wants to be or to have but cannot. He wants to be a person who can receive attention and control events—in other words, to be like the man he wishes to kill. Rather than emulating the public figure, however, he hates him in order to protect himself from fear and anxiety that might be stimulated if he were to adopt a constructive orientation toward the government: if he thought positively about the government he would have to think negatively about himself, admit that there might be something wrong with him. His feelings of hate are stimulated because the leader or the head of the government is able not only to release hope but is also capable of releasing hate in the assassin. Under the guise of political or social conviction, therefore, he directs and often acts out his hostility toward the governmental leader to whom he has displaced his childhood hate.

In examining the records of the eleven threat cases described earlier, we find parallels to the life histories of Lee Harvey Oswald and John Wilkes Booth. Most striking, fundamentally, is the pattern of dependency relationships all of the would-be assassins had with their mothers, the maternal deprivation, and the power the mothers exerted over their children. Even in cases where it appeared that an individual was kept or kept himself at a distance from his mother, he was emotionally overwhelmed by her. In all of the would-be assassins we find emotional disturbance, sometimes to the point of psychotic involvement. More important, perhaps, is the presence in most of them of suicidal tendencies, or attempts at suicide, indicating their frustrated rage against themselves. Those who were eager to be apprehended were unconsciously asking for help and punishment.

The other dominant pattern is one of anger at male authority. Two individuals had fathers who were policemen, but often, as in the case of Lee Harvey Oswald, the rage was directed basically against the mother figure with a superimposed father figure, the act of threat being an act of revenge and self-punishment. Central to this rage was a confusion of identity resulting from the absence or lack of a father. This was expressed in latent homosexuality and alcoholism, through which hostile aggression was displaced from women to men. It is noteworthy that several of the would-be assassins had joined various branches of the military service in an attempt to find masculine identification. Often an individual enlisted to emulate an older brother who had had military service (a double-barreled attempt at identification); more important, however, was his need to get himself out of the clutches of the woman by joining an organization that would take care of him. But since the service could not fulfill the would-be assassin's expectations, could not, in other words, become his father, he became frustrated and directed his anger toward the head of the government the service represented.

We may ask why these would-be assassins direct their anger and threats against the President or other government officials rather than against other glamorous figures who are in the limelight. The reason, of course, is that society figures and stars of the theater, movies, or the sports world who are making the headlines do not satisfy their displacement needs.

Assassination in most other countries is truly political in nature; in the United States, however, where the structure of our government prevents totalitarianism, it is usually the act of an emotionally unstable individual. Potential assassins in our country are preoccupied with their own fantasies and dreams. Hating the world around them, they long for their own world, which they have created in their own image, and therefore strike out when their regressive fantasies of carrying out grandiose deeds reach their peak. Because they desire perfection in their lives, they feel easily threatened and become vulnerable to changes in their environment; they wish for change, but only insofar as they can dictate it. Reality for them is dreamlike, something that must be controlled in accordance with their fantasies—even if the means to their control be murder.

The American Dream— Inspiration or Deception?

In order to explain further why our frustrations and our innate aggressive drives have produced in America so fertile a soil for violent acting out, we must consider one essential influence to which I alluded previously, the influence most peculiar to our environment—the American Dream. It is a dominant force affecting the unconscious —the wellsprings of behavior—in all of us. To understand it is essential because of its bearing upon our life and behavior as a nation of people, all of us either immigrants or descendants of immigrants. Along the line of our national development into a violent society lies the American Dream—the dream of a Promised Land.

Although the term "American Dream" did not come

into being before the early twentieth century, the wish contained in it has existed in one form or another as long as man himself. The perennial dream of man, which lies at the root of the American Dream, is of the same nature as our personal dreams. In the dream and fantasy world, perhaps more than in any other sphere of human activity, the individual and the group merge; hence, the individual in the dream world is the prototype of the group, and for this reason *the American Dream expresses every man's personal dream.*

Any deeply satisfying dream a country offers is, of necessity, joined with the personal desires and dreams of each of its citizens. The American Dream, therefore, embodies our wishful fantasies as individuals and projects them into the fabric of our country. Among them is the desire for strength, which is instinctual in all men. We want to feel powerful, to think of ourselves as in command of any situation. Even when we suspect the desire for unalloyed power to be contrary to reality, we are predisposed to a further "show of strength." When we are not in command of a painful situation, we very often resist acknowledging our weakness by rationalizing that what we need is an even more forceful solution to it.

Our hopes for and demands upon the future, more pronounced here than in any other country, lie in our inborn desires stimulated by the abundance of our land. And our future-oriented insistence on their fulfillment is continually activated by the age-old Messianic mirage of a land where milk and honey flow and every need is instinctly fulfilled—a land which is, of course, Paradise. A substitute for immediate gratification, the Perennial

Dream is a childish desire symbolizing the instinctual needs of man.

While the American Dream has created different images in us, it has always been emotionally charged with utopian ideas. Thomas Wolfe eloquently described the promise it has held out to us:

So, then to every man his chance—to every man regardless of his birth, his shining golden opportunity—to every man the right to live, to work, to be himself, and to become whatever thing his manhood and his vision can combine to make him— this, seeker, is the promise of America.[1]

This was precisely the dream of the Mayflower people and of all our immigrants.

"American history is the most romantic of all histories. It began in myth and has developed through centuries of fairy stories," wrote Bernard DeVoto.[2] The myth he referred to, present as a psychological influence, is an obvious point from which we may begin to study our unconscious beginnings, the feelings involved in the emotional childhood of our country, in order to discover some of the origins of our attitudes in general and of our violent behavior patterns in particular.

The myth is almost primeval in origin, universal, deep in the unconscious of all of us and endlessly recurrent, and when America was discovered, the fantasy of a Paradise began to seem real. Here, inspiring the first settlers' feelings of adventure and imagination, in contrast to their own often miserable existence, was a glorious fantasy indeed—a land that, like a good mother, would give them everything they wanted. It would be a place of pleasure without pain, rich and wonderful. We easily recognize here much of the American Dream—and realize how little it has changed despite disappointments and trial.

In these representations, of course, we see the ideal of childhood. To be taken care of, to have everything given to him, is the need of the dependent child. In the concept of Paradise lies the adult's yearning to return to his childhood, a time when, since the child is dependent emotionally as well as in fact, if his needs are not satisfied, he knows only that he is frustrated and becomes angry.

When we feel let down or rejected, we try somehow to pull ourselves out of our frustration, and one way to do this is by using our fantasy to conjure up wishful, pleasant things, anticipating that these may come our way. In this way our fantasy serves as a defense against our troubled situation. This is not particular to Americans alone, since all people use the same psychology. But where there seem to be more opportunities, this conjuring up of fantasies seems to be more prevalent.

In all fantasy we find the possibility of glorified existence, in Nirvana, in a life hereafter, in any way which promises to improve our lot, and of course, in the dream of life in a new land. Fantasies and dreams augment yearning. They encourage us to attempt a fusion between the imagined and the real. If, in a dream, people discover a desired place, they attempt to find it on earth.

The American Dream, then, began as fantasy. Its vital source was the unconscious; its stimulus, tales of new lands; its motivation, a blissful existence. We must understand the unconscious impetus, the power of fantasy and dream, in order to understand our past and present violence.

It is customary, with good reason, to look to the past for indications that may, in part, explain the present. While data collected from our American past is easily available, the unconscious underlying emotions that motivated and still motivate the American people have not been given special attention. Yet these are determinants in a very real sense, as tangible as our geography, our climate, and our economy.

The Puritans were a small clan. We know from whence they came, their names, their thoughts, and their feelings because they faithfully recorded them. Their struggles, their sadness and joy, their hopes and their frustrations, their prejudices, and their singlemindedness and steadfastness have been made clear. From William Bradford's diary, which clearly records the Puritans' experience, we can approximate an interpolation of their reactions, particularly their fundamental fear, which bred hatred and violence against the "savage and brutish men" who were part of the landscape.

We can well imagine that as fears of their overseas voyage and what they might expect to find in America began to enliven their minds and their fantasies, they were overcome alternately by hope and dread. These were traumatizing experiences, which consciously or unconsciously intensified their already considerable anxiety about their undertaking.

We admire the Puritans—and rightly so—for their courage, steadfastness, and imagination throughout the inhuman suffering they had to endure in their efforts to secure their footing on American soil. Their perseverence brings to mind Lord Tennyson's words from Ulysses: "To

strive, to seek, to find and not to yield." Feeling they
were God's chosen people, doing everything in His service,
reinforced their conduct.

The fearful and hostile feelings which they brought
with them to these shores were reinforced by their hardship, just as the carryover of our early childhood experiences affects our attitudes in adulthood when we go
through traumatic experiences. They were fighting for
their survival—in psychological as well as physical terms.
Their instinct for self-preservation became a need to master a great many new situations. For most it was a drastic
change from a relatively secure life to a hazardous existence—like the change a newborn baby experiences when
he leaves the womb to enter a new, threatening environment. As a consequence, force became the preferred, even
if not always the effective, instrument of survival; attack
became the means of defense.

Under stress, all of us tend to regress to the early
stages of our childhood, to resume our earlier patterns
of behavior and become dependent again; we demand to
be loved and accepted, expect immediate gratification,
and when our wishes are not fulfilled, feel frustrated—and
become angry. For the Puritans to live up to their ego-
ideal demanded strength and self-discipline. Being consciously aware that they would not return to England,
they felt they had to succeed. But their desire for success, which had something of a compulsive quality,
intensified their fear of failure. Whenever there is a need
to *prove* one is successful, we can be sure that it stems
from a *fear* of not succeeding. This was the case with the
Puritans. While not always consciously aware of that fear,
they would be anxious and fearful about their undertak-

ing and feel threatened. Therefore they resisted any infringement upon their way of life. In their insecurity, they rejected and, when possible, suppressed any idea or belief that was alien or considered dangerous to their own. As Perry Miller expressed it, "Piety was the inspiration for the Puritan heroism. . . . It also made sharp the edge of Puritan cruelty and justified the Puritan in his persecution of disagreement. . . . It inspired Puritan idealism and encouraged Puritan snobbery." [3]

A person's tendency to put his forceful impulses into action is conditioned by the way he is brought up to handle his personal and physical environment, and we may surmise that such a conditioned tendency is transmitted from generation to generation. The Puritans' use of force, therefore, which despite their repressive efforts did become a way of life, has influenced our present national attitude.

How can the historical experience of a group remote in time, occupying only a small corner of the country, and despite the claims of many people, generating only a tiny proportion of our present population, have such great influence on our contemporary life? It is not only the reality of their lives that has shaped the course of ours, but also the myth of their experiences, which has entered into our national mythology.

There is little doubt that the myth of the Puritans' influence lives on in our minds. They are revered and blamed for whatever misfortunes we go through or whatever violence we manifest. However, to establish a causal link between the fact that some Puritans held rigid, distorted views and the fact that some present-day Americans hold similar views is difficult, if not impossible to do because of the intervening centuries and the many other strands of influence operative on our national consciousness.

To understand the process we must turn to psychoanalysis. We have learned that a child adopts his attitudes and ideas from his parents, through the process of identification, which is mostly unconscious. The ego-ideal, which sees to it that we behave the way other people do, is the main factor in repressing our irrational desires.

The Puritan myth has served as a powerful and respected ego-ideal. To the nation the Pilgrims had the very real emotional function of serving as "superior" familial figures with whom to identify. In the same way, people often speak with quiet pride of some great uncle who founded the family business. They like when possible to keep a portrait of this ancestor; since he *began* the business, he did more in their opinion than those who *continued* it. The man who *saves* the family fortune—if a family is lucky enough to have one—is loved and admired, but the man who *first founded it* is respected most of all and becomes part of his descendants' superego and ego-ideal. Something similar may have taken place with our views of the Puritans.

We shall now leap into more recent history.

An exciting part of what later developed into the American Dream found strong expression in the life of the expanding frontier. It was here that our fantasies and dreams were first either transformed into reality or remained pipedreams.

In order to survive, the frontiersman had to fight against the overwhelming and impersonal forces of nature. And while he could use the plow or spade, his rifle and ax were at least as necessary if not more so. Such an attitude also colored his personal relationships. Through his own actions he could reap his own rewards, or by his own negligence he could cause his own death. The precariousness of his existence developed his adventurous and aggressive tendencies, and evoked his instinct for survival and his sexual drive, intensifying his fight for his own, most individual life. The man who survived, since many perished in the wilderness, laid down the standards for behavior, rules, and values. His ego-ideal became the accepted ideal of the frontier establishments.

Each man acted for himself. Rugged individualism was highly enterprising, egocentric, hostile, and narrow. This individualism, to some extent necessary and in a large measure practical, spurred the frontiersman to take things in his own hands. The frontier establishments were built by solitary people, each fiercely guarding his own settlement. Because of the often vast distances between the would-be farms, each man relied upon and kept to himself. Of course, when help was needed on the neighboring settlement, he could extend it, but once he had done so, it was usually all that he felt he ought to do. "I stand on my own, so my neighbor too should stand on his own," was common thinking. Noteworthy are Allan Nevins' words following a visit to Israel after the Second World War: "I could not but think how superior the genial and helpful atmosphere of the *kibbutz* settlement was to the rugged individualism and separatism of western Illinois." [4]

This type of separatism was in all probability at work all over the country. The frontiersman was an estranged individual, rugged and arrogant. If, as has been said, every American is a king, the frontiersman was foremost in ruling his own kingdom, the boundaries of which he himself had staked out. He was an isolated individual who wanted to be free, and he sought this freedom in the wilderness where there was no encroachment upon his individuality. The wish to build his own world drove him to seek faraway regions that nurtured his already existing need for loneliness. This loneliness, often arising from stubborn pride, was identified by the vast, boundless land. Out of this isolation arose, to the largest extent, the *American loneliness.*

Although a great deal of sentimentality was present in the frontiersman's loneliness, there was an aloofness in him that was instrumental in his often violent acting out of his fantasies with little or no concern for the law. *He* was the law because here he was master over an area even larger than what we think of as the frontier. The frontier, in fact, was a large fluctuating area. One side of it was settled, relatively old, and somewhat stable; the other side was open, empty land inhabited by native Indians, which, even with the obvious risks, offered unknown opportunities. It was natural for the frontiersman to become his own law, subject solely to his own whims. Only by ruling himself could he be sure to be able to pursue his goal. He was a self-governing person in an environment where the law of the strongest dominated.

Wherever new frontiers were opened, wherever new finds of minerals and oils were made, wherever new routes were established, cities and towns mushroomed without much plan or order, a deluge of people suddenly appeared—and a new battle for survival began. Conflicts between frontier people were prevalent and sharp.

To keep law and order, force was often necessary. The line that separated law enforcement from lawlessness was thin. Often the same individual maintained and broke the law—Wild Bill Hickok, for instance.

One of the most famous frontier law-enforcers was Roy Bean, known as "The Law West of the Pecos." In the 1880s Bean got himself appointed Justice of the Peace in Texas in order to be able to reap profits by presiding not only over the bar of justice but also over the barroom. That he was at the same time jury, judge, and executioner and kept most of the fines he imposed was not unusual in the West; there had been many such "lawmen." His method of meting out justice, however, was unique. The El Paso *Daily Times* reported on June 2, 1884:

Here is the latest on Roy Bean:

Somebody killed a Chinaman and was brought up standing before the irrepressible Roy, who looked through two or three dilapidated law books from stem to stern and finally turned the culprit loose remarking that he'd be d — — — — d if he could find any law against killing a Chinaman.[5]

During Bean's lifetime his myth had reached such heights that his brother Sam wrote:

You may have graduated at Yale or Harvard and carry a number of diplomas, but if you have not seen or heard of Judge Roy Bean of Texas you are groping in darkness and there yet remains a large space to be filled in your classical head.[6]

Frontier life was savage and cruel and led to rigid defense and attack, easily precipitating violence. The frontiersman, before he became settled, lived as a nomad or seminomad, "like Lincoln's father, fonder of fishing and hunting than of the steady toil of the peasant." [7] Many frontier people were boisterous and drank to excess. They identified themselves in much of their life with the roaming Indians; hunting the buffalo, at odds with those who had already settled.

Legends of the Wild West still live on in our minds and on our television screens. While men like Paul Bunyan or the boatman Mike Frick or Little John of the forest belong now to our history, it is such men of aggression as the James or Dalton brothers or Billy the Kid who still ignite and stir our fantasy and who, as an integral part of the acting out of the American Dream, nourish our repressed violent desires. Towns like Tombstone, with its Boot Hill Cemetery dedicated to those who were killed with their boots on, commemorate the lawlessness of frontier life.

The weak, the sleepy, and the do-gooder did not survive well on the frontier. The necessity for vigilance, resourcefulness, and swift action produced a continuing stress situation, exerting emotional pressure and coloring attitudes and outlook, that laid the foundation for a stress-sensitive (hypersensitive) society. One manifestation of sensitivity to stress is disregard for the law, and a measure of this disregard is the prominent role in frontier life played by killers.

We have been looking at what really took place on the frontier, but our fantasy of frontier existence as depicted over and over again in the many western films and television stories differs from reality, particularly in its concept of the hero.

The hero of the frontier life is never the man who plows

the land, feeds the cattle, or reaps the harvest. He is a young man, like a boy, a cowboy who has come upon the scene almost out of nowhere. He does not seem to have any parents; he is almost like another Moses, in the wilderness, and like Moses he maintains order of a sort. While Moses had the Ten Commandments, our hero has two guns and his horse, which is the only thing he cares about, his only love. Invariably he becomes involved with trying to find the bank robbers or the person who wounded or killed the old farmer. Although he does not know anyone, is a complete stranger to the local situation, he has a remarkable knack for meeting any danger squarely, so he knows instantly what to do and where to go. In this respect he is resourceful. In a pitched battle he shoots it out with the lawless people, and he is almost never hurt. As the story comes to an end, the old man is restored to health while his beaming daughter casts hidden glances at the cowboy hero. But he is emotionally blind to this, never admitting his sexual desires. He is, in a way, asexual. His only concern is to carry out his task. In contrast to the old folks—parents who brought about disorder—his mission is to restore peace, and he always succeeds.

The crime against the bank or the attempted killing of the old man is symbolically a reawakening of his own childhood fantasy of wanting to kill the father and rape the mother. Through his heroic deed on the ranch he revenges himself. He resolves everything as he wished it to be in his childhood fantasy. And then he leaves, riding on his horse, his faithful friend—two shadows lost in the mist of the prairie.

The Wild West story with all its variations is another

expression of the Oedipus situation. But in contrast to Oedipus, who felt guilty when he became aware that he had killed his father and married his mother, the cowboy is without guilt, and his death fantasies toward his father and yearning for his mother are completely hidden from him. Instead of planning his life around a goal, he lives in the present, basing his life upon a code of good-natured benevolence and expected justice. Being independent, he avoids any long-term responsibility or sexual involvement. Instead, he enacts his childhood glory over and over again in admirable adventures, without touching his unconscious, where his old unresolved conflict resides. This encounter is the most elementary struggle.

Therefore also the cowboy story is enjoyed by the child or adolescent left in us. We never walk into the forbidden territory. Maybe we would like to wet our feet, but we hurriedly retreat to safety. Like the cowboy we avoid the conflict. Instead of feeling anxious and guilty, we are excited and thrilled. Instead of finding out what is hidden in our childhood dreams and infantile fantasies about the primal scene, we are entertained by the bloody Wild West drama. We have regressed through our own daydreams back to the innocence of our childhood. The cowboy's sexual desires are acted out under the disguise of benevolent deeds. Even when he is fighting and killing, his violence takes the form of a certain innocence, as if it were without any social consequences. His behavior is a sort of play-acting where no reality is involved. Ignoring the girl who tries to make him aware of her love, he turns his sexual libido into shooting.

We may draw a parallel between the cowboy and the modern romantic hero James Bond. Bond too is a loner, performing unbelievable and fantastic deeds of derring-do. Nothing is impossible for him. He becomes involved with a whole procession of beautiful women, yet none of them has any real emotional meaning to him. While he appears to exist, he has no meaningful existence within family and friends.

There is little doubt that Americans consider the myth of the frontier extremely romantic. It obviously serves as an outlet for our aggressions, and the myth of the cowboy and his life gives us an easy escape from all realistic trouble. Behind these romantic devices lurks the American Dream with its promise of wish fulfillment.

Frederick Jackson Turner characterized the frontier as the most potent force in molding the character of the American people,[8] and Ray Allen Billington, referring to Turner, said, "The unusual environment and the continuous rebirth of society in the Western Wilderness, endowed the American people and their institutions with characteristics not shared by the rest of the world." [9] Prominent among these characteristics is the dream of a promised land.

Our feelings toward life have become in great measure conditioned by what I would term *the mental frontier* of the American people—their fantasies, drives, and aspirations, which stimulated by their new environment became the American Dream. As people saw this dream materializing through America's geographical abundance and its building democratic social structure, their optimism grew. America's promise of liberating man through equality, justice, and reason seemed to be reaching fulfillment and it reflected the hopes and needs inherent in every human being and appealed to all who had ever longed for a better way of life. It meant that they could practice their religion freely; it meant that the land they tilled could belong to them; it meant they could build businesses of their own; it means a chance for a voice in their government. Our Declaration of Independence, our Constitution, our Bill of Rights, and our striving to make these a reality singled out America as the central focus for gratification of man's dreams.

There is always a close tie between what people feel and fantasize as individuals and what their nation has at heart. The American Dream, therefore, lying at the root of both our individual emotional life and our national existence, has been a vital force in our evolution as individuals and as a people. It has come to form the foundation of our economic and political achievements so that we now have one of the highest standards of living in the world and have won the admiration and envy of many other people. We are justifiably imbued with a sense of pride. The power of the Dream lies in its underlying motivation for growth and expansion, expressed in its tremendous surging vitality, and reflecting the deep emotional need shared by all strata of our society.

Having observed how the constructive effects of the Dream came about, we may now ask, How did violence become part of the Dream itself, and how did the link come about in particular between the American Dream and our violent society?

While the American Dream has stimulated and made possible our great achievement in this country, it remains at the root of many of our unrealistic, negative, and destructive attitudes. Has it not nurtured our dreams of growing rich quickly, of being immune to failure, of convincing others that our way of life is the *only* way—attitudes that have brought about frustration and anger, crime and slums, and acting out to the point of force and violence? Has it not in its inexorable insistence on speed contributed to a fluidity of identification in our people? And above all, has not its emphasis on materialism led to exploitation of people, violation of their individual dignity, and disregard of their welfare, along with an almost insatiable desire to conquer everything within our reach? Has it not fostered in us a feeling that we are invincible and omnipotent—a feeling that, as we have seen in the case of the individual, leads to aggression? Hasn't our search for new individual accomplishments throughout our frontier life, a pattern fostered and handed down from generation to generation, emerged forcefully and ruthlessly whenever the competition and threats to our security become acute?

When we explore our individual dreams and fantasies, we will understand better why the American Dream with its promising future has come to have a disastrous effect upon us. The destructive aspect of the American Dream is fundamentally part of our death instinct.

Underlying our individual dreams are feelings of hope and fear. We dream at night or create daytime fantasies because we hope to achieve something, because we find it difficult to obtain the things we want, or because we are afraid that someone will deprive us of what we already have. The same feelings are at the bottom of the American Dream. It arises from the depth of our unconscious and expresses the hopes and fears, wishes and frustrations that have been intimately tied to our being since our earliest childhood.

Our dreams often help us to resolve our conflicts, giving us answers that our conscious minds have not perceived. They protect us, too: by helping to discharge emotional tension, to let off steam, they serve as a buffer between our inner selves and the frustrations we experience. Our dreams and fantasies reveal the struggle between our unconscious desires—either wish fulfillment or our fear of something threatening—and our personality, and the American Dream, being part of our yearnings, takes part in that struggle.

In the American Dream we find components of *both* the daydream and the night dream. It is partly a daydream or fantasy because we are frequently conscious of its content and because it contains certain specific and realistically attainable goals that prepare us for action. Its promise of opportunity embedded in the country's richness has lead us to anticipate, to expect something good in the future. It is object-centered, directed toward a definite goal—that of fulfilling our immediate needs in order to gratify us. Like our daydreams, it is flexible, adaptable to changing situations.

It bears a greater similarity to our night dreams, however, appearing intangible and elusive, continually waxing and waning, changing, and effecting a lingering hold upon us. It is essentially a wish fulfillment, and like all wishes it has utopian and idealistic features that are out of proportion to what we are able to achieve realistically.

The element of searching for a world without pain or toil, returning to Paradise (mother) that is strongly present in the American Dream is closely related to the perennial, continually returning dream in people. In wishing, we are actually hoping our desires will be fulfilled sud-

denly and without effort by the wave of a magic wand, for
all of us tend unconsciously to believe that some magic
power brings our wishes to fruition. When at times they
come true quickly, we tend to think of ourselves as possessing a part of the magic power, as being omnipotent
and invincible. And one of the American Dream's strongest effects upon us has been that it has fostered feelings
of invincibility and omnipotence.

These feelings have been essential to the mastering of
many of our difficult tasks. They have helped us to conquer and gain dominion of our physical environment
and have stimulated our desire to gain the upper hand in
whatever situation we find ourselves.

To a large extent our wishes have been transformed
into achievements. Driven by our desires and by the
American Dream, we have taken possession of this continent and made it into a flourishing land for most of our
people. Our successes have instilled in us the feeling that
we can have *anything* and *everything* we wish. Our wish,
neither unnatural nor abnormal under the circumstances,
has led to a desire to dominate and control, which in turn
has led to use of violence.

Our environment has unconsciously conditioned our
aggressive behavior. Because of its vastness we see ourselves as spectacular builders: our spanning of East to
West, our building of our sprawling cities where no cities
had been, our engineering of high bridges over roaring
rivers or deep canyons were awesome achievements to us.
I am inclined to believe that we have assimilated some
of the wildness we have tamed.

To prove such an idea is impossible; there is no evidence
anywhere in the social sciences that people living in

wild surroundings are more "wild" than people who live in tamer surroundings. What can be said, however, is that in all spectacular behavior there is a desire to display more drama than the actual situation requires. Acting out one's impulses can become more a selfish show to draw attention to oneself than a genuine desire for the act itself. This unconsciously motivated acting out is a means of relieving inner tension. When this is accomplished, new frustrations may set in and new tension accumulate, resulting in new acting out.

Through this process, and using the American Dream as an instrument, we have transferred our aggression from our physical environment to our culture, from nature to our society. From using violence in the raw, in nature, we have unconsciously succumbed to the use of violence in our daily lives.

Steeped as we are in our own culture and in all of its characteristic feelings, as every nation is in some measure, it is difficult if not impossible for most of us to step outside our own environment and look in. We look at ourselves not as observers but as participants, and therefore find our actions, whether domestic or national, most natural. We accept and approve of ourselves because this is the way we have come to form our ideas about ourselves. While the ego-ideal individually is observing and critical of the self, a people has a tendency to lose its individual critical grasp of its behavior. We have difficulty in seeing our blind spots, because all our behavior is directed by unconscious feelings, and governed by our self-image—the picture we have of ourselves as individuals and as a people.

Every country is a combination of its emotions and

geography. Our country constitutes a laboratory of emotions, people, and land, the bounty of which surpasses any other country. With bounty such as ours, materialistic desires are stimulated. The intensification of these desires frequently has brought to the fore hostile aggressions spurred greatly by the American Dream. Our materialistic desires have surpassed the idealistic feelings the Dream contained.

The promise of economic gain and security that made America a haven for the deprived and oppressed colored the Dream, and the fact that, as President Franklin Delano Roosevelt said, "All of our people—except full-blooded Indians—are immigrants, including even those who came here on the Mayflower," [10] has contributed to our tendency toward violent acting out.

The psychology of the immigrant is always the psychology of the uprooted man. As Oscar Handlin says, "Immigration altered America, but it also altered the immigrant." [11] Being uprooted, he was bound to feel uncertain, fearful, ambivalent, and often hostile toward his old or his new country, depending upon his childhood traumatic experiences and his unsatisfied needs. This ambivalence has expressed itself in almost as many different ways as there have been immigrants, although certain behavior patterns can be clearly discerned:

1. The immigrant may feel so uprooted and angry that he is determined to make his new life a success in order to prove that his leaving home was not a mistake.

2. He may accept America and what she stands for on the surface, and at the same time continue to dream about and glorify the "old country," forgetting the tribulations he may have endured there. By doing this, he

hides his feelings that his roots are founded in something that is undesirable.

3. He may try to do everything to support or cooperate with his new government, but at the same time keep comparing it with the regime in his native land and resent all new authority.

4. He may accede to hardship temporarily and be willing to work in order to realize his expectations, but unconsciously feel he should have more for doing less because he has suffered so much and expects that special consideration be given to him.

5. He may try to become assimilated, rejecting on the surface his own nationality, but be simultaneously clannish and cling to his own ethnic group.

6. He—and this would be almost as rare as it is ideal— may amalgamate what is good in the inheritance from his own country with what is good in America.

One predominant factor in the difficulty of identification was the isolation in which the majority of immigrants found themselves. Handlin has expressed this isolation well:

From the physical as from the religious experience with the New World, the immigrants had gained a deep consciousness of their separateness. It seemed sometimes as if there were only one street in the World, and only a single people, so that *I am in America and I do not even know whether it is America.* The street was apart as if a ghetto wall defined it. On other streets were other men, deeply different because they had not the burden of this adjustment to bear. This street and those did not run into each other; nor this farm into those. If the immigrants were to achieve the adjustment to their new environment, it had to be within the confines of the ghettos the environment created.[12]

This forced isolation brought out ambivalent feelings in the immigrants.

Ambivalent individuals are unable to separate themselves clearly from their surroundings. As a result of a blurred image of themselves, they develop a faulty identification.

There are three forms of identification distortion: identification may be completely lacking, as in several of the case histories we have examined; it may be underdeveloped; or it may be overdeveloped. The latter case results in too much loyalty to parents, family, or friends to the detriment of oneself—the man who "cannot" marry because he feels he must take care of his mother—or too much loyalty toward country, exemplified in superpatriotism. In all but the rarest of cases, the immigrant has a tendency either to overidentify or to underidentify with America. Whichever the case, his ambivalence places him in a tense and awkward relationship with his surroundings.

Inasmuch as immigrant parents are frequently anxious and insecure about their own identity, in particular because of their ethnic backgrounds, they will in most instances transmit this insecurity to their child. Since his first important identification is concerned with the image he has formed of them, quite naturally his own identification will be more blurred and ambivalent than that of a child of nonimmigrant parents, leading to perplexity and confused ideas about himself, his image, and his conduct.

This confused identification on the part of many immi-

grants and their children has affected their view of the
American Dream and their ability and willingness to
contribute to make it a reality. All the immigrants of
this country have sought for a new land, a new opportunity, a new life, which, even if they were unaware of it,
had to lead to a new identity. Each new group of immigrants has had to struggle against those who are more
established, and who in turn had to defend their new-
found status and identity. This new identity meant in
reality better work opportunities, better social status—
becoming, if you please, a "better American." The struggle
led to fustration, and frustration, as we have seen, results
in aggression and violence.

We know that a deep sense of belonging is particularly
essential to our well-being. Out of it develops our feeling
of identification—of being emotionally attuned to a person or group—which in great measure determines our
individual role and participation in life.

Healthy identification is one of the emotional pillars of
a mature attitude toward family, country, and life. This
begins developing *unconsciously* from the moment we
are born. We actually incorporate within ourselves the
mental picture of someone else so that through imitation
and empathy we think, feel, and act as he does and we
behave toward him as if he were our own self.

But the child's identification with his country depends
on whether the parents themselves have identified with
it. National identification is more important in the United
States than in any other country. Just as we need to feel we
belong to a family in order to be interested in it, we need
to feel that we belong to a nation in order to be concerned
about its present and future well-being. The child's identi-

fication is the *fundamental* link between himself and his family in the same way as identification is the fundamental link between the parents and their environment, and in the widest sense, their country. Identity is the link between the individual (intrapsychic forces) and his environment (interpersonal influences), leading to a feeling of belonging that requires a fusion of these two basic elements.

Today there is no longer any virgin soil, and this too has increased the immigrant's identification problems.

Few other countries have had to contend with the fluctuation and mobility of population and consequent fragmentation of identity and lack of belonging as has America. Consequently, few others have had to contend with so much frustration—such a contest between anticipation and the realization. Because of our prevalent feelings of frustration, impulsive hostility rises to the surface and is easily turned into violent acting out.

I repeat: This lack of, or distorted, identification leading to loneliness and ambivalence is a definite contributing factor to violence.

Frustration is the wet nurse of violence.

The double feelings present in the American Dream such as fear and hope, selfishness and generosity, stimulated in part from our environment, have been reinforced by our own ambivalent feelings. For example, although the Dream was formed from a desire for freedom, equality, and the pursuit of happiness, and we still express that desire, it has brought with it hidden or manifest intolerance toward other people.

This close relationship between the negative aspects of the ambiguity in the American Dream and our life is shown when, in tracing our history, we discover that the ambivalence of many Americans in the past differs but little from that of Americans today. The peculiarly ambivalent attitudes of some great American proponents of democratic freedom, such as Thomas Jefferson [13] and Woodrow Wilson [14] is surprising.

The question has even been raised whether Abraham Lincoln, whom generations of people have called "The Great Emancipator," really was an emancipator.[15] At least he was ambivalent. On the one hand he wished for the Negroes' freedom; on the other hand he was not completely alien to the belief in white supremacy. He issued the Proclamation with the greatest misgivings. The distinguished American historian James Shotwell remarks, "We have been essentially intolerant of varied creeds especially." He points out, "Americans are not by nature tolerant. They are more likely to be strong-minded on things, in line with American history in the past." [16] It becomes quite clear that the continuing thread of ambivalence and prejudice throughout our history has become a significant part of the fabric of our social life.

The intolerance as a result of ambivalence rooted in distorted identification has had to have a profound effect upon the many immigrants who have been unable to come to terms with their country. One reason, of course, was their immense numbers. To some extent, the same holds true for today:

According to the 1960 census, no fewer than 34 million Americans are either immigrants or the children of immigrants from Italy, Poland, Ireland, and a host of other countries. Racially the population includes not only Caucasians and 22 million blacks, but 5 million Mexican-Americans, and Puerto Ricans.[17]

While this large immigration in itself led to an inability to attain a strong sense of belonging, creating a preponderance of hostile feelings, another factor closely related to the American Dream was also significant. The difficulty the early and later settlers have had in identifying with the nation has been complicated by the gigantic scale and immensity of the country, which has made it almost impossible to develop a love for America as a *whole*. Interesting in this respect is Hawthorne's remark that he regretted that he himself was not "particularly patriotic . . . the limited sense of kinship he felt with the soil sprang from circumstances that 'we have so much country that we really have no country at all." [18] Merle Curti writes:

Hawthorne returned to this theme in "Dr. Grimshaw's Secret," in which the Englishman remarked to his American friend that if an American's heart were very large he might take in, he might come to know intimately and love, at the most, the soil of New England. The American agreed, adding; "Our space is so vast that we shall never come to know and love it, inch by inch . . . for where the land changes its ownership every few years, it does not become imbued with the personalities of the people who live on it. It is but so much grass; so much dirt, where a succession of people have dwelt too little to make it really their own.[19]

In contrast to these feelings, there is the boastful and expansive view of the geographical greatness of America compared to which the mountains of Europe are like hills, and European rivers like American brooks. Gertrude Stein once said, "In the United States there is more space where nobody is than where anybody is. That is what makes

America what it is." [20] When a nation of people identify too little or too much with their country, they become confused about their own self-image; this confusion, again, is intensified by their competitive and often frustrated search for personal accomplishments.

Through the forces of the American Dream interacting with our instinctual life, we have become victims of our own wishes and transformed part of a potentially creative dream into a destructive influence. The American Dream has traumatized us in that it has warped our outlook, made us set goals higher than we ever could achieve, and stimulated in us the search for power. While it has served as a fertile soil for the creation of America and constituted a storage of hope, it has also become a powder keg of violence.

Detecting the Potentially Violent Person

We have examined various forms of violence that manifest themselves in our society, and we have seen the part the American Dream plays in triggering the latent aggressive impulses we all possess. Now we must ask, Can we detect the potentially violent person in our midst?

Let us look at the young man Charles whom I mentioned briefly in Chapter IV. He was the third of eight children and could not get along with his parents. His mother described him as having been a difficult child, hypersensitive, a poor eater, who never wanted to go to bed. During his infancy and early childhood he had temper tantrums if he didn't get his own way. A chronic truant from school, he was a bedwetter until he was fifteen years old. He complained that his father, who worked at menial jobs and drank excessively, was abusive toward him.

Charles grew up in an unsettled home. Because of his many siblings he could never be close to his mother; instead he spent much of his pre-adolescent time with a sister. Because he didn't receive any attention from his mother, he thought constantly of running away.

A rather adventurous boy, Charles was accident prone. He fell out of a tree, fell off a cliff, and injured himself with some glass. At school he was belligerent and rude, talked back to his teachers, and became quite a showoff in class. For this reason he was sent to an institution, then transferred to a psychiatric hospital. Later he was admitted to a training school, but he ran away.

When he was eleven years old, he and a sister became involved in a burglary. By the age of fifteen he had begun to drink and smoke marijuana. He become involved in stealing a car, a charge he denied, and was arrested. When he was sixteen years old he assaulted his father.

Throughout his childhood and adolescence Charles displayed uncontrolled violent impulses manifested by threatening and attacking other boys and torturing and killing animals. While in the institution, he removed the feathers from a parrot and placed the bird in a toilet bowl. Another time he killed a cat by hanging it from a tree.

His mother described him as being nonchalant about everything. "He has asked me why I cry, and he said 'Don't worry about me.' He doesn't realize that he is the cause of all our troubles."

When I examined him in prison after he had killed three people, I asked, "Did you feel guilt or remorse?" "To me, authority means nothing," he responded. Asked how he felt when he killed, he replied, "It doesn't bother me to kill. It doesn't result in emotions. It's like an animal instinct." His primitive egocentricity was reflected when I asked if he would go so far as to kill his wife and child. "Oh, no," he answered, "I wouldn't kill them because they are me."

In discussing his early thefts, he said, "When I had stolen there was a feeling of impending punishment. It made it more of a challenge. It didn't seem to stop. Just kept on coming. . . . As long as I didn't get caught, it wasn't wrong. When I got caught, then it was wrong. I operated mostly by myself. I did just what got into my head. I first did the thing and then thought about it afterwards." When I asked if criminal activities gave him a feeling of adventure, he answered, "Yes, it was stimulating, it kept things from getting boring. As a boy we used to play at the cemetery. We would play tag on the tombstones."

Asked whether he realized that killing people was wrong, he answered, "I realize, yes. But I look at it in a different way. Nine-tenths of conscience is religion. If you are going to die, it is your time."

In his fantasy life he thought of himself as a man who was going to amount to something.

In psychological examinations made several years before his murders he was found to be withdrawn, lacking in self-control, and given to acting out his deep-rooted hostile impulses. Interesting in this respect were his drawings of depressed-appearing men who were small and rigid in contrast to his drawings of women, who were mobile, aggressive, and large breasted. Along with his homosexual conflict, this clearly showed his dependency features. Psychological tests carried out before and after the murders indicated that he was superior in intelligence, showing a discrepancy between the lower verbal score of 118 and the higher performance score of 142. The findings suggested emotional and intellectual deprivation in an alert person distrustful of his environment.

Charles felt inadequate about personal and social responsibilities and saw authority as arbitrary. It is highly significant that he expressed his feelings of distrust particularly against the female, indicating his distortion of reality. During the interview I observed his hidden feelings of anxiety, fear, and agitation, which he tried to ward off by smiling and laughing. When the Rorschach test was administered, he continuously rotated the cards, making little effort to structure and organize the stimulus material in spite of his high intelligence. Cards IV and VI, popularly referred to as the "father or male cards," were seen as tropical flowers. He identified primarily with the female, yet he believed women to be unreliable. While his hateful and distrustful feelings had become indiscriminate and global, they were directed more against women than against men. Identifying with the female, he had become passive; impulsive and destructive acting out was his way of denying this passivity.

Could Charles have been detected before he committed his three murders? Before answering this question, let us examine another case history.

Early one morning Joe called a law enforcement agency in New York and said, "I am going to kill the President. I have a high-power rifle. I don't like Johnson and I am sick." He called several times again, repeating his threat and virtually asking to be arrested by giving his whereabouts and description. When apprehended, he said that he had made the calls because he had been drinking. Under psychiatric examination he was found to be well oriented, without psychotic signs, able to fully understand the nature of his threats, and competent to stand trial.

Joe's only previous offense was having turned in five false fire alarms in one night. He had been drinking, and when he awoke the next morning and realized what he had done, he told a policeman whom he had known since boyhood. Five years prior to his threat against the President, following excessive use of alcohol, he was admitted for a few days to a psychiatric hospital. While there, he was confused, delusional, and hallucinating.

In the interview, Joe, who had a dull normal intelligence, described his father as strict, always controlling his children. The father was a policeman for almost three decades. While on the force he drank, and on one occasion he attempted suicide. Joe's mother appeared to be a pleasant person, rather talkative and motherly. At least of average intelligence, she had throughout her life tried to help her son, for whom she felt a great deal of compassion. He attributed his emotional difficulties and his drinking to the fact that his three brothers were in the military service while he was rejected because of his poor vision. He was told that as an infant he had had some form of convulsions. He did poorly in school. Considered a troublemaker and a nuisance by his teachers, he was the brunt of jokes because of his behavior and poor vision, and felt alone and isolated.

Joe was married once. His wife divorced him after he physically assaulted her. He blamed the divorce on his drinking and the fact that he wanted to have children and his wife did not. He complained that she was compulsively clean around the house and always had a dustcloth in her hand. He later kept company with a divorced woman with whom he had normal sexual relations. Believing his poor vision to be his only trouble, he had little insight into his own problems. He minimized his alcoholism, arguing that for the last three years he had had a good job. During the interview he stuttered slightly, but claimed to do so only when he got excited.

The "black sheep" of the family, Joe was kept at a distance from his brothers, and from his own mother, who nevertheless tried to make up for his shortcomings by giving in to his whims. His resultant frustration, spurred in part by his physical inferiority and by alcohol, became so pronounced that it elicited his violent impulses into threats.

In Joe's childhood there were harbingers of future difficulty—poor school record, strict home, faulty eyesight—but many children grow up under similar conditions without becoming violent; most of them, in fact, become lawful citizens.

Why did Joe threaten the President of the United States?

Part of this answer may be found in his early background. His father, we have learned, drank, and at one time attempted suicide. His strictness reflects a rigidity that made itself felt in his children's personality reaction to him. Joe's reaction to his father's strictness and what he unconsciously considered his mother's rejecting him was in the form of hidden frustration, loneliness, insecurity, and attention seeking. But these symptoms do not indicate that Joe was dangerous. Only when he acted them out by alcoholism, pulling five false fire alarms, indicating deep-seated revenge feelings, and threats against the President of the United States did he become a menace to society.

Another case is that of Paul, who at twenty-five years of age threatened the President in a letter to a professional person:

I will go on writing letters and sending cards to you until I die. . . . I am so very lonely and I am a nobody. But when I do something spectacular, I won't be lonely no more. *I am going to kill our beloved President, Mr. Johnson. It's no joke. . . .* My friend and myself stole two German Lugers and ammunition from a store we burglarized. I sent a letter to Mr. Johnson saying I was going to kill him. I will have to be stopped but I won't. I am too ingenious to be stopped. I am sorry to do this but all my life I've been a shy, sad, lonely boy who is forever getting hurt. Now I believe I have to hurt LBJ. . . . I will probably get killed but I don't care. I was in and out of the stupid psychiatrist's hands. They don't know who they had. I will be better than Oswald sad to say. Pray to God . . . that I don't get killed doing it. My mother died at 28. I will die at 27. Isn't that nice of that bastard God in heaven. . . . I belong in Washington, dead or alive. Please don't warn officials. They won't stop me. I love you . . . but not myself.

Paul admitted that he had written the letter, but said that it was only a fixation of his imagination, that he hadn't burglarized a store, that he was not violent by nature and never intended harm to the President. He admitted though that he had written another threatening letter to the President himself.

When interviewed at the time of his arrest, Paul appeared lucid, coherent, and alert. There was no clinical evidence of delusions or hallucinations. His memory was poor. He was able to understand the charges against him and to confer with a lawyer, and was found able to appreciate the nature of his acts.

Paul's mother died five days after he was born. Two-and one-half years later, his father remarried. He was a seaman until the time of his death in 1963, and because of his work, he was away from home a great deal of the time. As a result Paul grew up without his father and without his natural mother. Until his father's remarriage he lived in a foster home. A son, Paul's stepbrother, was born as a result of the second marriage. The stepmother showed a preference for her own son, and Paul felt neglected and rejected. He did, in fact, undergo a great deal of deprivation. His stepmother frequently beat him up and locked him out of the house. Since the father was absent from the home most of the time and therefore kept unaware of his wife's mistreatment, Paul was helpless.

He attended school through the eighth grade and then went to an out-of town high school because at that time he was living with a cousin. When he was fifteen he was charged with stealing bicycles on two different occasions and placed on probation. At sixteen he was charged with sexually assaulting a four-year-old girl and placing a rope around her neck, which he eventually removed. He was arrested for this and sent to an institution, where he remained for three years. One year after his release he was sentenced to prison for burglary and possession of burglar's tools. When he came out of prison in 1963, he attempted suicide and was placed in a psychiatric hospital, where his case was diagnosed as a schizophrenic reaction. He was released a year later, but having broken parole, was returned to prison, where he stayed until 1966.

Throughout his short life Paul was never able to develop any identification with a male figure. Apparently he never established a relationship with a member of the opposite sex. Although in his fantasies he imagined himself being in love with various girls, these fantasies never came to fruition. Being tall and wearing his hair long, he thought of himself as a writer of philosophy and poetry, but he had very little of his work to show. His working and living habits during the years preceding his arrest were irregular. Not having a home, he stayed with friends, on the street, or wherever he could find a place. Records from psychiatric hospitals indicate that he harbored self-destructive and suicidal thoughts.

Outstanding in Paul's case is an unusually damaging family background with a sadistic stepmother and a frequently absent father. Paul as a result was lonely, an outcast from society. He reacted by becoming suicidal or by expressing violence through threats toward the President. His most outstanding symptoms are his violent behavior dating back to his adolescence, attempted suicide, threats against public officials, loneliness, and feelings of revenge. While at times he was considered to be schizophrenic, at the trial he was found to be competent and was sentenced with the condition that he receive psychiatric treatment.

It is noteworthy that all three of the individuals described showed manifest or hidden early signs of violent behavior prior to their murders or their threats against the life of the President. However, the signs or symptoms vary from person to person. The question we have to raise is whether or not we can determine with some degree of certainty who may commit violent acts. When we examine persons suspected of violent acts, we do find a common background pattern of symptoms or signs that may indicate a future probability of violent behavior.

Based upon study of hundreds of adults and adolescents who have threatened to kill or have killed, I am setting down as an orientation the following list of danger signs found in the potentially violent person.

TABLE V
DANGER SIGNS IN THE POTENTIALLY VIOLENT PERSON

1. Excessive aggressiveness, temper tantrums
2. Feelings of paternal or maternal deprivation, mother domination
3. Loneliness, withdrawal, isolation
4. Excessive shyness and fearfulness—model child
5. Exposure to violent behavior in family
6. Intense and recurrent fantasies of revenge and of omnipotence which may stimulate acting out of violent impulses
7. Excessive truancy
8. Sexually stimulating situations and witnessing parents' sexual relations
9. Inability to withstand frustration and to develop stable identification
10. Self-destructive—suicidal—tendencies, accident proneness, psychosomatic symptoms
11. Speech and spelling errors
12. Bedwetting
13. Lying, petty stealing, firesetting, or other antisocial, criminal, or violent acts
14. Sex-chromosome abnormalities

We don't always find all of these signs present in one individual prior to his committing a violent act, but where there is a pronounced incidence of two or more, we may suspect that he may be prone to act out his violent impulses. The important feature here is not the various symptoms, but the behavior pattern they form.

One important and easily detectable external sign is habitual truancy, which is found in about 70 percent of all criminal and violent cases. An easily measurable manifestation, it is always a strong measure of undue rebelliousness, hate, or defiance, symptoms indicating an unstable personality.

Another external sign is speech or spelling errors. This, too, when present, seems to be a measurable symptom. Because an individual does not know how to spell, he uses his fantasy to think that the word might be spelled out the way it sounds. This tendency, which can be discovered early by a child's teachers, is related to faulty pre-Oedipal development.

Focus on this symptom is comparatively recent. I strongly believe, however, that if confirmed in large-scale research data, it can be used as a means of detecting the potentially violent person.

I must stress that this misspelling is only one sign. Its presence is *not* enough, of course, to indicate a child may become violent or criminal. If, however, the possibility of organic brain impairment has been excluded, and if there are other danger signs present, one has to be on the alert. If an otherwise intelligent person makes spelling errors, we must not suspect that he does not spell correctly because he cannot spell, but because he would like to spell words as his own imagination tells him to. His spelling errors are emotionally motivated, as we have seen demonstrated in Lee Harvey Oswald's case.*

---

* It is noteworthy that spelling errors have also been found in the writings of Sirhan Bishara Sirhan, who shot Senator Robert F. Kennedy to death in 1968. When he testified, Sirhan "appeared to be more embarrassed by the misspellings in the page than by the contents." [1]

Another finding that has recently attracted much attention is the presence of sex-chromosome abnormalities in some murderers. A case in point is that of the young man mentioned earlier who killed eight nurses in Chicago. The impetus for testing this factor in criminals was the fact that a higher incidence of sex-chromosome abnormalities was found in mentally deficient individuals than in the general population. Present observations indicate a high incidence of chromosome abnormalities in mental defectives, schizophrenics, criminals, and "hard to manage" individuals. It seems possible that both XXY states in men and the XXX states in women result in a high level of psychosocial disturbance, and may directly or indirectly be causally related to an individual's emotional illness. Some external signs present in the people who have or display chromosome abnormalities have been said to be acne and extreme tallness. At the present time, however, our knowledge about these abnormalities is so limited that it can only be used with caution.[2]

Bearing in mind these danger signs, would it have been possible to prevent the violent acts described here? Lee Harvey Oswald showed practically all of the signs of a probable killer. He was psychiatrically examined when he was thirteen years old and advised to seek treatment, but his mother didn't think there was anything wrong with him and took him to New Orleans. The lay public usually ignores such symptoms until they become manifest and dangerous. And usually a parent has more than the usual difficulty in admitting that a child is sick and needs help. This was obviously the case with Lee's mother. Still we must ask: Why was he not detected?

How about Charles? He too had a variety of danger

signals that should have alerted whoever was dealing with him. But no one cared enough to take notice. It is noteworthy that he was on probation when he killed his victims. Charles had no obvious need for psychiatric help, and therefore was not forced to have it, although our experience has frequently confirmed that the court can compel an offender to take psychiatric help, often with good results. Fortunately, Joe and Paul gave themselves away so that they could be caught, but suppose they had not been detected: what then?

Of course, I am using hindsight here. It is easy to say now that they all had the earmarks of a murderer. The difficulty we are faced with is that there are many people walking around in society who may show a few signs but never become dangerous. Furthermore, even if a person becomes psychotic, it does not necessarily mean that he will become dangerous or violent. The percentage of dangerous people at large is rather small—in contrast to that of prison inmates, who already have a record of violence. I would estimate that 20 to 25 percent of our prison population must be considered dangerous, and therefore, even if it sounds idealistic, should be kept within walls for psychiatric treatment until rehabilitated.

One important fact that to some extent minimizes the importance of these early signs is that they can also be present in emotional or mental disturbances where no violent acting out takes place. A person does not need to become deranged in order to become violent, although of course sometimes he does. Half of our hospital beds are occupied by mentally ill people, but few of them commit violent acts.

Under what circumstances, then, are violent tendencies

acted out? In other words, can we explain satisfactorily the mechanism that transforms violent impulses into violent acts? Our knowledge here is inadequate, but it is significant, I feel, that in the earlier mentioned research project on sex offenders[3] it was found that those who had actually committed rape, in contrast to those who had merely attempted or fantasized it, displayed a greater gap between their impulses and their control of them. It was also found that those men who used violence had weaker motor control than those who only attempted it.

It would seem, then, that the violent acting out would depend upon an individual's control of his impulses, whether by suppression, repression, or long-term sublimation. In other words, the central focus for overcoming individual violence would be *ego control.*

The mechanism through which any action, be it violent, antisocial, or criminal, is carried out is composed of the individual's impulses, his individual and social situation, and his resistance against the act. Thus we may put an individual's violent acting out into a formula (V stands for violence, T for violent tendencies, S for total situation, and R for resistance):

$$V = \frac{T + S}{R}$$

Whether or not an act of violence will grow out of a pressure situation, then, depends upon the outcome of the struggle between an individual's violent tendencies and his resistance.

Since there are numerous personality types, various forms of resistance, and almost limitless situational possibilities, the outcome of our formula is always in question. Possibly the most difficult factor to determine is the amount and type of resistance a person may show to committing a violent act in any given situation. Resistance arises from emotional, intellectual, and social roots, all three of which are intimately associated with the super-ego formation, its relation to the ego, and the person's individual and cultural situation.

A violent act may be due to situational pressure, emotional disturbance, or both. This is one reason why one individual may turn to violence while his siblings, who apparently experienced the same background, grow up normally, marry, and live useful lives.

Interesting in this connection are the following excerpts from the Hearings of the National Commission on the Causes and Prevention of Violence, for which I testified.

MR. JAWORSKI: I am interested in Robert Oswald, brother of Lee Harvey Oswald. It so happens that I had occasion to talk with him several times. The Attorney General of Texas worked with the Warren Commission on the investigations and the hearings, and I had occasion to serve as his special counsel in that matter.

I heard the testimony of all the Oswalds before the Commission, all the testimony that they gave and I had, as I say, the opportunity of talking with this young man, Robert Oswald, on several occasions. I never talked with a man I considered to be better adjusted. He was a great help to the Attorney General of Texas and to the officials in Dallas in connection with a matter that arose that was rather delicate involving Marina Oswald and some others. He was of great help and showed not only splendid character but excellent judgment.

He was employed by a large concern near Forth Worth, Texas. He had a very responsible position and had the finest of commendations of his employers. He was, as I recall it, maybe three or four years younger than Lee Harvey Oswald. But would you please help me?

DR. ABRAHAMSEN: Are you, sir, talking about Robert Pic or John Pic?

MR. JAWORSKI: I'm talking about a situation where you have two brothers who grew up in exactly the same environment. They had the same mother.

DR. ABRAHAMSEN: No, they did not. This is the trouble. Robert and John Pic were born before Lee Harvey Oswald was born. At least Robert and John Pic, they had some sort of father figure around them while Lee grew up without a father.

Furthermore, there was more stability in the early family life of John and Robert Pic than there was with Lee Harvey Oswald because at the time when Lee was born, Marguerite, his mother, was without a husband. She had to make a living by herself.

When Lee was three years old he had to be put into a foster home, a very small home where also both his brothers were, so I do think that in the family consideration or in the upbringing of the children, there was a great deal of difference between the upbringing of John and Robert Pic on the one hand and that of Lee Harvey Oswald.

Of course, this is not the complete explanation of it because one thing is how these children were brought up. Another thing is what were the personality reactions actually of Lee Harvey Oswald to his surroundings; these personality reactions may to a large extent possibly have been responsible for his fateful development.

MR. JAWORSKI: Doctor, there were two bothers. One brother did not have the same father. As far as Robert was concerned, he had the same father and mother as was true with Lee Harvey.

Now it is true, of course, that there was some change undoubtedly in Mrs. Oswald's employment and I don't know exactly when the divorce occurred, but certainly generally speaking, the environment—there was the same mother, the same failures of the mother, I would assume certainly the mother's characteristics. Her own nature did not change any. Her characteristics didn't change any, did they?

DR. ABRAHAMSEN: No, but I must say this, though, that since her husband died, certainly one has the right to assume that the mother's difficulties were intensified. She had to start making a living and she was troubled by having this little child around her. . . .

There also was no male figure for Lee Harvey Oswald to identify with although later on, as you know, his older brother went into the Army and Lee himself later on joined the Marines, so on that point there was some identification.

May I read for you here something from my own study about Lee Harvey Oswald?

Although we have no specific information about Lee's development from eighteen months to three years of age, the impressions of his half-brother, John Pic, from the years in the children's boarding home are interesting. . . . [John said:]

"Robert and I enjoyed Bethlehem. Things for myself became worse when Lee came here. They had a ruling that if you had a younger brother or sister, the older brothers would clean them up. And they would yank me out of classes in school to do this, and of course this peeved me very much. . . ."

Which means really, although this is only one statement we had, that a great deal of resentment was expressed on the part of his brother and half-brother against Lee Harvey Oswald.

DR. MENNINGER: I think for the benefit of Mr. Jaworski, too, it should be pointed out that there are many instances observed where one sibling in a family will get into considerable difficulty, will develop antisocial behavior, while other siblings are apparently law-abiding and don't get into trouble, and that there are a number of studies of these kind of situations indicating special interactions between the parent, one parent or both parents, and that child that is acting that may be also involved here.

In other words, it is not unusual to have situations where one child somehow becomes, if you will, the black sheep.

MR. JAWORSKI: Yes, and I have seen that, Dr. Menninger, in some of our very finest citizens who have had a brother or a sister that has gone awry. I am mindful of that.

But what I felt though was considerable reference to this young man's past life, Lee Harvey Oswald's past life that related to his mother and inasmuch as these two boys had the same mother, I was wondering how the situation was explained and rationalized.[4]

The mind and its actions are not always open to us. Too frequently we are surprised when the so-called model person commits an act of violence. However, general signs of passivity are often warnings that a potentially violent character may be developing. A shy, withdrawn, submissive, passive person may often act out his hostile aggressions when the pressure is too much for him. In a study I conducted of 102 sex offenders,[5] it was found that fourteen of them had been "model children" and at least thirty-two seemed to be good boys. Altogether, forty-six were considered to be "nice" people. Yet they had been violent.

One common sign that stands out in the symptomatology of violent people is their loneliness and isolation, usually growing from their inability to be close to their mothers. Although this loneliness exists in all potentially violent individuals, it is most outstanding in the murderer.

The most piercing thorns in the side of the violent person, shown most explicitly in the murderer, are his loneliness, his sense of helpless impotence, and his preoccupation with revenge, carried over from early childhood. Intertwined with this nucleus of feelings, which color and distort his view of life and all his acts, are certain other often-detectable traits.

Perhaps the most obvious are his irrational hatred for others, his suspiciousness, and his hypersensitivity to injustices or rejection. Hand in hand with these go his self-centeredness and inability to withstand frustration, expressed by frequent, uncontrollable emotional outbursts and impulsive indulgence in angry acts. We recognize these symptoms most readily in the person who kills in a fit of passion, who is so unable to bear the intensity of his tortured feelings that he must discharge them immediately. But the same current of twisted feelings is operative, though much more disguised, in murderers who seem more withdrawn and calculating.

The violent person is unable to curb his hostile, aggressive tendencies; they continue to build and he continues to seek outlets for them. Through repressing any awareness of his intolerable reality situation, he avoids experiencing the real emotional content of his feelings. The danger level is reached when all outlets for his aggression have been exhausted. If at this point gratification in some form becomes impossible, his locked-in emotions are apt to burst through and engulf him.

Homicide, then, is due not so much to murderous impulses in themselves as to the persistent, intense conflict between the killer's impulses and his environment. Obsessed with vengeful feelings against his mother—or his father—he loses emotional interest in the outside world.* His fixated or regressed fantasies find an outlet in revenge.

Since we have found violent acting out to be closely associated with loneliness, we must ask whether these two factors are causally related to each other. If they are, we may find one fundamental reason for the extent of violence in America.

The loneliness here did not only arise from the newness of the American environment. It goes back to the earliest times of our history. The immigrant, as mentioned, was in part a rebel against his old country which he had left. Coming to this land, he was disowned, alone, and on his own, relying on himself and his own resources. Now, he had no environment that could give him emotional support. While living in Europe, whether or not he liked it, he was protected—not only by his family and his class, but also by his environment in the widest sense: his neighborhood, his town or village, the customs and traditions. All these elements in his old surroundings served as a cushion on which he could lean, providing him with protection and security. And with this security came a sense of belonging and identification. This is in sharp contrast to his coming to an unfamiliar country, often without his family, to a strange environment without customs or traditions, a type of existence that intensified his loneliness. As one man said to me, "All I have is me."

Social and cultural influences affect us in two ways: they produce a change or a shift in the personality structure, evoking a powerful reaction from the superego, a

---

* This process is also operative in depressed patients.

reaction formation; or they affect the more superficial personality traits, effecting changes in our defensive responses, such as a rationalizing or explaining away our behavior, or disguising our unconscious hostility. A social yielding to, or a "social compliance," to use Hartmann's term [6] (similar to Freud's concept of "somatic [body] compliance"), occurs during which our environmental influences stimulate or inhibit our instinctive or learned aggression. Among these environmental influences we may count the American Dream, immigration, our country's physical abundance and rapid national development, and our freedom of action due in part to our lack of a feudal past—all of which, with some variations, have been constant and have reacted interdependently with our personalities.

These influences, which to a large extent may have determined our behavior patterns, can be considered to be specific for the American environment; and in addition to evoking damage in the area of identification and consequent ambivalent feelings, they have stimulated the loneliness that underlies most of our violent acting out.

Having provided a masculine self-image in our culture, the American male has been inclined to assert his masculine character traits and minimized or even disregarded his feminine ones.

Our most predominant characteristic is, perhaps, our readiness to go into action and, if necessary, to use force to satisfy our desires so that we can become powerful. As Van Wyck Brooks said, "Americans love the ability to do something, as they love power also, far more than they can ever love mere living." [7] We are determined, adventurous, and forceful, and can be tough even when it is

not called for. Our history is filled with action. Throughout it, muscle and strength were needed to overcome
everyday obstacles. The swashbuckling, fast-gun-draw-
ing, justice-meeting Westerner became an ideal. Our
admiration, then and now, for his masculinity and
strength is dramatically reflected in our movies.[8] Today
many Americans believe that to have a brain is to be
effeminate—to use Dore Schary's words, "lacking in masculine character. . . . There's something almost un-
American about him." [9] This is in contrast to the man of
action who does not sit around and talk, but is a strong
believer in American destiny.

Very few men admit to being shy or modest, mild or
sympathetic. Yet, in a curious way, we like to see modesty
in special cases, apparently as an expression of our ambivalent feelings toward the masculine ideal. This very
ideal the woman, too, has adopted through imitation. She
has, in many instances, become aggressive and domineering, forceful, controlling. A process of equalization of the
sexes has taken place with little regard for the biological
and emotional natures of men and women. In the United
States, the glorification of the male ideal became intensified through our frontier development, when women were
scarce and were put on a pedestal by admiring men. On
the other hand, they had to play a decisive part in the
family, particularly in regard to the children. The tumultuous and often rootless life did not allow much opportunity for a father and mother to share in the family's joys
and burdens, particularly when it came to rearing their
children.

We have seen that in many cases the violent person was
raised in a family where the mother was strong and ag-

gressive and the father, when he was not absent from the home altogether, was weak and unassuming. Many of the traits we have discussed are ultimately traceable to the child's emotional hurt when deprived of his mother. The role of the father is also highly significant, particularly in the development of healthy identification and superego functioning in a male child. If the father is absent or weak, a boy has no chance to relinquish or diminish his omnipotent fantasies that provide much of the soil for his violent acting out.

The same result occurs when, because of the father's brutality or his frequent emotional outbursts against his son, there is no bond between them. This emotionally loaded family atmosphere has the same effect as if there were no father present in the home: it leads to disturbed identification. The fledgling criminal's fantasy of achieving limitless power arises from lack of a strong male figure with whom to identify.

Bearing this fact in mind we meet Otto, the thirty-five-year-old son of an Irish father and a German mother, who came to see me because of his marital quarreling, during which he frequently became violent with his wife. He frankly admitted that on many occasions he had been unable to control himself and had struck her.

Otto grew up in a home with an aggressive mother who had her own successful business and therefore had neither the time nor the inclination to take care of him. He had a meek but shrewd father who during World War I had been drafted into the Army and had to fight on the side of the English, whom he abhorred. He constantly talked about this to his young son. Having been wounded, he received a small pension, returned to the United States, and in the course of a few years amassed a great deal of money, only to lose it in the Depression of 1929. He never overcame this loss and remained bitter and lonely for the rest of his life, preoccupied with the American promise, the dream that once had come true but now was only fantasy.

Throughout Otto's childhood he was secretly ashamed of his mother's heavy German accent and his father's clipped British accent. Yet on the other hand, he unconsciously imitated both. He lived in a rough neighborhood of Italian and Jewish children who teased him for his accent; as a consequence he was regularly forced to fight them. One of his recurring memories was of being repeatedly beaten up by them, defenseless simply because they outnumbered him.

Otto did not do well in school, mostly because of the poor relationship he had with his parents. Moody, sullen, and angry at his mother, he had nightmares in which he killed or he himself was killed. Often during his temper tantrums he hit his mother with his bare fists. These fights with her always precipitated bitter quarrels between his parents. Living in this tense family atmosphere, he had no sense of belonging and became confused about himself.

When Otto finished high school, his mother wanted him to work in her business, but he refused and, against her advice, pursued an engineering career, in which he managed to become moderately successful. After a brief and hectic engagement, he married a woman ten years his senior. From the first day they were married, they quarreled about everything, particularly money matters. When she didn't give in, he often beat her severely. "She was impossible, a bad housekeeper—I never had a home," he said to me. This lack of identity with her reflected his own childhood-blurred identity with his parents.

Eventually Otto joined an extreme-right-wing patriotic organization and began to spend more and more time with their activities. There he found the security he could not find at home. But since he himself was chronically threatened, he began to fear that America, too, was in danger. It became important to him to get rid of those who menaced his country—and him. Therefore he utilized every opportunity to "protect" America through violent actions. Once while picketing he took part in an assault; this gave him a great thrill.

Otto's every political reaction graphically reflects his lack of identification with his family and consequent withdrawal. His fear for America's security was the same fear he had felt for his own since childhood. His unstable identification became the foundation for his confused patriotism.

The interaction between his own fear and the influence of the right-wing group determined his violent behavior pattern. In the face of frustration, a carryover from his childhood rejection by his mother, he was unconsciously seeking power—a male ideal to regain the power he once had lost. In a healthy situation, a boy is able to transfer his omnipotent feelings to some male person, thus recognizing that there are other people who have more power than he.[10] Otto, however, could not. His father was too weak to be a healthy model for him. Consequently, he carried his Oedipal fantasies of omnipotence into adulthood and became prone to acting out his hostile aggressions.

Because of shifting identification, emotional isolation, and weak ego, a person like Otto follows in the footsteps of someone else, emulating his ego-ideal, pretending to be something he is not—deceiving himself and others. Richard Hofstadter [11] has brilliantly delineated people like Otto as pseudo-conservative. This type of person is just a pseudo. Because of his inability to sustain an identity, he is always changing, assuming one role after another.

Such a person, for instance, may firstly identify with an engineer and become one, or secondly he may identify with a political demagogue and become politically active and continue to change, unconsciously setting his aim in accordance with his weak identity. In each role he hopes to obtain complete superiority. When he fails, he is forced to switch. His goal, however, is imaginary. His emotional need is to attain power, if necessary through violence. These people are in fundamental respects like the "as if" people, those displaying neurotic and psychotic manifestations or character disorders resulting in violent acting out. Whatever emotional bonds they try to establish are brittle.

Otto's mother was tremendously important to him. He wanted to show her how strong and powerful he was. This need is one of the results of an unresolved Oedipal situation. Since the Oedipus Complex is universal, we may ask whether the American Dream has played a significant role in intensifying it in our society. The answer to this question to some extent lies in the particular environment that the American Dream has been instrumental in creating. Our affluent environment with its inexhaustible opportunities constitutes a basis—realistic or unrealistic—for fulfillment of everyone's wishes. It is there for everyone. The only thing is, how to get it? And that, how to get it, is part of what everyone in this country dreams about. The possibility of possessing part of this rich land must, naturally, produce in people cravings, which when not satisfied, and when satisfaction is considered a "right," may lead to frustrations strong enough to keep them tense, but still nurture in them an unrealistic feeling that they will always succeed. Such optimistic feelings are apt to be more pronounced in an affluent country than in one with meager opportunities. Our country's natural endowments reinforce the desire to be strong and powerful, and this feeling dovetails with the unresolved Oedipal situation where the battle between father and son for the mother takes on the show of power.

The son, as would be his fate, will naturally lose the battle, and if mature enough, will be able to overcome his loneliness and fear and find himself his own wife. But more often than not he will feel rejected by his mother. Overcome by his loneliness, he will feel helpless and sensitive, believing that the world is against him. And being defensive, he will easily react with violent acting out, showing his mother consciously or unconsciously that he is not insignificant, that he has power and is strong.

We do find, then, a causal connection between a person's loneliness and his violent acting out, which in all probability is associated with his mother's domineering relationship during his childhood and intensified through his social and cultural environment. It may be possible—and I express it as an idea only—that because of our specific environment, the dominant-mother situation with an absent or weak father is more pronounced here than in any other Western country, leading more often to a child's feeling threatened and powerless and consequently acting out his hostile impulses. This does not mean that the mother alone can be blamed for this lopsided situation. Blame—if blame is appropriate—must also be put on the father.

Since any boy or man—particularly one feeling insignificant and powerless—consciously or unconsciously strives for power, it is natural that a tendency to violence, as stressed by Marvin E. Wolgang,[12] is predominantly present in that part of our population which considers itself to be out of the mainstream. These are people whose primary feelings are of insignificance and powerlessness: minorities, unskilled workers and laborers, youngsters or adults who feel that they are not making their mark— people who feel rejected and lonely, but who in truth, because of emotional and social influences, may be repressed.

Thus, the strongest motivating factor in the life of the potentially violent person, whatever form his aggression may take, is an unresolved Oedipal situation continually intensified by the environment. We must understand and learn to work with this conflict. Detecting the potentially violent person and taking appropriate steps to cure him of his emotional disturbances is a must—a *conditio sine qua non*—for the redemption of our society.

Are We Able to
Prevent Violence?

The American is not given to contemplation. He is a man of action.

We have observed that violence and aggression are part of our national origins which have all merged together to create specific environmental influences that in turn have brought about a climate of hostile aggression and violence.

America, as mentioned earlier, has had an almost explosive increase in violence and crime. It is interesting to compare the incidence here with that of other countries. *The World Handbook of Political and Social Indicators* [1] uses a violent-death-by-group indicator to determine the incidence of violence in most of the countries of the world. It covers all forms of group violence for a twelve-year period (1950–62) except murder and execution committed by individuals. Out of seventy-four countries, the United States ranks fifty-eighth. It has less group violence than Poland, East Germany, Israel, Greece, Portugal, Belgium, the U.S.S.R., France, Italy, Spain, Japan, and West Germany, but more than the Scandinavian countries and several other European countries. Domestic violence, according to the *World Handbook,* correlates highly with inequality of income distribution. The United States ranks thirteenth out of twenty countries on income inequality before taxes. We have less inequality than Mexico, West Germany, the Netherlands, Denmark, Italy, and Sweden, but somewhat more than Canada, Norway, the United Kingdom, India, Israel, and Australia. After taxes the United States ranks eighth out of twelve countries, with little change in the order.[2]

It is significant, however, that the *World Handbook* statistics do not, as mentioned, include murder and execution. Although its rate of group violence as opposed to individual one-to-one violence is not extremely high, America has the highest murder rate of all civilized nations. Our individual violence, then, may be seen as a functional alternative for group violence.

In order to find another measure of violence, Ivo K. Feierabend and his associates have compiled a seven-point index of political instability in which various political events are assigned scores from zero to six—general election, for instance, is scored zero and civil war is scored six.[3] In a later report Feierabend examines politically aggressive behavior and assassination figures within a total complex of such violent manifestations as civil wars, revolutions, mutinies, executions, acts of sabotage and terrorism, riots, demonstrations and strikes, political suicide, imprisonment, exiles, dissolutions of cabinets, and resignations of office-holders—all of which reveal aggressive turmoil and crisis situations within a nation.[4] In Feierabend's most extensive study, covering the eighteen years from 1948 to 1963 and including eighty-four nations, all independent since 1948, some eight thousand aggressive events are recorded.[5] In the seven-year period from 1955–1961, the United States was ranked in Group Three out of seven groups. If current statistics indicating a high degree of internal turbulence were taken into account, the United States would probably be in Group Four today.[6]

There are drawbacks in Feierabend's methodology. In compiling his data he does not evaluate the specific frustrations experienced by black people that lead to riots. Also, while finding that the United States has had a high number of political assassinations, he overlooks the fact that they were usually committed by mentally deranged people, whereas in Europe assassinations have usually been politically motivated.

Even if the data from the field of political science may not be conclusive as to the prevalence of violence in America as compared with other nations, the overwhelming and increasing incidence of violent acting out here dovetails with my own psychosocial and psychoanalytical findings and interpretations. As we have seen, ours has been a bloody past—first in our decimation of the Indians and our establishment of Negro slavery and now in our hidden and open crime and political violence, much of which is celebrated by the entertainment media. The explosive continuity of violent acts that we have experienced in recent years has become so much a part of our lives that we can justifiably say that violence has become normalized in our society.

It has been said that one reason for this normalization is that we live in a time where violence is widely and highly publicized, but we have seen that the impetus to violent acting out does not lie in the news media, but in the individual. The media provide a channel, an outlet through which violent impulses can be expressed, resulting in widespread publicity. Because of the conscious and unconscious fascination people have for violence, it feeds on publicity, which in turn feeds on violence.

By exerting violence, an individual or a group obtains power—and the wish for power is universal. As shown earlier, from childhood on we all dream of power and strength, the craving to dominate and outdo our fathers. It is the old, and yet new, story of parricide repeated in each generation. This search for power, which continues throughout life, is lodged in each individual's Oedipus situation—the old confrontation between father and son—which serves as the prototype for all social and political conflicts. Through violent acting out an individual can, at least for the moment, achieve power over the representatives of his mother, his father, or his whole family. And once the appetite for power is whetted by violent action, such action, which derives from unconscious, instinctual sources, becomes as a pattern of behavior. Biology is stronger than rationality.

I have previously mentioned that there is drama in all acting out. By the same token, violence dramatizes the action which tries to ward off whatever grievances are present. Violence, therefore, dramatizes injustices and brings them to the awareness of the public. Violent acts, then, have the seeds of power within them and can through their dynamics promote causes—but only to a point, since power has a tendency to consummate itself.

In order for power to stay alive—be it in the struggle for domination in interpersonal relationships or in a social or political conflict—it has to feed upon itself through further acting out. It cannot stay static; it has to grow, to spread. In order to remain potent, it has to expand through violence at the expense of others.

In our modern society the average citizen has no or little means of acting. Little room is left for him to participate. Federal, state, and city governments have assumed more and more power, and government today has become anonymous. Who, for instance, were the white people who had the power to keep the Negroes down? Who were the university administrators who dictated all aspects of the students' lives and curricula? Why do administrators in all fields have so much power, while those under them feel frustrated and helpless, unable to voice an opinion or to be heard?

People are beginning to rebel against all power structure, all administration—against those undefined enemies "the bureaucrats." Through this rebellion black people and students are begininng to feel that there is something they can do. They are united in action, and their action creates a mutual bond among them and gives them hope. By assertive and aggressive acts they achieve the power to meet and to discuss their grievances.

Because of this country's bigness and its massive population, the American culture has become vulnerable to the anonymity of power more than any other. David Brion Davis has written, "There is a tacit recognition that American society is characterized by a weakness of authority and an unregulated competition for power." [7]

The authority is not weak, though; rather it is we who have little respect for it, mainly because we are afraid that authority will interfere with our wishes involved in our undertakings. We like to be on our own, and this always spurs on our competitiveness. Life here has always been competitive from top to bottom.

The ways we compete are examples of the American pattern of progress through action. Such action, as we have seen, has throughout our history been violent. Sometimes I wonder whether we would have ever been able to solve any of our great domestic problems without having to resort to violence.

Strangely enough, though, most of us are not yet aware of this central characteristic of our society. We loudly assert that the current national turbulence is only a flareup that will subside in time. Yet over one hundred years ago the Boston merchant, scholar, wit, and abolitionist John Murray Forbes, who tended to the American investments of the widow of Alexis de Toqueville, had a letter from her from the Old World cheerfully closing: "Tell me the probable result of this conflict [between the North and South]. . . . You are a most volcanic people, and when one fancies you are in a dead calm, out bursts a tremendous storm." [8]

Our attitude toward our violent society leads me to believe that we suffer from cultural amnesia. Like any other emotional or social phenomenon, violence is contagious. Those trying to resist their own aggressiveness give in more easily to their impulses when the environmental climate is tuned to them.

Although we see violence in and around us, most of us seem to react as if it didn't exist. In spite of overwhelming evidence that it has become a way of life for us, many deny its presence. To be sure, every time a violent crime takes place, the ire of the citizenry is aroused—but it is short-lived. After a few days or a week, it is forgotten until new acts of violence occur. We may attribute our amnesia to the fact that we are apparently so steeped in our culture that violent acting out is taken almost for granted. But there is more to it than that. Our fascination with violence and our readiness to condone it indicate that deeper emotions than we are aware of are at play. We cannot wholeheartedly condemn violence because somehow we are entangled in it and feel part of it. Because of our own emotions, therefore, we *resist* admitting that we are violent. This is the reason that many of us put up resistance when it come to changing the pattern of our society constructively.

An example of our astonishing resistance is the reception given to the proposal for effective gun control. Our arguments against such control are obviously rationalizations; we have found from experience that where control of firearms is enforced—Boston, New York versus Dallas or New Orleans—the murder rate goes down.

Under the pretext that firearm-control laws only disarm law-abiding citizens, leaving the criminal free to arm himself, a great deal of pressure has been exerted by gun and sporting interests, particularly the National Rifle Association, against enforcing such regulations. The facts about the comparative rate of murder in cities with and without gun regulations show the real story. When the sportsmen and lobbyists claim the right to bear arms, one wonders against whom. People who like to carry guns somehow feel threatened and insecure. Deep down they are afraid something might happen to them—that they might be attacked. They feel that they have to defend themselves. If stricter laws controlling the sale of firearms had been enforced, many murders would have been avoided.

Throughout our history the gun has been a primary instrument of defense and attack. Action with a gun was swift and often final. There was no ambiguity in shooting; it was masculine, virile, potent. Our country grew up with the gun, and it is now one of the last vestiges of the power of the individual. Most people want that power because it represents the way of life that had been theirs and that they had hoped to pass on to their children.

We can understand, then, their emotional outbursts when they are threatened with having their guns taken away from them. It is almost as though they were being deprived of their birthright. They have always claimed and are still claiming their misunderstood Constitutional right to bear arms. Because of their emotional resistance they are unable to see the danger guns represent to the citizenry at large.

When we ask, *Are we able to prevent violence?* the question is not whether we *want* to rid ourselves of violence. It is, rather, whether because of our emotional and environmental structure we are *emotionally able* to do so. The cause is deep-rooted, in part beyond our reach because it lies in our instinctual life, in our destructive impulses. The extent of our resistance to coping constructively with violence may indicate that our destructive tendencies are consciously or unconsciously directed against ourselves. The case histories we have seen show people who needed to carry out violent acts—and thereby to bring about their own downfall. No act is purposeless, although many purposes lie beneath the surface of consciousness. There is far more to us as human beings than we know, or care to know, because much of what we see, or try not to see, disturbs us. We refuse, therefore, to confront our perplexities. Western movies soothe us because the people in them are one-dimensional—either good or bad. Their clear-cut actions, set against a backdrop of lone farmhouses and rickety towns and accompanied by the sound of horses galloping, provide an outlet for our own complicated—and repressed—fears and anger and free us from the contemplation of them.

When deprived of an outlet for our aggressions, we become upset. White Americans ought to feel thankful to the Negroes for providing, since the earliest days of slavery, handy targets for their hostile aggressions.

There is obviously something wrong, however, when people have to carry out violent acts in order to gain gratification. Such people, I repeat, do not necessarily need to suffer from psychosis or character disorder, or even deep-seated neurosis. What they exhibit is a deviant pattern of behavior, which they have to maintain in order to enjoy some emotional well-being.

Under the pressure of our American culture, many of us have become deviated or neurotic in our behavior. This is because in order to live peacefully with other people, we have as children had to learn through identification and sublimation to curb our hostile aggressions, to postpone gratification of our instinctual needs. In order to obtain satisfaction tomorrow, we have to delay gratification today. Our culture has been built upon the renunciation of instinctual gratification. When our instincts are suppressed or repressed, elements of our innate aggression produce in us feelings of guilt that make us feel uncomfortable and often cause overcompensation in our actions.

The civilizing process of man is, in the language of

Freud, "naturally more of an abstraction than is the development of the individual." We have seen the growth process of the individual superego, and we may speculate that the same form of superego may also be developed in our culture. Even if this is the case, it is only a rudimentary form of a superego, which, judging from our experience, is too weak to check the instinctive hostile, aggressive impulses of the group or the individual.

The assumption of a social superego brings us into the problems of national characteristics, which cannot be discussed here in detail, since such a discussion would require another volume.[9] For our purposes it should be mentioned that the presence of our different ethnic, religious, and social backgrounds, which many idealists would like to believe have been amalgamated into a melted unit, has created many subgroups with diverse and rather contrary outlooks. Nevertheless, we can discern in them certain prevailing attitudes rooted in their instinctual life. While for a long time we have thought our America to be a melting pot—although in actuality it is sometimes more of a pressure cooker—this melting pot is not really a pot of amalgamation where all people have blended together and become unified without streaks or dots.

As a people we are distinctly heterogeneous, separating ourselves into ethnic, economic, religious, and social groups. But our aspirations, feelings, fantasies, wishes, fears, and values, as reflected in the American Dream, transcend the boundaries of these groups. All of us strive for "the good life." Our many million people who live in poverty and hunger, or who have been kept out of the mainstream of American life, still hope for better days. Although we live in many highly diversified subcultures,

we are exposed to the same fantasies of becoming successful, powerful, and rich; consequently we have a common inheritance of value judgments. Our different ethnic
backgrounds merely provide us with different means of
obtaining our goals.

The shared unconscious image of what we would like
to be has helped to form our character and behavior. But
since environmental forces interfere with the fulfillment
of our desires, we become frustrated. Much of our behavior in society becomes deviated or neurotic.

Each society because of its collective values and specific frustrations develops its own unique form of neurosis
or deviance. The predominant characteristic of the American social neurosis, as we have seen, is the tendency toward acting out, which often manifests itself in violence.

Violent acting out is directed against others or oneself,
and we must suspect that a large, if not the largest, element of this destructiveness is directed against the self. In
the same way as the individual attempts to destroy himself, he tries to do the same to society. We must then ask,
Does the fact that we have so many deviated people indicate that we are a sick society?

To answer it with a yes or a no would indeed be simplistic. Before we can understand the question, we must
first define what a sick society is and then see whether
the United States (or any other nation) fits that defini-
tion. Otherwise the statement means only: "Are you unhappy and do you blame your environment for your un-
happiness?"

We know that the life of every citizen is self-limiting.
His instinctual life has seen to that. So too, as history has
shown, every society, by existing for a longer or shorter

period of time and then perishing, has been self-limiting.

When every citizen of a society lives under stress and strain, it is clear that his society does not function well, since it is unable to provide him with emotional and physical satisfaction. To what degree is our society able to furnish the individual with the comforts that make life meaningful and satisfying to him? Since large masses of our people toil to their day's end not only in sweat and tears, but also in fears, we must admit that our legendary plethora of opportunities is not there for them. The "have people" do not believe that our society is an overly rich one. They accept our affluence as natural. The "have nots," on the other hand, do believe our society is a rich one.*

Because of our emotional and social structure, I venture only as a thought that our violent tendencies provide much of a foundation for some deviation of our behavior. One predominant reason for my thought is the destructive and self-destructive tendencies ingrained in us, which because of our environment, seem to have received a wider and deeper play than in any other Western society.

Against the argument that our society is sick, it has been stated that we only have neglected problems which have to receive attention. Unfortunately, the problem goes deeper than that because we must ask, Who created our social problems and who left them unattended? Can we not here observe our resistance to recognizing the

---

* Interesting in this respect is a survey made by *The New York Times* (July 2, 1968), indicating that the majority of people did not agree that the United States is sick. The largest segment of those who disagreed were college-trained men. Sixty-seven percent disagreed and 30 percent agreed; while 3 percent had no opinion. Nationally, 48 percent of the black population agreed that the United States was a sick society; while the opposite view was held by 60 percent of the white population.

existence of violence? Acknowledging a problem is the first step in counteracting it.

To admit that there is anything wrong with us individually is extremely difficult. To admit that there is something wrong with most of us is still worse. Our pride prevents us from seeing our drawbacks because, being the human beings that we are, we resist looking at our darker side. Then too, we are a people of optimists; thus we feel that there is nothing wrong with us—and even if there is some slight unadmitted flaw, we will always be able to fix it.

While it is good to be optimistic when the situation calls for it, we should try, rather, to be realistic, particularly in dealing with the crucial problems of violence. We all need to face the fact that the American society is a violent one. To delude ourselves into thinking otherwise would be self-defeating. If we do not admit to ourselves that violence is ubiquitous in our society, and if we do not understand the forces that mobilize it, we will never be able to reduce it to a reasonable level, let alone eliminate it. To admit that our society is violent would not at all mean that we had become victims of defeatism; it would mean, rather, that we were realistic in our appraisal of the situation.

In view of our emotional resistance, are we able to put up a dedicated fight with all our heart and mind against our violence? Undoubtedly, our fight under those circumstances will be half-hearted, mechanical. But it is mandatory for our survival as a society!

The fundamental question, of course, is, Can we reduce or change our own hostile aggression? Before we can answer this question we must be aware of one basic psychological law: No feeling or emotion can be reduced or withdrawn from our minds unless something else is put there to replace it. The economy of the working of the mind demands that it be kept in equilibrium.

One way to effect a change would be to encourage the constructive aspects of aggression, but this would meet with severe obstacles because the process would only work in a mature, integrated personality.

Another method of change would be to try to inhibit our hostile aggressions, but such inhibition would at best be only temporary: if pressure becomes strong enough, fear and anxiety will break through into hostile acting out.

Strange as it may sound, it would be fine to be aggressive if we did not always suppress or repress our aggression. The suppression or repression would, however, reactivate our aggressive tendencies.

To eliminate our violent impulses would of course be desirable, but this is an impossible task. We do not have power over our id impulses. No matter how consistently we tell ourselves to love other people, our instinctive hostility must at times emerge from the id. Reason is of little avail because our actions are directed by our feelings.

We cannot control our violent impulses unless we are able to control those feelings that underlie them: fear, frustration, and anger. But these emotions permeate our unconscious and our environment. This same environment cannot primarily eliminate them, as some rather optimistic or naive "cultural environmentalists" believe. Because our violent destructive tendencies are instinctual, the fundamental change has to come from within each one of us.

We cannot sit on our hands, withdraw from the battle. This would be out of character—"un-American." We must, however, be consciously aware of our difficulties and expect to encounter stumbling blocks at every turn of our uphill fight.

It has been said that we Americans are experimenters. If we do not have the exact remedy in an emergency situation, we experiment, we try to find the best means to a necessary end. Let us therefore follow this positive cultural tradition in our quest for the elimination of violence.

One means to our desired end would consist of recognizing and treating those individuals who are apt to act out their hostile aggressions. But these measures are symptomatic only. Unless forced to by the courts, many of these people rarely submit to psychiatric treatment because they feel no need for it. Among them are borderline cases of many emotionally disturbed people manifesting character disorders, but not psychotic in the legal sense, for which reason they cannot be committed to a psychiatric hospital unless voluntarily. Many of those whose prevalent behavior pattern is hostile and destructive exhibit such closed minds that their consciousness is diminished or narrowed, which may indicate a diminished responsibility. Within this category, for instance, fall dangerous leaders who are not psychotic, but manifest, rather, a character disorder. Since society has to protect itself against disruptive and destructive influences, special treatment and rehabilitation centers for patients suffering from diminished consciousness should be established.

Keeping in mind the overwhelming number of people who are shot to death each year, we must question who should possess a gun. Drs. I. A. Rotenberg and Robert L. Sadoff have written:

It is interesting to note that state mental hospital patients often cannot drive automobiles while they are inpatients and may not drive if they are on certain amounts of medication as out-

patients. However, no restriction is placed on them with respect
to possession of weapons.[10]

Some states—Pennsylvania, for example—do bar the sale
of weapons to the mentally ill and potentially violent or
dangerous, but again, the question is, Who is mentally ill
and potentially dangerous?

The correlation between emotional disturbances and
crime makes us wonder, in light of America's crime statistics, whether we have a greater preponderance of mental
illness than any other country. To judge this is, unfortunately, impossible, since its incidence is dependent upon
too many variables such as social conditions, living standards, proximity to hospitals, the quality and number of
diagnostic and treatment facilities, and hospital insurance.
In a national study I undertook of 2.75 million children
in public and private schools in the United States, I found
that about 10 percent of these children in public schools
were emotionally disturbed and in need of treatment,[11]
whereas the percentage in private schools was 11.7 percent.[12] This discrepancy, rather than indicating that there
are more mentally ill children in private schools, may only
indicate better psychiatric or psychological care and testing in those schools.

Discovering the early signs of the potentially dangerous
person is in itself intricate, and is complicated by the
fact that a child exhibiting some or even many of the
danger signals often might not end up with a violent
temperament. However, we must be aware that children
or adults exhibiting fear and anger are prone to acting
out their violent impulses. We must therefore institute
a broad mental hygiene program with outpatient or community clinics where people overcome by fears, hatred,

and violent acting out can be treated on an emergency basis.

On the Federal level we must establish a research institute for the study and treatment of violence and social pathology. The two destructive manifestations that have become prominent in American life warrant extensive studies whose findings can be applied to the prevention and curbing of violence.* Any such research center should be based on cooperation between such medical and sociological disciplines as psychology, psychiatry, sociology, law, political science, anthropology, economics, law enforcement, and all community health programs. Through individual clinical and family studies in the community, problems such as warning signs in individuals potentially capable of committing violent acts, the origins of intense hostile aggressiveness, or the channeling of violent impulses into constructive ones could be investigated closely. The institute would serve as a training place for students, as an observation and examination center for those people in need of psychiatric help, and as a center for information. In the same way we have trained doctors to utilize scientific data to bring about a cure in the many ills of the mind and body, so also we can here train social scientists to use sociological data in alleviating destructive social problems and ills. Here we can collect data with innate predictive value on the emotional and social derange-

* It is gratifying that Brandeis University established in 1966 the Lemberg Center for the Study of Violence, with Dr. John Spiegel as Director, which is mainly sociological in its approach, and that the Mental Health Center in the Department of Psychiatry at Roosevelt Hospital, New York City, directed by Dr. Harley Shands, has established a Research Center for the Study of Social Changes, which offers an institutional framework for a variety of research efforts, including investigations into the nature of violence.

ments so prominent in our society. While the control of potentially violent people lies in the hands of the lawmakers, psychiatrists can make a real contribution in predicting and preventing violent behavior.

But all these measures—along with better housing and training and work programs for unskilled and skilled workers of all races—are in the main palliative ones. The most successful and basic means of counteracting violence is to develop healthy feelings within the family. Constructive relationships depend fundamentally upon correct child rearing. While this subject is outside the scope of this book and would require a volume in itself, I shall give a few examples. Let me say at the outset, however, that to give advice is easy, whereas to carry it out and follow it up is difficult.

Parents often slap children at the slightest provocation without realizing that it inadvertently sets an example of violence as an immediate means of settling arguments or venting anger. Alarming is the fact that in order to gratify their own violent impulses, they unwittingly often encourage violent criminal actions in their children. A mother who disciplines her child too severely may, without realizing it, be developing sadistic and punishing tendencies in him. Parents themselves have to go through an inner education whereby they can learn in time to understand their own violent tendencies, which is the first step in counteracting them.

As we have seen, though, the real genesis of violence as it arises in the family is the mother's dominating role over her son. Her role has become so pronounced of late, and the father's role so insignificant by comparison, that we may well describe our society as matriarchal.

It is easy to say that parents should raise a child with due consideration to his individual emotional and intellectual capacity, and when justified give him the opportunity to express his anger. Unfortunately, though, much of the process of child rearing is unconscious and is transmitted from generation to generation without much thought, and people therefore have a tendency to repeat the practices by which they were reared. Mother and father, nevertheless, should be acutely aware of their personal roles in the family and act as two equal partners.

It is essential that we as parents are cognizant of the fact that failure to behave correctly does not lie so much in our actions as in the motivations behind them. Our desires, whatever they may be, are not so much a question of *what* we want as one of *why* we want it.

Since it is easier to change the mind of a youngster than that of an adult, the other important source for counteracting violence is the schools. They provide a valuable avenue through which the parents can be reached. However, the teacher must be aware of his own feelings and attitudes so that he can understand the emotional problems he meets in the classroom.

The influence of television and film programs upon the child's mind and behavior has been debated endlessly. Some thirty years ago I pointed out that regular radio listening led people to become passive and dependent, storing up energy within them that could eventually explode into hostile action. Their egocentricity is stimulated to the point where they may lose interest in other people.[13] This holds true perhaps to a higher degree in regular television watching, since visual impressions are usually stronger than auditory impressions. When children or adults watch television for many hours at a time, normal aggression, denied a constructive or creative outlet, turns into violent energy. By passively entertaining themselves instead of actively creating their enjoyment or education, they become so wrapped up with themselves that they may have difficulty forming relationships with other people. This particular danger of television has consequences that have not received sufficient attention.

The influence of television upon children and adults becomes more serious when the programs deal with violence. The aggression witnessed on television may serve as a stimulus, as a triggering point for hostile actions in those people who because of weak inhibitions are unable to check their violent inclinations. Of particular danger in this respect is the observed violence on television or on the screen that is *not* condemned. While many children may not be affected by violence shown on television or in the movies, those who are fearful, anxious, or lonely will react strongly. It is possible that the more normal child will also adopt some distorted feelings and values regarding violence that indirectly might make him more prone to hostile acting out.

The degree of the effect, however, depends upon the parents' emotional interest in their child. If they have sense enough to ration the time during which he sits before the television screen, some of the hostile aggression shown may serve as a vicarious outlet for his fantasies. But the time *must* be rationed, and he must be encouraged to engage in active endeavors to counteract the passivity of his television viewing.

The only way to overcome violence is to eliminate that which nourishes it. We must eliminate the frustrations and fears that turn into hate and acting out. Such a measure, however, would require a basic change of our attitudes and outlook and a consequent change of our institutions. The odds against this are overwhelming, since we categorically resist any emotional change in ourselves. And our emotional climate of violence does not give us much understanding for coping with such a task.

Nonetheless, if we ever hope to overcome the violent impulses that have taken such a high toll of destruction to our society, we shall have to begin with ourselves. We shall have to look inward. Out of the agony we have experienced, we shall have to try to understand the emotional forces that have been released and have brought us to the brink of disaster. Changing our emotions is a task of the greatest magnitude, and in this respect, I am a reluctant pessimist and a dubious optimist.

Our human nature shows itself when confronted with our present greatest dilemma. We thought that we could involve the twenty million Negroes in our country as partners in our working social-economic order through some mechanical means, failing to realize that our reforms were peripheral compared to the central conditions of life for our Negro population. We have kept the American Dream—and whatever it has given us—for ourselves and prevented most of the Negroes from partaking of its promise. As Floyd B. McKissick expressed it:

Although slavery as a recognized legal institution has been abolished, economic slavery, economic exploitation, has not. Black people in this country have never been allowed to share in the economic riches of America. A few get in—here and there—a few get rich, but their success has no effect on the masses of black people.[14]

While we reluctantly have come to realize that we will have to correct the miserable conditions of our ghettos through concerted efforts, it is obvious that these or similar measures will fall short of the goal, since they do not touch the core of the race violence: the prevailing fear and hate of the Negro, and his hate of himself and the white man.

We must cease believing, as Martin Luther King, Jr. did, that our race conflict will resolve itself as the inevitable result of progress. While King most certainly brought about some progress, time seems to have run out for his nonviolent ideas. As much as we would hope that nonviolence would be the right way, it does not seem to fulfill the present needs of the Negroes.

Emotionally balanced between their own anger and the fear of white power, Negroes would rather listen to SNCC, to the deposed Stokely Carmichael or to his successor, H. Rap Brown—the heroes of Black Power. Nonviolence, the old SNCC, and CORE have lost their meaning for an important segment of the black population. Antipoverty programs, aid to education, swimming pools, and similar constructive programs have not as yet alleviated the situation. Having developed a taste for violence, as we have developed a taste for apple pie, we have girded ourselves for the anticipated clash as if we almost unconsciously wished it.

Since the black man has been cut off from the mainstream of American life, he has, to a varying degree, experienced an emotional and social isolation and withdrawal resulting in indifference and apathy, which explode periodically into aggressive acting out. Interesting in this respect is Eldridge Cleaver's observation:

Prior to 1954 [the United States Supreme Court decision about school integration which caused such upheaval] we [Negroes] lived in an atmosphere of novocain. Negroes found it necessary, in order to maintain whatever sanity they could, to remain somewhat aloof and detached from "the problem." . . . I was soon aflame with indignation over my newly discovered social status, and inwardly I turned away from America with horror, disgust and outrage.[15]

The overspecialization, mechanization, and departmentalization of our society have caused many people to become alienated, estranged from the vital ideas and ethical concepts rooted in society. This alienation has become more pronounced in Negroes than in any other ethnic group of people. The National Advisory Commission on Civil Disorders states in this connection:

Another and equally serious consequence is the fact that this course would lead to the permanent establishment of two societies: one predominantly white and located in the suburbs, in smaller cities, and in outlying areas, and one largely Negro located in central cities. We are well on the way to just such a divided nation.[16]

In conjunction with this study, it is noteworthy that in a follow-up report, *One Year Later*, it is stated that "we are a year closer to two societies—black and white, increasingly separate and scarcely less equal." [17]

The simple fact is that we *are* a divided nation. Emotionally and socially the Negro in all probability has never had a deep-rooted identity with America or what she stood for, although most certainly we have proof that he wanted to belong but was not allowed to. He became at best ambivalent, at worst depersonalized, robbed of his ego. He had no meaningful ties with his white masters.

Harriet Tubman, a former slave who became a spy behind the Confederate lines, helping hundreds of slaves to
escape to Canada by the Underground Railway,[18] said
when she herself became free, "I was free, but there was
no one to welcome me to the land of freedom. I was a
stranger in a strange land." [19]

Alienation, as well as being imposed by the social environment, may be formed to a large extent within the
individual himself. Anyone estranged from himself and
others, whatever the reason, will live in a fantasy world
of his own—and under sufficient pressure act out his
fantasies aggressively, lawlessly.

The black man has detoured from his previous nonviolent path into a violent one that is right in the American
tradition of using force and power. He has always witnessed violence in one form or another, although he may
not have participated in it—except as a victim. For him the
smell of violence has always been in the air, and the impetus he now feels to use it in solving his conflict with
society is more than understandable.

But we must not see the revolt of the black people
purely as a desire to use violence. They are trying to throw
off the white people's yoke, to gain their manhood and
dignity and their real selves much in the same way as a
child growing into adolescence tries to liberate himself
from his resisting parents. Just as the parents fight with
their child over who is going to be master, so also white
society resists the Negro's attempt to grow up into independence.

We have always told ourselves that the trouble between
whites and blacks was due to the Negroes themselves—
that it was really a "Negro problem." Such an attitude

indicates our inherent animosity and prejudice. In fact, the problem is as much, if not more, our own. But our prejudice does not permit us to recognize this fallacy.

If white society continues to resist the Negro's liberation, he will be forced to continue along the desperate path of violence upon which he has embarked. Prejudice and hate cannot be forbidden by law. Nor can they be eradicated from a society that places intolerance and fixed ideas high on its priority list. There will be no solution to the basic problem unless there is a *fundamental* change in our feelings toward people of a different origin.

Again, I am doubtful that any fundamental change will take place in the white people's emotional attitude toward the Negro. Habits on which our emotional attitudes are built are deeply entrenched within us and do not easily give way, since they are perpetually rationalized as correct and just. Yet in the face of heavy odds we must try to rise to the task.

On the positive side of the ledger, constructive tendencies are emerging. People attempt to be tolerant; they try to cooperate, and at times they show great neighborly kindness, interest, and concern. Some are contained emotionally, feel happy about their wives and children and their lots in life. Some seek and find consolation and meaning in religion. Others work faithfully for the public good. There are signs that a new sense of social responsibility, particularly on the part of some of our youth, seems to be in the offing. Many people feel guilty about racial discrimination and have tried in their own meager ways to remedy it. Some have become aware that insufficient medical care is a stigma and that agonizing poverty is degrading in a country as affluent as ours.

The total picture, though, is discouraging. Our inertia and emotional resistance impede fundamental changes in society.

We cannot all be psychiatrists or undergo psychoanalysis. But we can begin to examine—each of us individually—the attitudes we express in our behavior, and question our own motives in acting or refraining from action, rather than becoming complacent and apathetic about what is happening around us. Because what happens *around* us eventually happens to us. And what happens *within* us, eventually happens *around* us.

It would be tempting to suggest that if psychoanalytical principles were applied to society in areas of child rearing, education, and political science, a more mature outlook would follow, promoting emotional and social well-being and lessening violent acting out. Our awareness, for instance, that political conduct is intimately connected with the vicissitudes of the personality makeup would make us more discriminatory in selecting leaders who would be better able to formulate mature domestic, national, and political aims, and thereby counteract our own individual wishes, fears, and frustrations.

Yet in spite of the obvious benefits psychoanalysis has upon many people, society has not accepted it, and it is not likely that it will. Arising from our feelings, our assumed collective superego is unable correctly to appraise our cultural level. Our life is a thin disguise for our instinctual behavior, which gives rise to our bent to violence. Ironically, we have to a large extent utilized scientific data from such fields as biology, medicine, chemistry, and physics that have brought many of us physical satisfaction but less than satisfactory emotional gratification. But data from psychoanalysis have been in large measure neglected by our dominant interests in society. And this bodes ill for us. Not wanting to do something is one matter. But being unable to act for our own emotional benefit—and thereby for the benefit of mankind—because of ignorance is deeply wrong.

If society would permit itself to take cognizance of the contribution psychoanalysis could make to the universal emotional good, a new foundation could be laid, upon which a new common future could be built. Such a change would undoubtedly alter the course of our development as individuals and as a nation.

Although we are all concerned about what we are, more important is the *direction* in which we are going, and the direction will depend upon our ability to see our life in a new perspective.

Some hope may be derived from the attitudes of young people at home, on the battlefield, and on the campuses of our universities. Tempered by war and exposed to a cold, embittered peace, they feel their problems acutely and intensely. Being sensitive, many of them have lost their sense of belonging to their elders. Many people, not only in the United States but all over the world, think that our youth are wrong in their protests, sit-ins, and demonstrations. I am of the opinion that even if they have at times gone overboard in their demands, many of them at least have the idealism most of their elders have lost.

The uproar at our universities is of course another expression of the Oedipus situation, in which the younger generation is fighting the older one. Their rebellion against the old institutions and establishments is in many ways a symbolic overthrow of the father's and the mother's tyrannical regime. There are many realistic grievances, however, that accompany—and often overshadow—the instinctual tendency. The young people have discovered that their elders have alienated themselves from commitment to much of that which is worthwhile in life.

In blaming the younger generation, we of the older generation have in reality projected onto it many of our own frustrated hopes and agonizing failures. To a large extent, we ourselves are responsible for their assumed weakness. So we blame them for their protests, for their lawlessness, for their lack of discipline, when in fact it is we ourselves who are lawless and lacking in discipline. It is the students who have brought protests and demonstrations into our daily lives, giving rise to political action leading to dialogue and change.

It would be wrong to say that young people have directed their anger solely against the universities; these have only served as a vehicle for their frustrations. Their protests are really directed against society, which they strongly feel has maintained the inequities of the people while leaving them with little or no emotional gratification.

Fundamentally, this is a power struggle, which, because violence is ingrained in power, has led to overreaction and radicalization. But this polarization of power only reflects the polarization that has gone on in our society at large. For instance, we have long praised our political system as being one of the best, if not the best, in the Western world. But the fact is that our cities with their underprivileged and underrepresented minorities have had little to say in a political system that has been dominated by the conservative communities in our rural areas.

The students on the university campuses have tried to change their own setup. By dramatically demonstrating their often violent actions, they have been able to assert their frustrated, aggressive feelings and have transformed them into a weapon to achieve power. In many ways this process has served as a prototype for other groups, such as teachers, nurses, and doctors, seeking redress for their grievances.

Through much of their idealism our university students have shown what seemingly powerless people can do when they band together and work toward a common goal. Obviously, emotional factors have played a great role in their search for power, but they have played an equally important role in the older generation's refusal to give it up.

The old father-son situation is the motor behind the motivations of both the generations. Let it be clearly stated, though, that in the same way that many of us protested lawlessness in police violence in the South, and in Chicago in 1968, we must also raise our voices against violation of academic freedom. The often brazen actions by students, particularly Students for a Democratic Society, who occupy university buildings, request control over curricula, and protest professorial appointments reflect in part long-buried hateful emotions against their elders. But mixed with these emotional elements are social and political ones. Many students consider the university an important part of a social system that maintains war, racial and material inequality, and slums. What must not be forgotten is that the students' onslaught against academic freedom at the university means that they deprive these universities of the same freedom they demand for themselves. And freedom requires responsibility. It should be said that many of the student movements, as has been demonstrated so well by Lewis Feuer,[20] have sometimes ended up in killing, apparently because this satisfied the hate of the younger generation toward the older one. We frequently find that some of the student leaders, both here and abroad, have had deep conflicts with their fathers.

I would characterize today's youth as the *turbulent generation*. But in looking beneath their turbulence, we can detect an almost chaotic, despairing behavior pattern and this is quite unconscious—*a cry for help*.

It is therefore highly disturbing that the prevailing opinion among the public and most university administrators is that the only way to meet the students' protests is with suppression or punishment. Such overly zealous repressive measures as forbidding public meetings and the use of police, tear-gas, or antiriot weapons only increase the frustrations of the protesters and urge them on to retaliating with violence. In their eagerness to exercise control through repressive measures, whether protests or riots take place on or outside university campuses, the public or law-enforcing authorities come to rely upon coercion and thereby prevent dialogue and airing of the grievances.

I may here remind you that the history of our universities is filled with violence and that ever so often violent protests by students lead to reforms. In the violent outburst in the thirteenth century, for instance, a formal constitution at the University of Paris was instituted, and the same happened at Oxford. At that time there were students' protests, boycotts, and closing of the university. It was in this way, for instance, that Cambridge University

in England was established after Oxford University had been closed.*

Any irrational show of force, be it against students at universities or other civilians, reduces respect for law enforcement. The police officer under such circumstances is prone to become indifferent to the protestors' and rioters' needs. Often against his own will he becomes the judge and executioner who metes out punishment at once, without due process of law. Such occurrences only enforce the protesters' belief that the law does not guarantee their Constitutional rights.

The police must therefore be educated in how to control crowds and riots, in how to modify the excitement of a crowd before it reaches the point of violence. Policemen under pressure become aggressive, angry, and tough, and therefore need training in how effectively to overcome riots without giving in to their own aggressive impulses. To find the balance between permissiveness and firmness in handling such situations is, of course, difficult. Each has to be judged by itself. While it is wrong to go too far in one direction, it is equally wrong to go too far in the other. As in child rearing, permissiveness and firmness must go hand in hand. But it has to be handled intelligently. The most effective way to deal with riots and protests is to prevent their outbreak. This necessitates quick action and serious attention on the part of the governmental or administrative authorities to the underlying causes of unrest.

As statistics have indicated, youth plays a large role in committing violent acts. If it were possible to eliminate

* Hasting Rashdall, *The Universities of Europe in the Middle Ages.*

juvenile violence and delinquency, much of our violence
would be reduced. But as we have seen, this can only be
achieved when we are able to detect the early signs and
symptoms in those youngsters who are most likely to
commit violent acts. However, to claim, as has the National Commission on the Causes and Prevention of Violence, that crime by youth is the key to the violence in the
United States[21] is indeed exaggerated and simplistic. It
is another example of our projection of our own frustration—in this case because we feel unable to deal with the
problem of violence—upon the younger generation. In
fact it is we, the older generation, who nurture the soil
for violence and crime among our young people through
maintaining frustrations and fears in our society.

We are developing many millions of frustrated and
frightened young boys and girls. How many of them
would like to kill a President or another public citizen
nobody knows. But if he does not kill a President or another human being, each one will still kill something—
some love or affection—in himself or in others, because of
the pressure of his fear and because *nobody really cares*.

The fact that we disregard or oversimplify to a large
extent the real scope of our domestic and national difficulties indicates that we do not have the ego strength to
identify with these difficulties in order to cope with them.
In order to lessen our indifference to the needs of our
people, then, it is necessary to develop a national empathy, a *national identity*. This is more important for us
than for people in any other country, because we do not
have a strong class system. In most of the European
countries, the citizen's class—worker, industrialist, physician, etc.—gives him a sense of identity. Our fluid society

does not permit such a class identification; a dock worker or an accountant today may tomorrow become, for instance, an industrialist, or as the saying goes, "Anyone may become President of the United States." The valuable element of family or ethnic identification is missing for us, too, since too many people in their haste to become Americans are anxious to forget their native origins. This holds true not only for recent immigrants, but for many of the second- and third-generation Italians, Poles, Scandinavians, Negroes, Jews, and Catholics who make up a significant part of the American people. In order to form a genuine identification, and thereby self-esteem, minorities must undertake an emotional rooting back to their origin, as the Negroes have recently done.

E Pluribus Unum is a noble motto, but history so far has not yet shown us one society where many different groups of people have lived together and been able to retain their own distinct identities. The destiny of all minority groups has been to disappear through annihilation, expulsion, or assimilation. Our attempts to unify our people have shown success, but our fragmented national identity shows that it has been far from complete.

If we can manage to attain a stable identification, we will feel more secure, less frustrated, and less fearful. We will also be able to reduce the frustrations and fears of the younger generation by showing them that we care. The only way we can give them hope and faith is by being true to ourselves and true to the best in us.

Our life is a steady development. If we don't have an identity, we try to seek one. But we do not find our identity as we find a garment to clothe us. Genuine identification has to be created in accordance with one's true self.

If our society is to win its long and arduous battle for survival, it will have to change its emotional attitude toward all men, regardless of color, creed, or race. This can only be begun when each of us acknowledges his own humble origin and remembers once we were all immigrants seeking a land that gave promise for a better future.

Thus may we grasp the real meaning of the American Dream, which we have misunderstood and distorted through our childish demands for instant gratification. The Dream never meant to imply that *everyone* would be wonderfully wealthy, continuously successful, and supremely happy. Nor did it mean that each one of us, and all of us together, would be omnipotent. It did promise that each of us could be free to choose his own way of life and could "become whatever thing his manhood [his maturity and capacities] and his vision can combine to make him." But to attain this freedom of choice we must seek our goals not only from without but from within. Changes—and they are important for the survival of our society—have to come from within. Can they be peaceful?

Peaceful, constructive changes in society will depend on the level of emotional maturity on the part of those who are at the helm and those who are aggrieved.

The only avenue left to our violent society is to scrutinize ourselves, lay bare our faults, no matter how painful, and upon a foundation of enlightenment build a life meaningful for everyone. Maybe then, through our violence, through that by which we have fallen so deep, we may also rise above our frustration and fear.

Until each one of us learns to understand ourselves and

others—which will bring change in our America—until that time, Tennyson's comforting words are noteworthy.

He gave the people of his best.

His worst he kept, his best he gave.

Notes

I

1. Bess Furman, "Hearing Tuesday on Youth Crimes," *The New York Times* (March 15, 1965).

2. *Uniform Crime Reports—1965*, Federal Bureau of Investigation, United States Department of Justice, p. 106.

3. *Ibid.*, p. 8.

4. *Ibid.*, p. 11.

5. *F.B.I. Law Enforcement Bulletin*, Federal Bureau of Investigation, United States Department of Justice (June, 1968).

6. *Uniform Crime Reports—1968*, p. 6.

7. *Ibid.*, p. 7.

8. Murray Schumach, "F.B.I. Crime Data Called Misleading by Sociologists," *The New York Times* (March 22, 1965).

9. *The New York Times* (August 27, 1968).

10. Lloyd Cutler, "The National Commission on the Causes and Prevention of Violence Report," *The New York Times* (October 10, 1968).

11. *Time* (June 20, 1968), p. 14.

12. "Crime Is a World-Wide Problem," *F.B.I. Law Enforcement Bulletin* (December, 1966), p. 8.

13. *Uniform Crime Reports—1966*, pp. 60–64.

14. *Ibid.*, p. 5.

15. *Uniform Crime Reports—1967*, pp. 6, 8.

16. *Ibid.*, pp. 80–93.

17. Knut Hamsun, *The Literary Life of Modern America* (1889), quoted in *Nordisk Tidende* (February 29, 1968).

18. *The New York Herald Tribune* (April 12, 1965).

19. *Uniform Crime Reports—1966*, p. 7.

20. *The New York Times* (September 3, 1967).

21. H. G. Earl, "Ten Thousand Children Battered and Starved, Hundreds Die," *Today's Health* (September, 1965).

22. Joan C. Holter and Stanford B. Freedman, "Principles of Management in Child Abuse Cases," *American Journal of Orthopsychiatry*, Vol. 38, No. 1 (January, 1968).

23. Paper, "The Child-Killing Mother," delivered at American Psychological Association Meeting, September 2, 1967.

24. *Uniform Crime Reports—1961*, p. 165.

25. *F.B.I. 1970 Appropriation*. Testimony of John Edgar Hoover, Director FBI, Before the House Subcommittee on Appropriations on April 17, 1969, p. 42.

26. *Uniform Crime Reports—1967*, p. 1.

27. *F.B.I. Law Enforcement Bulletin* (June, 1968).

28. Ralph Slovenko, ed., *Crime, Law and Correction* (Springfield, Illinois: Charles C Thomas, 1966).

29. *F.B.I. Appropriations—1968*. Testimony of J. Edgar Hoover, Director, Federal Bureau of Investigation, before the House Subcommittee on Appropriations (February 16, 1967), p. 12.

30. Truman Capote, *In Cold Blood* (New York: Random House, 1966).

31. *Medical News* (October, 1966).

32. James McCague, *The Second Rebellion: The Story of the New York City Draft Riots of 1863* (New York: Dial Press, 1968).

33. Paul M. Angle, ed., *The Lincoln Reader* (New Brunswick, New Jersey: Rutgers University Press, 1947), pp. 363–64.

34. Carl Sandburg, *Abraham Lincoln: The War Years*, Vol. 1 (New York: Harcourt, Brace and Company, 1939), p. 34.

35. *Harper's Magazine* (October, 1950), p. 108.

36. *Saturday Review* (June 17, 1967), p. 32.

37. *F.B.I. Appropriations*, p. 65.

38. E.M. Rudwick, *Race Riot at East St. Louis, July 2, 1917* (Carbondale, Illinois: Southern Illinois University Press, 1964), p. 217.

39. *F.B.I. 1970 Appropriation*. Testimony of John Edgar Hoover, Director, F.B.I., Before the House Subcommittee on Appropriations on April 17, 1969, p. 40.

40. *Life* (September 8, 1967), p. 98.

41. David Abrahamsen, *Who Are the Guilty? A Study of Education and Crime* (New York: Grove Press, Inc., 1958), p. 201.

42. *The New York Times* (April 1, 1951).

43. *Ibid.* (June 10, 1967).

44. Estes Kefauver, *Crime in America* (Garden City, New York: Doubleday, 1951), p. 20.

45. Norman Douglas, *The Honored Society*, (New York: Putnam, 1964).

46. *Life*, September 8, 1967, p. 103.

47. *The New York Times* (June 1, 1967).

II

1. Fred Powledge, "Rankin Reports 'Many Oswalds,' " *The New York Times* (December 13, 1964).

2. A.M. Rosenthal, *Thirty Eight Witnesses* (New York: McGraw-Hill, 1964).

3. *The New York Times* (July 19, 1965).

4. Andrew Turnbull, "Perkins' Three Generals," *The New York Times Book Review* (July 16, 1967), p. 25.

5. *The New Yorker* (June 3, 1967), p. 25. Author's italics.

6. "Reporting from the World of Television and Radio," *New York Herald Tribune* (August 1, 1964).

7. *The New York Times* (July 16, 1967).

8. *Report of March 1964,* The American Jewish Committee, New York, New York.

9. *Ibid.,* p. 2.

10. *Ibid.,* p. 3.

11. *The New York Times* (June 28, 1965).

12. *The New York Times* (November 30, 1967).

13. *Newsweek* (August 10, 1964).

14. *The New York Times* (February 6, 1966).

15. *The New York Times* (October 8, 1960).

16. Raymond E. Wolfinger, Barbara Kay Wolfinger, Sheila H. Rosenhack, Kenneth Prewitt, "Crusaders for the Right," *Trans-Action,* Washington University, St. Louis, Mo., July, 1964, pp. 23–27.

17. "The Fearmongers," *Life* (February 7, 1964).

18. *Encyclopedia of American History,* ed. by Richard B. Morris (New York: Harper & Row, 1966).

19. Charles Y. Glock and Rodney Stark, *Christian Beliefs and Anti-Semitism* (New York: Harper & Row, 1966).

20. Richard Hofstadter, *Anti-Intellectualism in American Life* (New York: Alfred A. Knopf, 1963).

21. *Ibid.,* p. 28.

22. Stewart H. Holbrook, *The Age of the Moguls* (New York: Doubleday & Co., 1953), p. 16.

23. Caroline Bird, *The Invisible Scar* (New York: David McKay Company, 1966), p. 24.

III

1. Bayard Rustin, "The Watts 'Manifesto' and the McCone Report," *Commentary,* Vol. 41, No. 3 (March, 1966), p. 29.

2. *The New York Times* (October 2, 1964).

3. William H. Grier and Price M. Cobbs, *Black Rage* (Basic Books, 1968).

4. William Miller, *A New History of the United States.* Introduction by Frank Freidel (New York: George Brasiller Inc., 1958), p. 71.

5. Oscar and Mary Handlin, "Origins of the Southern Labor System," *William and Mary Quarterly,* 3 Ser., VII (April, 1950), pp. 199–220.

6. Richard B. Morris, *Encyclopedia of American History* (New York: Harper & Bros., 1953), p. 513.

7. Carl N. Degler, *Out of the Past: The Forces That Shaped Modern America* (New York: Harper & Bros., 1959), p. 29.

8. Kenneth M. Stampp, *The Peculiar Institution: Slavery in the Ante-Bellum South* (New York: Vintage Books, 1956), p. 24.

9. Morris, p. 513.

10. Catherine Drinker Bowen, *John Adams and The American Revolution* (Boston: Little, Brown & Co., 1950), p. 207.

11. Stampp, p. 18; *see also,* Ulrich B. Phillips, *Life and Labor in The Old South* (Boston, 1929).

12. Degler, p. 31.

13. Stampp, p. 22.

14. Oscar and Mary Handlin, pp. 199–222; *see also,* Ulrich B. Phillips, *American Negro Slavery* (New York, 1933).

15. Degler, p. 36.

16. William Styron, *The Confessions of Nat Turner* (New York: Random House, 1966, 1967), pp. 53–54.

17. Degler, pp. 165–66.

18. Stampp, p. 127.

19. *Ibid.,* p. 127; *see also,* Stanley M. Elkins, *Slavery: A Problem in American Institutional and Intellectual Life* (Chicago, 1959).

20. Stampp, p. 127.

21. Arnold Forster, "Violence on the Fanatical Left and Right," *The Annals of the American Academy of Political and Social Science, Patterns of Violence* (March, 1966), pp. 141–48.

22. Martin B. Duberman, *In White America* (Boston: Houghton Mifflin Co., Cambridge: The Riverside Press, 1964), p. 50.

23. Frederick L. Hoffman, *The Homicide Problem* (Newark: Prudential Press, 1925), p. 78.

24. Morris, p. 332.

25. Forster, p. 144.

26. *The New York Times* (August 1, 1965).

27. Forster, p. 142.

28. *Ibid.*

29. Federal Bureau of Investigation Press Release dated January 5, 1967. Washington, D.C.: U.S. Department of Justice, p. 15.

30. *F.B.I. Appropriations—1968,* p 65.

31. William Pierce Randel, *The Ku Klux Klan: A Century of Tyranny* (New York: Chilton Books, 1965).

32. David Danzig, "Rightists, Racists, and Separatists: A White Block in the Making?" *Commentary*, Vol. 38, No. 2 (1964), p. 29.

33. Simeon Booker, *Black Man's America* (New York: Prentice-Hall, 1964), p. 120.

34. *Ibid.*, pp. 121 ff.

35. *The New York Times* (August 10, 1964).

36. Booker, pp. 121–26.

37. Gunnar Myrdal, *An American Dilemma, The Negro Problem and Modern Democracy* (1944).

38. Louis Jolyan West, "The Psychobiology of Racial Violence." Paper given at The American Psychiatric Association Convention, May 4, 1965.

39. Eldridge Cleaver, *Soul On Ice* (New York: McGraw-Hill Book Company, 1968), p. 14.

IV

1. Martin Grotjahn, M.D., *Beyond Laughter: Humor and the Subconscious* (New York: McGraw-Hill, 1960).

2. Sigmund Freud, "Analysis Terminable and Unterminable," *Collected Papers*, Vol. V (London: Hogarth Press and the Institute of Psychoanalysis, 1950), p. 355.

3. John E. Snell, Rosenwald, Richard J., and Roby, Ames. "The Wife Beater's Wife: A Study of Family Interaction," *Archives of General Psychiatry*, II, 1964 pp. 107–112.

4. George F. Willison, *Saints and Strangers* (New York: Reynal & Hitchcock, 1945), p. 319.

V

1. Sigmund Freud, *New Introductory Lectures on Psycho-analysis* (New York: W.W. Norton & Co., Inc., 1933), p. 147.

2. Konrad Lorenz, *On Aggression* (New York: Harcourt, Brace & World, Inc., 1966).

3. Robert Ardrey, *The Territorial Imperative* (New York: Atheneum Press, 1967); Anthony Storr, *Human Aggression* (New York: Atheneum Press, 1968).

4. Rene A. Spitz, "Aggression: Its Role in the Establishment of Object Relations," *Drives, Affects, Behavior,* edited by Rudolph H. Lowenstein (New York: International Universities Press, 1953), p. 126; *see also* H. Hartmann, E. Kris, and R.N. Lowenstein, "Notes on the Theory of Aggression," *The Psychoanalytic Study of the Child*, III/IV (New York: International Universities Press, 1949).

5. From *"Le Neveu de Rameau"* as quoted by Sigmund Freud, *An Outline of Psychoanalysis* (New York: W.W. Norton & Company, 1949), p. 97.

VI

1. Sigmund Freud, *Leonardo Da Vinci, A Study in Psychosexuality* (New York: Random House, 1947), p. 118.

2. Sigmund Freud, "Psychoanalysis and the Ascertaining of Truth in Courts of Law," *Collected Papers*, Vol. II (London: Lund Humphries, 1924), p. 18.

3. David Abrahamsen, "The Dynamic Connection Between Personality and Crime and the Detection of the Potential Criminal Illustrated by Different Types of Murder," *The Journal of Criminal Psychopathology*, Vol. V, No. 3 (January, 1944), p. 482.

4. Phyllis Greenacre, *Trauma, Growth and Personality* (New York: W. W. Norton Co., 1952), p. 227. This point has in general been emphasized by Dr. Greenacre in the genesis of acting out.

5. *Hearings Before the President's Commission on the Assassination of President Kennedy*, Vol. VIII (Washington, D.C.: U.S. Government Printing Office, 1964), p. 122.

6. *Ibid.*, Vol. I, pp. 231–32.

7. *Ibid.*, Vol. VIII, pp. 51–52.

8. *Ibid.*, Vol. VIII, pp. 7, 13.

9. *Ibid.*, Vol. I, p. 311.

10. *Ibid.*, Vol. VIII, p. 47.

11. *Ibid.*, Vol. I, p. 254.

12. *Ibid.*, Vol. VIII, p. 47.

13. *Ibid.*, Vol. I, p. 37.

14. *Ibid.*, Vol. I, p. 254.

15. *Ibid.*, Vol. VIII, p. 47.

16. *Ibid.*, Vol. VIII, p. 95.

17. *Ibid.*, Vol. I, p. 252.

18. *Ibid.*, Vol. VIII, p. 98.

19. *Ibid.*, Vol. I, p. 145.

20. *Ibid.*, Vol. VIII, p. 42.

21. *Ibid.*, Vol. VIII, pp. 98–99.

22. *The New York Times* (September 28, 1964), p. 39a.

23. *Hearings*, Vol. VIII, pp. 51–52.

24. *Ibid.*, Vol. VIII, p. 55.

25. *Ibid.*, Vol. VIII, p. 57.

26. *Ibid.*, Vol. XI, p. 17.

27. *Ibid.*, Vol. XI, p. 75.

28. *Ibid.*, Vol. VIII, p. 48.

29. *Ibid.*, Vol. VIII, pp. 50–55.

30. *Report of the Warren Commission on the Assassination of President Kennedy* (New York: McGraw-Hill Book Company, 1964), p. 368.

31. *Hearings*, Vol. XI, p. 94.

32. *Report of the Warren Commission*, p. 601.

33. *Ibid.*, p. 357.

34. David Abrahamsen, *Mind and Death of a Genius* (New York: Columbia University Press, 1964), p. 156.

35. Private communication.

36. Donald Jackson, "The Evolution of an Assassin," *Life* (February 21, 1964), pp. 70–71.

37. *Report of the Warren Commission*, pp. 369–70.

38. *Hearings*, Vol. I, p. 331.

39. *Report of the Warren Commission*, p. 601.

40. *Ibid.*, p. 602.

41. *Ibid.*, p. 603.

42. *Hearings*, Vol. VIII, p. 353.

43. *Report of the Warren Commission*, p. 599.

44. *Ibid.*, p. 353.

45. *Ibid.*, p. 356.

46. *Hearings*, Vol. VIII, p. 223.

47. *Ibid.*, Vol. VIII, p. 224.

48. *Ibid.*, Vol. VIII, p. 9.

49. *Ibid.*, Vol. I, p. 23.

50. *Ibid.*

51. *Ibid.*, Vol. I, p. 22.

52. *Ibid.*, Vol. I, p. 212.

53. *Ibid.*, Vol. I, p. 201.

54. Lee Harvey Oswald, "Historic Diary," *Life* (July 10, 1964), p. 29.

55. *Hearings*, Vol. V, p. 229.

56. *Ibid.*, Vol. I, p. 34.

57. *See also:* David Abrahamsen, *Men, Mind and Power* (New York: Columbia University Press, 1945), pp. 90, 91.

58. David Abrahamsen, *The Psychology of Crime* (New York: Columbia University Press, 1967), pp. 164–65; *see also* Rose Palm and David Abrahamsen, "A Rorschach Study of the Wives of Sex Offenders," *The Journal of Nervous and Mental Diseases*, Vol. 119, No. 2 (February, 1954).

VII

1. Personal communication.

2. Records of the Probation Department of the U.S. District Court, Southern District of New York.

3. David A. Rothstein, "The Presidential Assassination Syndrome," *General Archives of Psychiatry*, II (1964), pp. 245–54.

4. David Abrahamsen, *The Psychology of Crime* (New York: Columbia University Press, 1967).

5. L. Vernon Briggs, *The Manner of Man that Kills: Spencer-Czolgosz-Richeson* (Boston: The Gorham Press, 1921), p. 243.

6. Philip Weissman, M.D., *Why Booth Killed Lincoln.* A Psychoanalytic Study of a Historical Tragedy. Psychoanalysis of the Social Sciences, edited by Warner Muensterberger, Ph.D., and Sidney Axelrod, D.S.Sc. Vol. V. (New York: International Universities Press, Inc., 1958), p. 107.

VIII

1. Thomas Wolfe, "Epilogue: The Promise of America," *America Remembers,* edited by Samuel Rappaport and Patricia Schartle (Garden City, New York: Hanover House, 1956), p. 669.

2. Catherine Drinker Bowen, "Bernard DeVoto: Historian, Critic, and Fighter," *The Atlantic Monthly* (December, 1960), p. 75.

3. Perry Miller, *The New England Mind: From Colony to Province* (Cambridge, Massachusetts: Harvard University Press, 1933), p. 5.

4. Allan Nevins, "The Limits of Individualism," *Saturday Review* (November 25, 1967), p. 26.

5. *A Treasury of American Folklore,* edited by B.A. Botkin (New York: Crown Publishers, 1944), p. 131.

6. C.L. Sonnichsen, *Roy Bean, Law West of the Pecos* (New York: MacMillan, 1943), p. 46.

7. D.W. Brogan, *The American Character* (New York: Alfred Knopf, 1944), p. 12.

8. Frederick Jackson Turner, "The Significance of the Frontier in American History." Paper read at meeting of the American Historical Association in Chicago in 1893. See also the collection of Turner's essays, *The Frontier in American History.* (New York: 1921.)

9. Ray Allen Billington (with the collaboration of James Blair Hedges), *Westward Expansion, A History of the American Frontier* (New York: The Macmillan Company, 1952), p. 3.

10. Franklin Delano Roosevelt, Speech Accepting the Nomination for a Fourth Term as President (July 20, 1944).

11. Oscar Handlin, *The Uprooted: The Epic Story of the Great Migrations that Made the American People* (New York: Grosset & Dunlap, 1951), p. 4.

12. *Ibid.,* p. 169.

13. From "Notes on Virginia," in the *Writings of Thomas Jefferson* (Washington: 1903), II, as cited by Thomas F. Gossett, *Race, the History of an Idea in America* (Dallas, Texas: Southern Methodist University Press, 1964), pp. 42, 44; and Martin B. Duberman, *In White America. A Documentary Play* (Boston: Houghton Mifflin Company; Cambridge: Riverside Press, 1964), pp. 85–91.

14. Gossett, p. 292.

15. *The American Treasury, 1455–1955, Prose, Poetry and Song Drawn from our Life, Laughter and Literature,* selected with commentary by Clifton Fadiman, assisted by Charles Van Doren (New York: Harper & Brothers, 1955), p. 379.

16. *The New York Times* (August 6, 1964).

17. Murray Friedman, "Is White Racism the Problem?" *Commentary,* Vol. 47, No. 1 (January, 1969), p. 61.

18. Nathaniel Hawthorne to Henry Wadsworth Longfellow, October 24, 1854, in *Hawthorne, Critic of Society,* edited by Laurence S. Hall (New Haven: 1944), p. 71; *see also,* Merle Curti, *The Roots of American Loyalty* (New York: Columbia University Press, 1946), p. 32.

19. Curti, p. 32.

20. Gertrude Stein, *The Geographical History of America,* quoted from *The American Treasury, 1455–1955.*

IX

1. *The New York Times* (March 6, 1969).

2. Janet N. Anders, M.Sc., Georgianna Jagiello, M.D., Paul E. Polani, M.D., F. Gianelli, M.D., John L. Hamerton, B.Sc., and D.M. Lieberman, M.D., "Chromosome Findings in Chronic Psychotic Patients," *British Journal of Psychiatry,* 114:1167–1174 (September, 1968); *see also* William M. Court Brown, *Human Population Gytogenesis,* Frontier of Biology Series, Vol. V (Amsterdam, Holland: North Holland Publishing Company, 1967).

3. David Abrahamsen, *The Psychology of Crime* (New York: Columbia University Press, 1967), p. 167.

4. *Hearings of the National Commission on the Causes and Prevention of Violence* (October 3, 1968), pp. 966–71.

5. David Abrahamsen, "Report on Study of 102 Sex Offenders at Sing Sing Prison," *State Hospitals Press* (March, 1950), p. 20.

6. Heinz Hartmann, *Essays on Ego Psychology, Selected Problems in Psychoanalytical Theory* (New York: International Universities Press, Inc., 1964).

7. Van Wyck Brooks, "A Writer's Notebook," *The Nation* (November 14, 1953).

8. Dory Schary, "Our Movie Mythology," *The Reporter* (March 3, 1960).

9. *Ibid.,* p. 40.

10. K.R. Eisler, "Ego-Psychological Implications of the Psychoanalytic Treatment of Delinquents," *Psychoanalytic Study of the Child,* Vol. V (New York: International Universities Press, 1950), p. 97.

11. Richard Hofstadter, *The Paranoid Style in American Politics and Other Essays* (New York: Alfred A. Knopf, 1964) p. 58.

12. Marvin E. Wolfgang, *Patterns in Criminal Homicide* (Philadelphia: University of Pennsylvania Press, 1958), as cited by Jackson Toby, "Violence and Masculine Ideal: Some Qualitative Data," *The Annals of the American Academy of Political and Social Science, Patterns of Violence* (Philadelphia: The American Academy of Political and Social Science, March, 1966), p. 19.

X

1. Bruce N. Russett, Howard R. Alker, Jr., Karl W. Deutsch, Harold D. Lasswell, with the assistance of Robert Bunselmeyer, James Einstein, Robert Grey, Russell Murphy, John Shingler, Seth Singleton, Stephen Stephens, *World Handbook of Political and Social Indicators* (New Haven: Yale University Press, 1964), Table E29, pp. 99–100.

2. *Ibid.*, Table E71, p. 245, and Table E72, p. 247.

3. Ivo K. Feierabend, Rosalind L. Feierabend, and Betty A. Nesvold, "Correlates of Political Stability." Paper presented at the 1963 Annual Meeting of the American Political Science Association, September 4–7, 1963.

4. *Report of the National Commission on the Study of the Causes and Prevention of Violence* (October 2, 1968), pp. 776–828.

5. *Ibid.*, p. 777.

6. *Ibid.*, pp. 779–80.

7. David Brion Davis, "Violence in American Literature," *Patterns of Violence, The Annals of the American Academy of Political and Social Science* (March, 1966), p. 31.

8. Carl Sandburg, *Abraham Lincoln: The War Years*, Vol. I (New York: Harcourt, Brace & Company, 1939), p. 4.

9. *See* Alex Inkeles and Daniel J. Levensohn, "National Character: The Study of Modal Personality and Socio-cultural Systems," *Handbook of Social Psychology*, Vol. II (Cambridge, Massachusetts: Addison-Wesley Publishing Co., Inc., 1954), Chap. 26, pp. 997–1020.

10. I.A. Rotenberg and Robert L. Sandoff, "Who Should Have a Gun? Some Preliminary Psychiatric Thoughts," *American Journal of Psychiatry*, Vol. 125, No. 6 (December, 1968), pp. 841–43.

11. David Abrahamsen, "Status of Mental Hygiene and Child Guidance Facilities in Public Schools in the United States," *Journal of Pediatrics*, Vol. XLVI, No. 1 (January, 1955), p. 107.

12. David Abrahamsen, "Mental Hygiene Services in Private Schools," *Mental Hygiene*, Vol. 43, No. 2 (April, 1959), p. 282.

13. David Abrahamsen, "Mass Psychosis and Its Effects," *Journal of Nervous and Mental Diseases*, Vol. XCIII, No. 1 (January, 1941), pp. 63–72. (Paper published originally in Norway, 1938.)

14. *The New York Times* (July 30, 1967).

15. Eldridge Cleaver, *Soul on Ice* (New York: McGraw-Hill, 1968), pp. 3–4.

16. *Report of the National Advisory Committee on Civil Disorders* (New York: Bantam Books, 1968), p. 398.

17. Report to President Lyndon B. Johnson, January 9, 1969.

18. *Black Protest—History, Documents and Analyses— 1619 to the Present,* Edited by Joanne Grant. (Greenwich, Conn.: Fawcett Publications, Inc. 1968) p. 103.

19. *Report of the National Advisory Commission on Civil Disorders* (New York: Bantam Books, Inc., 1968) p. 398.

20. Lewis Feuer, *The Conflict of Generations.* (New York: Basic Books, 1968).

21. Report to President Lyndon B. Johnson, January 9, 1969.

Bibliography

ABRAHAMSEN, DAVID, *The Mind and Death of a Genius* (New York: Columbia University Press, 1946).

———, *The Psychology of Crime* (New York: Columbia University Press, 1967).

———, *The Road to Emotional Maturity* (New Jersey: Prentice-Hall, 1968; paperback ed. Pocket Books, 1966).

ALMOND, GABRIEL A., and VERBA, SIDNEY, *The Civic Culture. Political Attitudes and Democracy in Five Nations* (Boston and Toronto: Little Brown and Company, 1965).

BALDWIN, JAMES, *The Fire Next Time* (New York: The Dial Press, 1963).

BARBER, JAMES D., "Classifying and Predicting Presidential Styles: Two 'Weak' Presidents," Yale University *Journal of Social Issues,* Vol. XXIV, No. 3, 1968.

BENDINER, ROBERT, *Just Around the Corner, A Highly Selective History of the Thirties* (New York: Harper & Row, 1967).

BILLINGTON, RAY ALLEN, *Westward Expansion, A History of the American Frontier* (New York: The Macmillan Company, 1949).

BIRD, CAROLINE, *The Invisible Scar* (New York: David McKay Company, Inc., 1966).

BOOKER, SIMEON, *Black Man's America* (New Jersey: Prentice-Hall, Inc., 1964).

BOTKIN, B. A., Ed., *A Treasury of American Folklore* (New York: Crown Publishers, 1944).

BOWEN, CATHERINE DRINKER, "Bernard DeVoto: Historian, Critic, and Fighter," *The Atlantic Monthly* (December 1960) p. 75.

BRODY, SYLVIA, and AXELROD, SIDNEY, "Anxiety, Socialization and Ego Formation in Infancy" (Lecture at the New York Psychoanalytic Institute, 1966).

BRUCKBERGER, R. L., *Image of America* (New York: Viking Press, 1959).

BURNS, EDWARD MCNALL, *The American Idea of Mission* (New Jersey: Rutgers University Press, 1957).

CARMICHAEL, STOKELY, and HAMILTON, CHARLES V., *Black Power, The Politics of Liberation in America* (New York: Random House, 1967).

CLEAVER, ELDRIDGE, *Soul on Ice* (New York: McGraw-Hill Book Company, 1968).

COMMAGER, HENRY STEELE, *The American Mind* (Connecticut: Yale University Press, 1959).

CONANT, RALPH W., "The Future of Black Protest in Civil Disorders and Riots," Reprinted from *The Police Chief*, Vol. XXXVI (April, 1969), Reprint Series Lemberg Center for the Study of Violence, Brandeis University, Waltham, Massachusetts.

CURTI, MERLE, *The Growth of American Thought* (New York: Harper & Bros., 1951).

————, *The Roots of American Loyalty* (New York: Columbia University Press, 1946).

DEGLER, CARL N., *Out of Our Past, The Forces That Shaped Modern America* (New York: Harper & Bros., 1959).

DeVoto, Bernard, *The Year of Decision, 1846* (Boston: Little, Brown and Company, 1943).

Duberman, Martin B., *In White America* (Boston: Houghton Mifflin Company; Cambridge: The Riverside Press, 1964).

Erikson, Dai T., *Wayward Puritans, A Study in the Sociology of Deviance* (New York: John Wiley & Sons, Inc., 1966).

Fadiman, Clifton, and Van Doren, Charles, Eds., *The American Treasury, 1455–1955* (New York: Harper & Bros., 1955).

Feuer, Lewis, *The Conflict of Generations* (New York: Basic Books, 1968).

————, *The Character and Significance of Student Movements* (New York: Basic Books, 1968).

Freud, Anna, *The Ego and the Mechanisms of Defense* (New York: International Universities Press, Inc., 1964).

Freud, Sigmund, *Civilization and Its Discontents* (London: Hogarth Press, Ltd., and the Institute for Psychoanalysis, 1946).

————, *Group Psychology and the Analysis of the Ego* (New York: Liveright Publishing Corp., 1951).

Goldman, Eric F., *The Crucial Decade—And After, America 1945–1960* (New York: Vintage Books, 1960).

Gossett, Thomas F., *Race, the History of an Idea in America,* (Dallas: Southern Methodist University Press, 1964).

Grant, Joanne, Ed., *Black Protest, History Documents and Analysis 1619 to the Present* (Connecticut: Fawcett Publications, Inc., 1967).

Greenacre, Phyllis, *The Quest for the Father* (New York: International Universities Press, Inc., 1963).

Gurr, T., *The Conditions of Civil Violence.* Princeton Center of International Studies (Princeton, N.J.: Princeton University, 1967).

Halleck, Seymour L., *Psychiatry and the Dilemmas of Crime* (New York; Harper & Row, 1967)

HANDLIN, OSCAR, *The Uprooted* (New York: Universal Library, 1951).

HARTMANN, HEINZ, *Essays on Ego Psychology, Selected Problems in Psychoanalytic Theory* (New York: International Universities Press, Inc., 1964).

The History of Violence in America, A Report to the National Commission on the Causes and Prevention of Violence Edited by Hugh Davis Graham and Ted Robert Gurr (New York: Praeger Press, 1969).

HOFSTADTER, RICHARD, *Anti-Intellectualism in American Life* (New York: Alfred A. Knopf, 1963).

———, *The Paranoid Style in American Politics and Other Essays* (New York: Alfred A. Knopf, 1965).

HOLBROOK, STEWART H., *The Age of the Moguls*, Ed. Lewis Gannett, Mainstream of America Series, (New York: Doubleday & Company, 1953).

———, *Dreamers of the American Dream*, Ed. Lewis Gannett, Mainstream of America Series (New York: Doubleday & Company, 1957).

INKELES, ALEX, and LEVENSOHN, DANIEL J., "National Character: The Study of Modal Personality and Socio-cultural Systems," in *Handbook of Social Psychology*. Vol. II (Mass.: Addison Wesley Publishing Co., Inc., 1954).

KNOPF, TERRY ANN, *Youth Patrols: An Experiment in Community Participation*, Approaches to the Study of Violence (Waltham Mass.: The Lemberg Center for the Study of Violence, Brandeis University, Waltham, Mass.)

LARRABEE, ERIC, *The Self-Conscious Society* (New York: Doubleday & Company, 1960).

LERNER, MAX, *America as a Civilization, Life and Thought in the United States Today* (New York: Simon and Schuster, 1957).

LEWIN, BERTRAM D., Ed., *On Character and Libido Development: Six Essays by Karl Abraham* (New York: W.W. Norton & Co., Inc., 1966).

LORENZ, KONRAD, *On Aggression* (New York: Harcourt, Brace & World, Inc., 1966).

LUPSHA, PETER A., "On Theories of Urban Violence," Paper delivered at the 1968 Annual Meeting of the American Political Science Association (Washington, D.C.).

MEAD, MARGARET, and WOLFENSTEIN, MARTHA, Eds., *Childhood in Contemporary Cultures* (Chicago: University of Chicago Press, 1955).

MENNINGER, KARL, *The Crime of Punishment* (New York: Viking Press, 1968).

MILLER, PERRY, *The New England Mind: From Colony to Province* (Mass.: University Press, 1933).

MORRIS, RICHARD B., Ed., *Encyclopedia of American History* (New York: Harper & Brothers, 1953).

MYRDAL, GUNNAR, *An American Dilemma, The Negro Problem and Modern Democracy* (New York: Harper & Row, 1962).

NOTESTEIN, WALLACE, *The English People on the Eve of Colonization, 1603–1630* (New York: Harper & Brothers, 1954).

PACKARD, VANCE, *The Status Seekers* (New York: David McKay Company, Inc., 1959).

Report of the National Advisory Commission on Civil Disorders (New York: Bantam Books, 1968).

Report: "Violence in America: Historical and Comparative Perspective," made to the National Commission on the Causes and Prevention of Violence, June 5, 1969.

RIESMAN, DAVID; GLAZER, NATHAN; DENNEY, REUEL, *The Lonely Crowd, A Study of the Changing American Character* (New York: Doubleday Anchor Books, 1954).

ROSENTHAL, A.M., *Thirty Eight Witnesses* (New York: McGraw Hill, 1964).

ROZWENC, EDWIN C., *The Causes of the American Civil War* (Boston: D. C. Heath and Company, 1966).

RUDWICK, ELLIOT M., *Race Riot at East St. Louis, July 2, 1917* (Carbondale: Illinois University Press, 1964).

RUSSETT, BRUCE N., and ALKER, HOWARD R., JR., DEUTSCH, KARL W., and others, *World Handbook of Political and Social Indicators* (Connecticut: Yale University Press, 1964).

SHOHAM, SHLOMO, "Culture Conflict as a Frame of Reference for Research in Criminology and Social Deviation," Offprints from *Crime and Culture:* Essays in Honor of Thorsten Sellin. Edited by Marvin E. Wolfgang (New York: John Wiley & Sons, Inc., 1968).

SKOLNICK, JEROME H., *The Politics of Protest,* A Task Force Report Submitted to the National Commission on the Causes and Prevention of Violence (New York, Simon & Schuster, 1969).

SNELL, JOHN E.; ROSENWALD, RICHARD J.; and ROBY, AMERS, "The Wife Beater's Wife. A Study of Family Interaction," *Archives of General Psychiatry,* II (Chicago: 1964).

"Sniping Incidents—A New Pattern of Violence?" *Riot Data Review,* Feb. 1969, No. 3 (Waltham, Mass.: The Lemberg Center for the Study of Violence, Brandeis University, Waltham, Mass).

SPIEGEL, JOHN, Six-City Study, A Survey of Racial Attitudes in Six Northern Cities: Preliminary Findings. (Waltham, Mass.: Lemberg Center for the Study of Violence, June 1967).

STAMPP, KENNETH M., *The Peculiar Institution, Slavery in the Ante-Bellum South* (New York: Vintage Books, 1956).

WECTER, DIXON, *The Age of the Great Depression 1929–1941* (New York: Macmillan Company, 1948).

WILLISON, GEORGE F., *Saints and Strangers* (New York: Reynal & Hitchcock, 1945).

Index

Adonis, Joe, 30 n
Affluence, and violence, 34
Aggression, instinctive and
    learned, 109–128
Alabama, 77, 78
Ambivalence, 125, 126, 205, 206
American Dream, 17, 20, 47, 55–
    57, 181–208
American Tragedy, An (Dreiser),
    16
Anal stage of development, 117–
    119, 132
Anastasia, Albert, 30 n
Andrews, Charles M., 26
Anti-intellectualism, 53–56
*Anti-Intellectualism in American
    Life* (Hofstadter), 53n
Anti-poverty bill, 126
Anti-Semitism, 44, 52, 53
Apalachin, N.Y., 32
Ardrey, Robert, 115
Arkansas, 18
Arnold, Matthew, 48

Arson, 29
Assassination, 5, 161–180
Association for the Advancement
    of Psychology, 129n
Astor, John Jacob, 57
Australia, 238
Austria, 59

Baptists, 52
Battered-child syndrome, 13, 14
Bean, Roy, 191
Beating, 28
Belgium, 237
Billington, Roy Allen, 195
Billy the Kid, 192
Birmingham, Ala., 11
Black Hand, *see* Mafia
Black Muslims, 80, 81
Black Power Movement, 28, 80,
    258
Black Rage (Grier and Cobbs),
    66
Bond, James, 194, 195

Bonus Expeditionary Force, 59
Booth, John Wilkes, 130, 164,
    174, 175, 176, 177
Boston, Mass., 10, 11, 30, 68,
    243
Brandeis University, 253n
Brooks, Van Wyck, 229
Brown, H. Rap, 90, 258
Brown, John, 61
Buchalter, Louis ("Lepke"), 29n
Buffalo, N.Y., 37
Bulletin, The (John Birch Society
    organ), 50
Bulletin of the New York Aca-
    demy of Medicine, The, 129n
Burning, 7, 28, 33

Canada, 30, 238
Capone, Al, 29
Capote, Truman, 15, 16
Carmichael, Stokely, 258
Catholics, 44, 50, 53, 78, 127,
    269
Charlotte, N.C., 11
Chessman, Caryl, 36
Chicago, Ill., 11, 21, 28, 29n, 32,
    61, 265
Child-battering syndrome, 13, 14
Choice Not An Echo, A (Scha-
    fly), 46n
Christian Crusade, 45, 46, 50, 51
Christians, anti-Semitism among,
    52, 53
Civil Rights Law of 1964, 62, 79
Civil War (Spanish), 23
Civil War (U.S.), 18, 20–23, 57
Clark, Ramsey, 166
Cleaver, Eldridge, 86, 258, 259
Cobbs, Price M., 66

Communism, 27, 28, 48–52, 55,
    56, 59
Confessions of Nat Turner, The
    (Styron), 70, 71
Congregationalists, 53
Congressional Record, 49n
Congress of the United States,
    59
Connecticut, 11, 70
Constructive Action, Inc., 46
Cooke, Jay, 57
Coordinating Committee for
    Fundamental American Free-
    doms, 79
CORE, 258
Cosa Nostra, 30, 32, 33
Coughlin, Reverend Charles E.,
    44
Crime: among children and ado-
    lescents, 7, 8; organized, 5,
    28–33, 38, 39; U. S. rate of,
    14–15
Curti, Merle, 207
Czolgosz, Leon P., 174, 175

Daily Times (El Paso), 191
Dallas, Texas, 11, 243
Dalton brothers, 192
Daughters of the American Rev-
    olution, 45
Davis, David Brion, 241
Death instinct, 114
Degler, Carol N., 68
Demonstrations, 5, 17
Denmark, 59, 238
Depression of the 1930s, 58, 59
Desegregation, 77, 79, 82
Detection of the potentially vio-
    lent, 209–236

Detroit, Mich., 28, 29n, 61, 62, 80
De Voto, Bernard, 183
Diderot, 123
Dies, Martin, 52
Dillinger, John, 29
Disciples of Christ, 52
Dreiser, Theodore, 16
Drew, Daniel, 57
Drowning, 7
Dulles, John Foster, 49

East Germany, 237
East St. Louis, Ill., 28
Ego, 118, 132, 133, 222
Eisenhower, Dwight D., 49, 50
Eisenhower, Milton, 49
Ekdahl, Edwin, 138–148
Ellsworth, Elmer, 21
England, 9, 10, 59
Episcopalians, 52
Evans, Myrtle, 134n, 135–140
Exhibitionism, 142
Extremist groups, 5

FBI, 8, 9, 12, 14, 28, 63, 79
Feierabend, Ivo K., 238–239
Feuer, Lewis, 266
Firearms, 9–11; control laws, 11
Florida, 78
Fontana, Dr. Vincent J., 13
Forbes, John Murray, 241
Force Laws, 74
France, 30, 47, 237
Frank, Robert, 106–108
Freud, Sigmund, 110–115, 119, 125, 131, 132, 151, 246
Frick, Henry Clay, 23

Garfield, James, 130, 174
Garrison, C. C., 56

Georgia, 76, 78
German-American Bund, 44
Germany, 44, 59
Gipson, Henry, 26
Glock, Charles Y., 52
Govan, Thomas, 72
Greece, 237
Grier, William M., 66
Grotjahn, Martin, 94n
Group Research, Inc., 45
Guns, see Firearms

Haley, J. Evetts, 45, 46
Hamsun, Knut, 11
Handlin, Oscar, 201
Hangings, 19
Hargis, Bill James, 50
Harper's Magazine, 24
Hartmann, Heinz, 229
Hate groups, 44–48
Hawthorne, Nathaniel, 207
Hay, John, 21
Haymarket Massacre, 23
Hemingway, Ernest, 39
Henry, Patrick, 26
Hickok, Wild Bill, 24, 25, 26, 56, 191
Himmler, Heinrich, 155n
Hobbes, Thomas, 115
Hofstadter, Richard, 53, 234
Holland, 59
Homestead Massacre, 23
Homosexuality, 41, 106, 107, 108, 121, 132, 148
Hoover, Herbert, 59
Hoover, J. Edgar, 28, 29, 63
House Un-American Activities Committee, 52, 78
Houston, Texas, 11
Humphrey, Hubert H., 164, 165

Ibsen, Henrik, 53
Id, 111, 118, 132, 250
Idaho, 19
Illinois, 18
Incest, 14
In Cold Blood (Capote), 15, 16, 39
India, 238
Indiana, 18
Indianapolis *Sentinel*, 22
Indians, 18, 47, 70, 82, 192, 201, 239
Instinct, 109–128
Integration, *see* Segregation
Invisible Circle, 74
Irish, 18
Israel, 237, 238
Italy, 30, 31, 237, 238

Japan, 237; resentment toward, 44
Japanese-Americans, 126
Jews, 16, 44, 71, 78, 269; *see also* Anti-Semitism
John Birch Society, 45, 48–51, 89
Johnson, Andrew, 174
Johnson, Lyndon B., 32, 45, 126, 164
Justice Department, 52

Kansas, 15
Kennedy, John F., 5, 129–160, 162, 163, 174
Kennedy, Robert F., 6, 219n
Kentucky, 18
Kidnapping, 29, 30
King, Martin Luther, Jr., 6, 258
Knights of the White Camelia, 74

Korean War, 16
Ku Klux Klan, 26, 27, 44, 60, 74–81, 89, 127

Labor unions, 23, 24, 30, 51, 58
Lansky, Meyer, 29
Lemberg Center for the Study of Violence, 253n
Leopold, Nathan, 106–108
Libido, 111
Life, 32
Lincoln, Abraham, 21, 130, 174, 206
Liuzzo, Viola, 79
Loeb, Richard, 106–108
Logan, Clara S., 42
Looting, 28
Lorenz, Konrad, 115
Los Angeles, 11, 42, 46n, 61
Louisiana, 76, 78
Loyalty Order, 52
Luciano, Charles ("Lucky"), 29n
Lutherans, 52
Lynching, 19, 28

MacArthur, General Douglas, 59
McCarthy, Joseph, 44, 55, 56
McKinley, William, 130, 174
McKissick, Floyd B., 257
McMullen, J. W. T., 22
Mafia, 30–33
Malcolm X, 80, 81
Maryland, 67, 69
Massachusetts, 11, 18, 50, 66
Memorial Day Massacre, 24
Menninger, Karl, 35, 225, 226
Mental Health Center, Roosevelt Hospital, 253n

Methodists, 53
Mexico, 238
Miller, Perry, 187
Minutemen, 27, 28, 89
Mississippi, 78, 79
Missouri, 18
"Molly Maguires," 23
Montana, 19
Morgan, Charles, 56
Movies, 42, 255, 256
Mugging, 9
Murder, 5–34
Murder Incorporated, 29, 30
Murret, Lillian, 134, 136, 138
Myrdal, Gunnar, 83

National Advisory Commission
on Civil Disorders, 259
National Association for Better
Radio and Television, 42
National Commission on the
Causes and Prevention of
Violence, 161n, 223, 268
National Rifle Association, 243
National Union for Social Jus-
tice, 44
Naziism, 16, 23, 44, 71, 90, 126
Negroes, 19, 22, 27, 28, 44, 47
53, 61–91, 110, 126, 206, 239,
241, 257–261, 269
Netherlands, 238
Nevins, Allan, 189
New Haven, Conn., 62, 63
New Jersey, 61
New Orleans, La., 11, 31, 243
New York Academy of Medi-
cine, 129n
New York City, 11, 12, 19, 20,
29n, 30, 37, 61, 81, 243
New York Herald Tribune, 42

New York State, 11, 57, 127
New York State Psychiatric In-
stitute, 161–162
New York Times, The, 248n
New Yorker, 39
Newark, N.J., 61, 62
Newport, R.I., 68
Nichols, George Ward, 24
None Dare Call It Treason
(Stormer) 46n
Nonviolence, 258
Norway, 59, 238

Oedipal situation, 55, 56, 86,
102, 103, 116–123, 133, 194,
219, 234, 235, 236, 240, 263
On Aggression (Lorenz), 115
One Year Later, 259
Oral stage of development, 116–
119, 132
Organization of Afro-American
Unity, 81
Osinski, Joseph, 37, 38
Oswald, Lee Harvey, 129–160,
164, 178, 179, 219–225
Oswald, Marguerite, 130–154,
224, 225
Oswald, Marina, 130–157, 223
Oswald, Robert, 130–150, 223,
224, 225
Otis, James, 26

Pain-pleasure principle, 112, 113
Paine, Bruce, 134n
Paterson, N.J., 13n
Penn, Colonel Lemeuel, 79
Pennsylvania, 252
Philadelphia, 18

Pic, John, 134n, 136–146, 224, 225
Pillaging, 19
Pistols, see Firearms
Pittsburgh, Pa., 23
Plato, 114
Pleasure-pain principle, 112, 113
Poland, 237
Police action, 5, 9, 33
Politician, The (Welch), 48, 49
Poole, Elijah, 80
Pope, Alexander, 43
Porter, Katherine Ann, 90
Portugal, 237
Poverty, 58, 59, 109
Presbyterians, 52
Press, 9, 36, 51
Prevention of violence, 237–271
Prohibition, 29
Providence, 68
Psychological capacity for violence, 129–160
Pullman strike of 1894, 23
Puritanism, 47, 185–188

Racial violence, 61–91
Radical right groups, 44, 45
Radio, 9, 46, 255
Rape, 14, 30
Rashdall, Hasting, 267
Reconstruction period, 27
Reles, Abe, 30n
Research Center for the Study of Social Changes, 253n
Revenge, 105
Revolts, student, 5
Revolvers, see Firearms
Riots, 5, 17
    draft, 19, 20
    race, 28, 61, 62, 63

Robber barons, 56, 57
Robberies, 9, 14, 18, 29, 30
Roosevelt, Franklin D., 26, 174, 201
Roosevelt Hospital, 253n
Rosenthal, A. M., 37
Rotenberg, Dr. I. A., 251
Rothstein, Dr. David A., 171n
Ruby, Jack, 130
Russia, 237

Sadoff, Robert L., 251
Sado-masochism, 94, 105, 106, 116, 117, 119
Salem, Mass., 68
San Francisco, Cal., 19, 29n, 61
Scandinavia, 9, 238
Schafly, Phyllis, 46n
Schary, Dore, 230
School Desegregation Law of 1954, 62, 79
Segregation, 44, 45, 50, 51
Senate Rackets Committee, 33
Sexuality, and violence, 14, 83–90, 92–108, 132, 172–173, 194, 218, 220; see also Homosexuality
Shands, Dr. Harley, 253n
Shays' Rebellion, 17, 18,
Shelton, Robert M., Jr., 78
Ship of Fools (Porter), 90
Shootings, 5, 8, 11, 28, 33
Shotwell, James, 206
Siegel, Benjamin ("Bugsy"), 29n
Sirhan, Sirhan, 219n
Slavery, 21, 22, 63–74, 110, 239, 257, 260
Smith, Alfred E., 127
SNCC, 258
Soul On Ice (Cleaver), 86

South Carolina, 17, 68
Spain, 237
Spiegel, Dr. John, 253n
Sports, 40, 41, 42
Springfield, Ill., 61
Stabbing, 7
Stark, Rodney, 52
Stein, Gertrude, 207, 208
Stevenson, Adlai, 54
Stormer, John A., 46n
Storr, Anthony, 115
Student protests, 264–267
Students for a Democratic Society, 265
Styron, William, 70, 71
Suicide, 15, 36, 133, 218
Superego, 118, 121, 133, 228 246, 262
Supreme Court, 44, 77, 78, 259
Sweden, 59, 238
Symbols, 111
Syndicates, see Crime, organized

Television, 9, 35, 41–43, 46, 255, 256
Tennessee, 18, 74
Tennyson, Alfred Lord, 185, 271
Texan Looks at Lyndon, A (Haley), 45, 46
Texans for America, 45, 46
Texas, 11, 76
Theft, 9
Thrill killers, 7
Tippit, J. D., 130, 164
Tompkins Square Riot, 23
Torture, 7
Toys, war, 41
Truman, Harry S., 174
Tubman, Harriet, 260

Turnbull, Andrew, 39
Turner, Frederick Jackson, 195

Un-American Activities Committee, 52, 78
Unemployment, 58, 59
Unions, see Labor unions
United Kingdom, 238
United Nations, 51
Universities of Europe in the Middle Ages, The (Rashdall), 267

Valachi, Joseph, 33
Vandalism, 28
Vanderbilt, Commodore, 56
Vietnam, 16, 39, 53
Vigilantes, 17, 18, 19, 28
Violence, and aggression, 109–128; and the American Dream, 181–208; as assassination, 161–180; among children and adolescents, 7; hidden, 35–60; incidence by country, 237–238; manifest, 5–34; potential, detection of, 209–236; prevention of, 237–271; psychological capacity for, 129–160; racial, 5, 61–91; and sex, 92–108
Virginia, 66–69
Voebel, Edward, 135

Wales, 9, 10
Walker, General Edwin A., 145, 155, 156
War, 16, 17, 109
Warren Commission, 131, 134, 162, 223
Warren, Earl, 49

298

INDEX

Washington, D. C., 13n, 59
Watts, L.A., 61
Welch, Robert, 48, 49, 50
West Germany, 237, 238
White, Joan, 37, 38
Wolfe, Thomas, 183

Wolfgang, Marvin E., 236
World Handbook of Political and Social Indicators, The, 237–238
World War I, 28, 59
World War II, 16, 28, 31, 71